ROYAL HISTORICAL SOCIETY
STUDIES IN HISTORY

GREAT BRITAIN AND INTERNATIONAL SECURITY
1920-1926

Other volumes in series

The Politics of Stability : A Portrait of the Rulers of Elizabethan London — *Frank F. Foster*

The Frankish Church and The Carolingian Reforms, 789-895 — *Rosamond McKitterick*

John Burns — *Kenneth Brown*

Revolution and Counter-Revolution in Scotland, 1644-1651 — *David Stevenson*

The Queen's Two Bodies : Drama and the Elizabethan Succession — *Marie Axton*

Copies obtainable on order from
Swift Printers., 1-7 Albion Place, Britton Street, London EC1M 5RE

GREAT BRITAIN AND INTERNATIONAL SECURITY 1920-1926

Anne Orde

Lecturer in History
University of Durham

LONDON
ROYAL HISTORICAL SOCIETY
1978

ISBN 0 901050 40 7

The Society records its gratitude to the following, whose generosity made possible the initiation of this series: The British Academy; The Pilgrim Trust; The Twenty-Seven Foundation; The United States Embassy bicentennial funds; The Wolfson Trust; several private donors.

Printed in England
by Swift Printers Ltd.
London E.C.1.

CONTENTS

PREFACE

This book originated in a thesis presented in 1972 for the degree of Ph.D. in the University of Durham, but has since been substantially revised. My interest in the international relations of the interwar period was initially derived from my father, and became settled when I worked on the publication of *Documents on British Foreign Policy 1919-1939.* I owe a great debt to the first editors, the late Sir Llewellyn Woodward and Mr. R. D. O. Butler, C.M.G., for their good training, and above all to the Hon. Margaret Lambert, C.M.G., for innumerable instances of help and encouragement then and since. When, after a period of work in the Cabinet Office Historical Section and elsewhere, I began teaching. Professor Douglas Johnson, then at the University of Birmingham, encouraged me to embark on research. After I moved to Durham, Professor W.R. Ward willingly took over the task of supervision and taught me a great deal about doing a kind of history which he still does not find particularly congenial. Professor H.S. Offler too and other colleagues have given me more help than they perhaps realise.

My thanks are also due to the librarians and staff of the Public Record Office, the Foreign and Commonwealth Office Library, the India Office Records, the British Library, the London Library, and the Direction des Archives et de la Documentation in the Ministère des Affaires Étrangères, Paris; and to the owners and custodians of the Baldwin, Chamberlain, Crewe, Curzon, Haldane, Lloyd George, Bonar Law, and MacDonald Papers. Crown copyright material is quoted by permission of the Controller of Her Majesty's Stationery Office; for other permissions I am grateful to the Librarian, Cambridge University Library (Baldwin Papers), William Collins and Sons Co. Ltd. (Stephen Roskill, *Naval Policy between the Wars*), the Clerk of the Records, House of Lords (Lloyd George Papers), Hutchinson and Co. Ltd. (L.S. Amery, *My Political Life*), and the Rt. Hon. Malcolm MacDonald, O.M., P.C. (J. Ramsay MacDonald, *The Foreign Policy of the Labour Party*).

Anne Orde
Durham, October 1977

LIST OF ABBREVIATIONS AND SHORT TITLES

(for full details of works see Bibliography)

AA	Auswärtiges Amt
ADAP	Germany, *Akten zur deutschen auswärtigen Politik 1918-1945,* Series B
CID	Committee of Imperial Defence
DBFP	Great Britain, *Documents on British Foreign Policy 1919-1939,* Series I, IA
DDB	Belgium, *Documents diplomatiques belges 1920-1940: La Politique de sécurité extérieure*
DDI	Italy, *I Documenti diplomatici italiani,* 7th series

Documents relatifs aux garanties = France, *Documents relatifs aux négociations concernant les garanties de sécurité contre une agression de l'Allemagne, 10 janvier 1919 - 7 décembre 1923*

FO	Foreign Office
FRUS	United States, *Papers Relating to the Foreign Relations of the United States*
HCDeb.	*The Parliamentary Debates, House of Commons*
HLDeb.	*The Parliamentary Debates, House of Lords*
MAE	France, Ministère des Affaires Étrangères. Archives
Petrie, *Life and Letters*	Sir Charles Petrie, *The Life and Letters of the Right Hon. Sir Austen Chamberlain*
Q d'O	Quai d'Orsay
Roskill, *Naval Policy*	Stephen Roskill, *Naval Policy between the Wars,* Vol. I

INTRODUCTION

This book is an account of British government policy on international security from the end of the Paris Peace Conference until, in appearance at least, a solution was reached in 1926 as regards the security of western Europe. The formulation of official policy – the decisions taken by Cabinets, the advice given to them by their professional advisers, and the considerations upon which the advice and the decisions were based – is a coherent subject which can reasonably be studied on its own. Parliamentary and public opinion, or what ministers and officials thought or said public opinion was, are of course important elements in the process; but the influence of pressure and attitude groups, although discernible in the positions taken by ministers and officials, is not here discussed as such.

It was a commonplace at the time that the world immediately after the First World War was a dangerous place in which almost all peoples craved for security. Even though they were not directly threatened, few had a greater stake in peace and security than the British. There was nothing very new about their situation or its causes. One could find many earlier parallels to the statement by a Foreign Office official in April 1926:

> We. . .have no territorial ambitions nor desire for aggrandisement. We have got all that we want – perhaps more. The fact is that war and rumour of war, quarrels and friction, in any corner of the world spell loss and harm to British commercial and financial interests. It is for the sake of these interests that we endeavour to pour oil on troubled waters. So manifold and ubiquitous are British trade and British finance that, whatever else may be the outcome of a disturbance of the peace, we shall be the losers.[1]

But although the basic policy was not new, the circumstances in which it was to operate were different from those known before 1914. The peace treaties were signed but the political, social and economic consequences of the war still gave trouble. The pre-1914 international order had disappeared and, since it was widely blamed for having caused the war, there was no desire to bring it back. A new and better order had to be constructed, and Britain was committed to playing a leading part.

1 *Documents on British Foreign Policy 1919-1939*, ed. E.L. Woodward and R. d'O. Butler, and others (London, 1947 ff.) hereafter cited as *DBFP*, Series IA, Vol. I, Appendix. This paper was prepared to assist the Chiefs of Staff in compiling their first annual review of defence.

For Britain, as one of the major victors and a great power with possessions and interests all over the world, security was a responsibility as well as a need. She was pre-eminently a 'producer' rather than a 'consumer' of security, one of those who were expected to 'give' rather than 'receive' under the Covenant of the League of Nations.[1] In some senses the position of Great Britain in the years immediately after the war was very strong. All her enemies had been defeated and she had suffered little material damage. But the war had imposed costs and burdens which would weigh heavily for two generations or more; her trade had been disrupted; her financial pre-eminence had gone; economic reorganisation and social improvement were imperative. To outside eyes Britain might appear powerful, but successive postwar governments were conscious rather of the severe limitations on her strength. Pacification seemed essential if the British economy were to recover: the desire fitted too the temper of a public determined never again to see such a war. But responsibility for security might be costly and might involve Britain in unforeseeable and unpopular commitments.

The problem was sharpened by the United States' abstention from membership of the League of Nations. The war had wrought a change in the relative power of the two countries. The United States was now a great naval power and Britain, although a net creditor in war debts, owed her £978 million. The possibility of war with the United States had been excluded from British defence calculations since 1904, and even after the rejection of the Covenant political co-operation with her, one of the hopes of the latter part of the war, remained a British goal; but it was not easy to obtain or keep. An important consideration in all official discussions of schemes of general security was the fear, not only that in the absence of the United States the British navy would have to carry the chief burden of enforcement, but that this responsibility might involve disputes with a United States possessed of a large navy and insisting on the freedom of the seas.

The Dominions too, during this period, acted as something of a brake on British policy. Their greater independence of Britain was marked by their separate membership of the League of Nations. Although the constitutional expression was not laid down until 1931, the practical implications of their independence were being worked out throughout the 1920s. The hope that it would be possible to construct and conduct an 'imperial' foreign policy in which the Dominions would have a

1 The term 'consumers of security' was used by the Canadian Senator Dandurand at the League Assembly in 1927: it is said to have been coined by Salvador de Madariaga. Cf. Sir Alfred Zimmern, *The League of Nations and the Rule of Law* (London, 1936), 325-32; J.R.M. Butler, in *History of the Peace Conference of Paris,* ed. H.W.V. Temperley, Vol. IV (London, 1924), 441.

voice and responsibility was defeated by Canadian, South African and Irish insistence on independent decision and refusal of responsibility; but since no one was yet prepared to face the consequences of separation the Dominions had something like a veto on fresh British commitments.[1]

In these circumstances Britain was neither willing nor able to provide for security in equal measure all over the world. The problem for British policy fell into two parts: international security in the broadest sense, and the security of areas of greatest interest to Britain and the Empire and Commonwealth. And by her defence policy Britain had to ensure the security of the Empire itself and perhaps make provision for general security.

International security in the broad sense was mainly a matter of the development of the League of Nations. During the war the creation of a new international order and some organisation to secure peace became one of the aims of many of the belligerents, especially on the Allied side; and its achievement was Woodrow Wilson's principal task at the Peace Conference.[2] The Covenant of the League of Nations drawn up there reflected mainly British and American conceptions of such an organisation. The elements of guarantee and conciliation, of coercion and tribunal of opinion, of obligation and free decision, were delicately and not altogether consistently balanced. Two elements on which the French member of the drafting committee, in particular, had set store – compulsory arbitration and an international military force – were not included. And although from the earliest British proposals, those of the Phillimore committee of 1917, sanctions were envisaged against a state refusing to use peaceful means of settling a dispute and instead resorting to war, the prevention of war by conciliation always featured more prominently in British thinking about the League than did collective action and guarantees. The absence of the United States enhanced but did not create the instinctive doubts of British Governments about the coercive obligations of the Covenant.

The two areas of the world the security of which, in international

1 The position of the Dominions in the 1920s is discussed in *Survey of British Commonwealth Affairs* (Royal Institute of International Affairs), Vol. I, *Problems of Nationality 1918-1936.* by W.K. Hancock (London, 1937), and Vol. III, *Problems of External Policy 1931-1939,* by Nicholas Mansergh (London, 1952).

2 For British thinking on the subject during the war see Zimmern, *The League of Nations and the Rule of Law;* H.R. Winkler, *The League of Nations Movement in Great Britain 1914-1918* (New Brunswick, N.J., 1952). The proceedings at Paris are recounted in D.H. Miller, *The Drafting of the Covenant* (New York and London, 1928). See also F.P. Walters, *A History of the League of Nations* (London, 1952).

terms, was of the greatest interest were Europe and the Far East. Of the two the problem of European security was the more immediate and the closer at hand. It was one aspect of, and at times seemed to be the key to the whole problem of the economic as well as the political recovery of Europe, and Britain, from the war. The problem of the Far East also arose to a large extent from the war, but was more a matter of the possible consequences of long-term changes in the relative strength of the powers concerned rather than of immediate difficulties.

A policy on security necessarily includes military considerations. Some connexion can be shown between defence policy and foreign policy in the Far East, but little in Europe. Since there was no expectation of a major war involving Britain for an ever-extended ten years, defence policy was determined above all by financial considerations.

The machinery for deciding and executing policy remained much the same as before the war. The Cabinet were responsible for deciding policy: the advice and information upon which their decisions were based were provided by the Foreign Office and the Service departments with the Treasury looming in the background. Within this constant framework practice and actual authority varied from one government to another. Until the end of 1922 Lloyd George took a more active part in the formation and conduct of foreign policy than many other Prime Ministers before and since. Frequent inter-Allied conferences gave scope for his particular talents, and his personal secretariat remained powerful. Curzon's lack of authority during Lloyd George's premiership, except in one specialised field, has often been described. For a year after Lloyd George's fall circumstances were against the taking of new initiatives by anyone.

In the first Labour Government MacDonald combined the posts of Prime Minister and Foreign Secretary. Before entering office the Labour Party had had ideas of introducing new blood and tapping fresh sources of advice to counteract the influence of the permanent officials. But although there is a different flavour about foreign policy in 1924 the officials were neither cold-shouldered nor often over-ruled. With the Conservatives' return to power the picture changed again to the one that was to last until 1929, with Baldwin as a generally non-interventionist Prime Minister and Chamberlain a Foreign Secretary more powerful than Curzon but yet not always able to get his way in the Cabinet.[1]

In defence policy too the framework remained much the same

1 Cf. Alan J. Sharp, 'The Foreign Office in eclipse, 1919-22', *History* 61 (1976), 198-218. There is an essay on the Foreign Office from Grey to

throughout the period, with the individual services, under more or less forceful political heads, contending more or less unsuccessfully for their individual needs. Some new co-ordination machinery was introduced, but the Committee of Imperial Defence remained the combined political and professional source of advice to the Cabinet.[1]

The Foreign Office conducted the day-to-day business of foreign affairs, even under Lloyd George; but since reparations were dealt with by the Treasury an important area of policy was almost wholly outside Foreign Office influence, and the Department of Overseas Trade was virtually independent. During these years, unlike those immediately before the war, senior Foreign Office officials did not exert great influence on the formation of policy. They were essentially executants: even if they had the inclination they had little leisure to reflect on or write about the long-term implications of the many problems with which they had to deal from day to day. But despite the upheavals let loose by the war, and the uncertainty introduced by the existence of a fundamentally alien regime in Russia, they still assumed that the state system would function in a generally rational manner. Adjustments through the League or by the exercise of direct influence might be required, but would work: it was not an international anarchy. And despite all Britain's difficulties she was still thought strong enough to apply the principles summarised by Gladstone more than half a century earlier:

> That England should keep entire in her hands the means of estimating her own obligations upon the various states of fact as they arise; that she should not foreclose and narrow her liberty of choice by declarations made to other powers, in their real or supposed interests, of which they would claim to be at least joint interpreters; that it is dangerous for her to assume alone an advanced and therefore an isolated position in regard to European controversies; that come what may, it is better to promise too little than too much; that she should not encourage the weak by giving expectations of aid to resist the strong, but should rather seek to deter the strong by firm but moderate language from aggression on the weak; that she should seek to develop and mature the action of a common, or public, or European opinion as the best standing bulwark against wrong, but should beware of seeming to lay down the law of that opinion by her own authority, and thus running the risk of setting against her and against right and justice, that general sentiment which ought to be, and generally would be arrayed in their favour.[2]

Chamberlain in Gordon A. Craig and Felix Gilbert, *The Diplomats* (Princeton, 1953). For the position before the war see Zara S. Steiner, *The Foreign Office and Foreign Policy, 1898-1914* (London, 1969).

1 See F.A. Johnson, *Defence by Committee* (London, 1960). For the period before the war see Nicholas D'Ombrain, *War Machinery and High Policy* (London, 1974).

2 Gladstone to General Grey, 17 April 1869: J.M. Morley, *The Life of William Ewart Gladstone* (London, 1903), Vol. II, 316-18.

1

THE NEGOTIATIONS FOR AN ANGLO-FRENCH PACT 1921-22

Relations between Britain and France in the two or three years after the end of the peace conference were confused and uneasy. The two countries were still closely bound together in completing and carrying out the terms of the peace treaties, a process which by no means ended with the departure of the last delegates from Paris. On the other hand there was no alliance between them. The only such formal agreement had been the declaration of September 1914 in which they, and Russia, bound themselves not to make a separate peace, and this had of course expired. Even during the peace conference French and British policies were seen to diverge in many respects, most notably on Germany; and thereafter they diverged on eastern Europe, the Near East, and Russia as well.

Differences over Germany were natural, for the interests of the two countries were not the same. Even before the popular passions expressed in the general election of November 1918 had died down, the Coalition Government believed it to be Britain's interest to execute the peace treaty as quickly as possible and thereafter to see Germany and Europe recover from the war together for the sake of British trade and the reduction of British responsibilities. The French Government believed that France's interests required the exaction from Germany in the shortest possible time of the maximum sums for the restoration of the devastated regions and the assurance of France's security against the possibility of German revenge. Both governments wished to see the Treaty of Versailles carried out, Germany disarmed and reparations collected; but the British soon came to believe that French methods were unlikely to be productive and likely to retard European pacification. By 1921 they regarded Germany as effectively disarmed, and although they did not contemplate allowing rearmament they did not think her disarmament could be maintained indefinitely. As for reparations, while they wished to receive the British share and were not prepared to make unilateral sacrifices, if it came to a choice between economic stability in Germany and the collection of reparations they would choose the former for the sake of general recovery. They underestimated the French need for money for reconstruction and were inclined to regard the French insistence on reparations as vindictiveness.[1] Since the two countries were so closely bound

1 The divergence between British and French policies has been the subject of many studies. Particularly useful are Arnold Wolfers, *Britain and France*

together it was impossible for them to go separate ways; but for two years, despite frequent inter-Allied meetings, no serious attempt was made to discuss their differences and reach a new understanding.

One element in French resentment at what was regarded as lack of due British support was the lapse of the guarantee of assistance against future German aggression, promised in April 1919 as part of the bargain over the peace terms on the left bank of the Rhine and embodied in a treaty signed, with a parallel Franco-American agreement, on the same day as the Treaty of Versailles.[1] Both agreements provided that they should only come into force together. The Anglo-French treaty was approved by Parliament and ratified. The Franco-American agreement was never brought before the United States Senate. So long as it was not rejected the British Cabinet had an excuse for refusing to think about the British treaty. In December 1919 Lloyd George told Clemenceau that there would be opposition in Parliament if the Government proposed a guarantee without the United States, but he refused in the House of Commons to discuss what the Government would do if the United States did not ratify.[2] Even when the Senate rejected the Treaty of Versailles Lloyd George still declined to commit himself so long as no decision had been taken on the Franco-American agreement.[3] Although occasional references were made to using the guarantee or a possible alliance as a lever with France, no real consideration was given to it until 1921.[4]

Shortly before an inter-Allied conference in London in February 1921 Sir Eyre Crowe, the Permanent Under-Secretary of State in the Foreign Office, suggested to Curzon that the Cabinet should consider a comprehensive policy of reconstituting the Entente and giving France a guarantee. Crowe feared a quarrel between the two countries if the conference did not reach a solution satisfactory to French opinion, a quarrel which could not be in Britain's interest since she had no other friends. He believed that an offer of security in the same terms as

between two Wars (New York, 1940); W.M. Jordan, *Great Britain, France and the German Problem 1918-1939* (London, 1943); B. de Jouvenel, *D'une guerre à l'autre,* Vol. I (Paris, 1940).

1 For the discussions at the Peace Conference see Harold I. Nelson, *Land and Power. British and Allied Policy on Germany's Frontiers 1916-19* (Toronto and London, 1963), Chapters VIII and IX.

2 S 5, 11 Dec. 1919, Public Record Office, London, CAB 23/35; *Parliamentary Debates, House of Commons,* hereafter cited as *HC Deb.,* 5th ser., Vol. 123, cols. 762-3. Documents in the Public Record Office are cited by their individual number and by the class and volume number - CAB, CO, DO, FO, for Cabinet Office, Colonial Office, Dominions Office, and Foreign Office respectively.

3 *HC Deb.*, 5th ser., Vol. 127, col. 865.

4 S 4, 10 Dec. 1919, CAB 23/35; CP 1782, 6 Aug. 1920, CAB 24/110; C 80 (20), 30 Dec. 1920, CAB 23/23.

the 1919 guarantee might make the French more conciliatory, both in their attitude to Germany and in their policy on the Near East, and that many sections of British opinion would support it.[1]

The London conference ended without progress on the Turkish problem. However there was no Anglo-French quarrel, and the two countries were united at the next conference at the end of April in presenting an ultimatum to Germany on reparations.[2] Crowe's suggestion was not brought to the Cabinet, but there was some discussion there in the early summer as to whether a new guarantee would, by reducing French fears, encourage French moderation towards Germany.[3] Whether an offer would be welcomed was not clear; and despite some urging from Lord Derby, who had been ambassador in Paris from 1918 to 1920 and advocated an alliance, no attempt was made to elucidate French wishes.[4] However the Dominion Prime Ministers were sounded at the Imperial Conference in the summer. Smuts was anxious for Britain to stand outside Europe as a mediater; Meighen of Canada was opposed to all alliances; W.M. Hughes of Australia and Massey of New Zealand were more favourable to a guarantee. The British ministers present did not propose an early decision; but it seems to have been tacitly agreed that in suitable circumstances an offer might be made.[5]

The genesis of the Cannes negotiations, November-December 1921

At the end of 1921 a discussion of Anglo-French relations became more desirable for both countries. The differences between them had become worse. The French had been angered by the British signature of a trade agreement with Soviet Russia in March; there had been a grave difference over Upper Silesia in July.[6] Now in the autumn they pursued negotiations of their own on matters closely affecting Britain. On 6 October the French and German Ministers for Recon-

1 *DBFP,* Ser. I, Vol. XVII, No. 38.

2 Proceedings of these conferences in *DBFP,* Ser. I, Vol. XV. An account of reparations to the beginning of 1923 in *Survey of International Affairs, 1920-1923;* British documentation to the end of 1921 in *DBFP,* Ser. I, Vols. X, XVI.

3 C 40(21), CAB 23/25.

4 *DBFP,* Ser. I, Vol. XVI, No. 634; *The Times,* 3 Jun. 1921; *Le Temps,* 6 Jun. ; Hardinge to Curzon, 13 Jun., Curzon Papers, India Office Records, Curzon Papers, MSS Eur. F. 112/200; Comte de St-Aulaire, *Confession d'un vieux diplomate* (Paris, 1953), 566-9.

5 E 2nd, 4th, 6th, 18th meetings, CAB 32/2.

6 On the Anglo-Soviet trade agreement see *DBFP,* Ser. I, Vol. XII: M.V. Glenny, 'The Anglo-Soviet trade agreement, March 1921', *Journal of Contemporary History* 5 (1970), 63-82; Richard H. Ullmann, *Anglo-Soviet Relations 1917-1921,* Vol. III, *The Anglo-Soviet Accord* (Princeton, 1973). On Upper Silesia see *DBFP,* Ser. I, Vols. XI, XVI.

struction, Loucheur and Rathenau, signed an agreement providing for direct German deliveries for the restoration of the devasted regions, which was thought in London to prejudice other countries' reparation interests. On 21 October a French representative, Franklin-Bouillon, signed an agreement with the Kemalist Turks which signified an open abandonment of Anglo-French co-operation in the Near East. Finally the Washington Conference on the limitation of armaments led to another quarrel.

The conference had been called to discuss the limitation of armaments without distinction. The British were prepared to discuss land and air forces, and in this connexion were ready to encourage American ratification of the 1919 agreement with France, which would bring the British guarantee treaty into effect. The French approached the conference almost wholly from the European angle and were prepared to demand security in return for a reduction of their army. The Americans, however, thought of arms limitation purely in naval terms and were determined to take and retain the initiative.[1] Briand, the French Prime Minister, pleaded at the plenary session on 21 November for Allied solidarity in the face of Germany's potential for revenge.[2] His eloquence won applause, but the speech was out of tune with the mood of the conference and provoked an angry reaction in London.

The Cabinet and the Committee of Imperial Defence, discussing Briand's speech, concluded that Germany, which could put only ten fully equipped divisions into the field, was no threat to France, which from the forces in the country itself could immediately produce forty-nine divisions. They did not try to estimate more accurately than Briand how long, once Allied control was withdrawn, it would take Germany to manufacture equipment for the manpower which was available. But when it came to the French naval programme they expressed great alarm about the future.[3] They therefore instructed

1 For the British position see C 83(21), CAB 23/27, and pp. 164-8 below. For the French position, and hopes of an agreement with the United States, see *DBFP*, Ser. I, Vol. XIV, Nos. 437, 438; Georges Suarez, *Briand. Sa Vie, son oeuvre,* Vol. V (Paris, 1952), 232; L. Archimbaud, *La Conférence de Washington* (Paris, 1923), 70-2. Soon after arriving in Washington Balfour gathered from two of the United States delegates, Senator Lodge and Elihu Root, that they did not expect the conference to deal with anything but naval limitation, and it was the sole theme of Secretary of State Hughes's opening speech: Hankey to Lloyd George, 14 Nov. 1921, Lloyd George Papers, House of Lords Library, London, F/62/1/2.

2 Suarez, *Briand,* Vol. V, 267-79; *Conference on the Limitation of Armaments, Washington, November 12, 1921-February 6, 1922* (Washington, 1922), 116-35.

3 C 88(21), CAB 23/27; CID 130th meeting, CAB 2/3; *DBFP,* Ser. I, Vol. XIV, No. 439.

Balfour, the leader of the British delegation in Washington, that land armaments must be taken up again:

> The position of this country *vis-à-vis* France will become impossible if British navy is to be restricted in accordance with American proposals while French army continues on the scale of at least a hundred divisions together with overwhelming aviation and the intention to build a very large fleet of submarines. . .Anxious as we are and have proved ourselves to disarm and to march hand in hand with the United States, we cannot contemplate a situation where Great Britain would be in a few years at the mercy of France if present happy relations were to deteriorate. We think that the Americans ought to be made to understand fully the gravity of the situation and to join with us in endeavouring to procure a general disarmament rather than disarmament by Britain alone. . .Finally, it is essential to take into account the influence of French armaments on Europe and the world in general. The possession of this overwhelming superiority by one power makes real settlement impossible. It keeps Europe in a ferment and provides minor powers, such as Roumania, Czechoslovakia, Yugoslavia and Poland with a standing excuse for maintaining proportionately large armaments which are a temptation to themselves and a menace to their neighbours. Europe is worse in this respect now than in 1914 and the main cause is the persistence of France in her present policy.[1]

Balfour, with an ironical reference to his lack of diplomatic training, deprecated these instructions and pointed out that it would be foolish to wrangle over land armament when French naval demands could still frustrate the main object of the conference. But Lloyd George telegraphed again that Briand must not be allowed to get away with 'faked and disingenuous figures', and the American public should be made aware of Germany's impotence lest they believe France to be in real danger.[2]

Land armaments were in fact not pursued, but the French naval position continued to cause difficulty. Their claim to capital ships upset the Americans in particular, since this was the central point of their proposals.[3] Submarines were a sore point for the British, who would have liked to secure their abolition, and further offence was caused when the First Lord of the Admiralty, Lord Lee, quoted in a speech a work by a French naval officer expounding in sympathetic terms German policy on submarine warfare.[4]

1 *DBFP,* Ser I, Vol.XIV, Nos. 442, 443.

2 Op. cit. Nos. 448, 452.

3 The British Ambassador in Washington wrote later to Curzon: 'France. . .has committed the heinous offence of interfering with the first great international conference held in America': A587/2/45, FO 371/7247. See also *DBFP,* Ser. I, Vol. XIV, Nos 505, 506.

4 The work was by Capitaine de frégate R.V.P. Castex, *Synthèse de la guerre*

Lloyd George was not solely responsible for the recrimination against France during the conference: his friend the newspaper proprietor Lord Riddell acted on his own in the United States, and both Curzon and Churchill included references to French militarism in speeches in England.[1] But Lloyd George seems to have shown particular excitement. His reasons are obscure, but some of his colleagues began to feel alarm at the quarrel. Lee sent messages from Washington that the prospects of the conference might be jeopardised, and suggested that a better way of inducing the French to abate their demands might be to renew the prewar undertaking to defend the French Channel coast.[2] And Churchill, who at Lloyd George's request had been responsible for at least one of the angry telegrams to Balfour, wrote to urge a reconsideration of Anglo-French relations. He thought that they, and Anglo-German relations, ought to be founded on British willingness to maintain the guarantee to France whether or not the United States took part. On this basis he would go to great lengths to stop the French building a large submarine fleet. Churchill also favoured bringing British policy on Turkey into line with the French, and thought that they should work for an understanding between Britain, France and Germany for the reconstruction of Europe. 'All these aspects need to be treated together. I am not at all in agreement with the way in which our relations with France are now being treated. It would be an enormous shock to the British public, who have 600,000 graves in France, if the statesmen were to tell them that we backed the wrong horse'.[3]

All these aspects, other than Turkey, were discussed when Briand visited London before Christmas. He had already indicated that he would like an opportunity for a general discussion,[4] although the immediate occasion of his visit was the reparation situation which was

sous-marine (Paris, 1920). The French delegation maintained at first that it only described German views: later a statement was issued saying that the author had been expressing a purely personal view.

1 *DBFP,* Ser. I, Vol. XIV, No. 517; Balfour to Jusserand, 19 Dec. 1921, CAB 30/31.

2 Lee to Lloyd George, 23 Nov. 1921; Balfour to Lloyd George, 18 Dec., Lloyd George Papers, F/31/2/67; F/10/1/70.

3 Churchill to Lloyd George, 28 Nov. 1921, Lloyd George Papers, F/10/1/48.

4 *DBFP,* Ser. I, Vol. XVII, No. 465; France, Ministère des Affaires Etrangères, archives, Europe 1918-1929, Grande Bretagne, Vol. 69, Quai d'Orsay to St-Aulaire, 4 Dec. 1921 (documents in the archives of the Quai d'Orsay are hereafter cited as MAE, with country and volume number, and Quai d'Orsay abbreviated as Q d'O); France, Ministère des Affaires Etrangères, *Documents relatifs aux négociations concernant les garanties de sécurité contre une agression de l'Allemagne, 10 janvier 1919-7 décembre 1923* (Paris, 1924), hereafter cited as *Documents relatifs aux garanties,* No. 17; Suarez, *Briand,* Vol. V, 356.

reaching one of its critical stages. The mark had fallen sharply in the last three months and the German Government informed the Reparation Commission on 14 December that they would be unable to pay more than a small part of the instalments due in January and February. In expectation of this announcement the British had been coming to the view that Germany would have to be given a moratorium, and were preparing to enlist Belgian and Italian support. The French were expected to oppose a moratorium unless some other concessions could be made, for instance on war debts. Lloyd George hoped that the United States would join in discussing economic problems; so having invited Loucheur to England for a preliminary talk he held out the prospect of virtual cancellation of the Allies' debts to Britain provided that the United States would co-operate.[1] This idea was perforce abandoned when enquiries in Washington showed that the United States Government were not prepared to take part in general discussions and when they announced on 11 December that there was no intention of cancelling Allied war debts. Lloyd George, who under the pressure of rising unemployment was seeking means of stimulating European recovery, also talked with Loucheur about international action for the reconstruction of Russia. The idea was current in Germany too, and Lloyd George had probably already discussed it with Rathenau.[2]

Briand's conversations in London were mostly taken up with reparations and plans for an international economic conference and Russian reconstruction, and it was agreed to hold an inter-Allied meeting on these subjects early in the New Year. Towards the end, however, Briand raised the question of an Anglo-French alliance. This had been suggested to Curzon on 5 December by the French Ambassador, who said that he thought the way to prevent war was not a British guarantee to France but a far-reaching defensive alliance covering indirect attack (for example a German or German-Russian attack on Poland) as well as direct invasion. St-Aulaire was acting without instructions and did not intend to make a formal proposal, but he said that he thought Briand

1 *DBFP,* Ser. I, Vol. XVI, No. 752; Hardinge to Curzon, 6 Dec. 1921, FO 800/153; Louis Loucheur, *Carnets secrets, 1908-1932,* ed. Jacques de Launay (Brussels and Paris, 1962), 185-8; Thomas Jones, *Whitehall Diary,* ed. Keith Middlemas, Vol. I (London, 1969), 183, 185.

2 Rathenau visited London twice in December. He accepted an invitation to meet Lloyd George at dinner on 2 December: Lloyd George Papers. F/53/3/12. Harry, Graf Kessler, in his biography *Walther Rathenau* (Berlin, 1928), 308, 311-2, suggests that it was on the second visit, when Rathenau met Loucheur and Horne, the Chancellor of the Exchequer, that the plan emerged; but he is inclined to conflate the two visits and references in *DBFP,* Ser. I, Vol. XV, Nos. 108, 109, and C 93(21), CAB 23/27, suggest that it had emerged in outline earlier. On the projects for Russian reconstruction see E.H. Carr, *The Bolshevik Revolution,* Vol. III (London, 1953), Ch. XXIX.

would share his views.[1] Before Briand arrived, however, the Cabinet still thought that the French were opposed to an alliance. They knew that Briand's ministry might fall if he returned from London empty-handed; but it was felt that his most likely successor, Poincaré, might be stronger and therefore better to deal with.[2]

Briand spoke of an alliance in general terms to Curzon,[3] and on 21 December opened the subject in greater detail to Lloyd George and Austen Chamberlain, saying that his idea was that Britain and France should guarantee each other's interests in all parts of the world and work closely together on all questions. Lloyd George said that British public opinion would not be ready for anything so wide. He thought it possible to give France a guarantee against direct German attack, but the public would not be willing to be involved in quarrels on Germany's eastern frontier. Briand replied that there was much to be said for a consultative pact like the four-power treaty on the Pacific which had just been concluded at Washington.[4] A European pact of this kind might include three or four countries: others, including Germany, might join later, but its nucleus should be a complete alliance between France and Britain. Lloyd George repeated that public opinion would not accept anything so wide, but a simple guarantee could be given. He said that he would consult his colleagues; Briand said that he would put his ideas in writing; and they agreed to continue the discussion at Cannes.[5]

When he got back to Paris Briand repeated to the British Ambassador much of what he had said to Lloyd George, and added the suggestion that Britain and France should form the 'secular arm' of the League of Nations, to enforce its decisions and maintain peace in Europe.[6] There is little evidence that he worked out these ideas much

1 FO to Hardinge, 5 Dec. 1921, W 12716/12716/17, FO 371/7000, printed in Cmd 2169 of 1924, *Papers respecting the negotiations for an Anglo-French Pact*. St-Aulaire did not report the conversation to Paris until 14 December, and was apparently annoyed when Hardinge took it up with Briand. He had previously mentioned an alliance to Chamberlain, but wrote later in his memoirs that he advised his Government not to take an initiative: St-Aulaire to Q d'O, 14 Dec., MAE, Grande Bretagne, Vol. 69; Hardinge to FO, 7 Dec., W 12728/12716/17, FO 371/7000; memorandum by Crowe, 30 Dec., W 50/50/17, FO 371/8249; A. Chamberlain to Ida Chamberlain, 1 Jan. 1922, Chamberlain Papers, Birmingham University Library, AC 5/1/222; St-Aulaire, *Confession d'un vieux diplomate*, 584, 749.

2 C 93(21), 16 Dec. 1921, CAB 23/27.

3 Curzon to Hardinge, 24 Dec. 1921, Curzon Papers, MSS. Eur. F.112/232.

4 See p.167.

5 *DBFP*, Ser. I, Vol. XV, No. 110.

6 Hardinge to Curzon, 26 Dec. 1921, Curzon Papers, MSS. Eur. F.112/200.

more fully before going to Cannes. A memorandum prepared in the Quai d'Orsay illustrates what he had in mind, namely an Anglo-French pact in which the two countries would undertake to concert their policies, give each other help in case of direct attack, and regulate their armaments by agreement; and secondly an agreement between France, Britain, Germany and Italy, under which the four countries would undertake to confer if peace were threatened by another country. There was no discussion of the relationship of such a pact to the Covenant, nor of whether Germany was expected to join the League.[1] St-Aulaire, who himself produced a draft Anglo-French treaty and suggested that Britain should be asked to maintain a specified size of army, thought that the idea of a two-tier alliance appealed to the British. But he warned Briand that Lloyd George was chiefly interested in economic reconstruction and that the Foreign Office were likely to insist on clearing up a number of political questions.[2]

Neither Lloyd George nor the Cabinet seem to have given the matter much thought. Apart from a brief discussion on 21 December the Cabinet did not consider it before Lloyd George left for Cannes; and he on the way through Paris simply repeated that British opinion would agree to a guarantee but not an alliance.[3] The Foreign Office put some work into the subject. Crowe on the whole favoured an alliance confining military help to the case of an unprovoked German attack on France and providing for consultation if the interests of either country were threatened from any quarter. Other countries, including Germany, could adhere to the latter agreement, which could follow the lines of the Covenant on methods of dealing with disputes likely to lead to war. Germany could also join the League. All this would offer substantial guarantees of peace. 'The alliance alone would keep any German aggressive designs on France in check; any danger from the Russian quarter, more particularly Russian or Russo-German movements against Poland, would be, if not absolutely prevented, at least rendered infinitely less probable, without at the same time finding England committed to go to war for Poland's sake in circumstances when Poland might be to blame'. The League would be strengthened, France would be enabled to reduce her armaments and to join in encouraging European recovery or at least to stop opposing Britain doing so. Crowe

1 Memorandum, 28 Dec. 1921, MAE, Grande Bretagne, Vol. 69.

2 St-Aulaire to Q d'O, 28 Dec. 1921, MAE, Grande Bretagne, Vol. 69; St-Aulaire to Q d'O, 31 Dec., *Documents relatifs aux garanties,* No. 19; St-Aulaire, *Confession d'un vieux diplomate,* 584-5.

3 Meeting of Ministers, 21 Dec. 1921, C 93(21), Appendix III, CAB 23/27 (no details are recorded); Hardinge to Curzon, 27 Dec., Curzon Papers, MSS. Eur. F.112/200.

concluded that Briand's proposal might lead to important and desirable objects. He should be encouraged to develop it and guided in the desired direction. Curzon on the other hand did not favour an alliance, and advised Lloyd George against even a guarantee without a settlement of the main questions dividing the two countries and an understanding on future policy. But he too recommended an agreement to consult in case of a threat to either country's vital interests, to which Germany and other countries could be invited to adhere.[1]

Cannes, January 1922

The purpose of the Cannes conference was an inter-Allied discussion of reparations and economic recovery. It achieved a measure of success, of the kind that conceals substantial differences, by hearing Rathenau (now German Foreign Minister), granting Germany a temporary moratorium, and laying down the bases for an economic conference to be held at Genoa in the spring and for extending relations with Soviet Russia. It was within this context that an Anglo-French pact was discussed, not by Curzon despite his presence at Cannes, but by Lloyd George alone with Briand. At their first meeting on 4 January Briand said that his proposal was not meant to involve Britain in military obligations in eastern Europe, but only in keeping the peace by such means as conferences at which she and France would act together. He admitted that a British undertaking limited to the protection of France might serve the same purpose. Lloyd George said that he thought the essential for France was a guarantee against German attack, and on this a stable peace might be built. Briand asked what conditions were proposed, and Lloyd George replied that certain questions must be cleared up between the two countries, France must co-operate in European reconstruction, and she must not arouse British anxiety by a submarine programme.[2]

After this conversation Lloyd George sent Briand his views in writing.[3] He described a close understanding between Britain and France as indispensable to European welfare and world peace. The

1 Memoranda by Crowe and Curzon, 26 and 28 Dec. 1921, W 13420, 13355/12716/17, FO 371/7000; *DBFP,* Ser. I, Vol. XVI, No. 768; Curzon to Lloyd George, 28 and 30 Dec., Lloyd George Papers, F/13/2/63-4.

2 *DBFP,* Ser. I, Vol. XIX, No. 1; MAE, Grande Bretagne, Vol. 69.

3 There are four versions of this memorandum: AJ 311(4 Jan.), AJ 321 (8 Jan.), AJ 323 (9 Jan.), and AJ 332 (probably 12 Jan. but published at the time and reprinted in Cmd 2169 of 1924 with the date 4 Jan.), CAB 29/35. Many of the differences between them are minor matters of wording; the chief differences of substance are described below.

problems facing the conference must be met as a whole, and the French anxiety about reparations and security, the British anxiety about unemployment and economic recovery, should be dealt with together. On reparations Britain was ready to recommend to the other Allies the arrangement discussed in London,[1] which was a sacrifice for her but would meet France's needs until a wider settlement could be reached. On security Britain was prepared to give France a 'guarantee that in the event of unprovoked German aggression the British Empire will put its forces at her side'. The undertaking could be given in the form of an alliance, but this would be contrary to British tradition and would not be generally supported. The British people 'would not willingly be committed to military liabilities for breaches of the peace in Eastern Europe, and they would not undertake responsibilities of any kind for the defence of countries in Eastern and Central Europe, in which their interest is necessarily small'. The alternative, which the British Government were ready to propose, and in which the Dominions would probably join, was a 'definite guarantee' that the British Empire would stand by France 'in the event of unprovoked aggression by Germany'.

The guarantee must, however, be accompanied by a complete understanding between the two countries and four problems must be cleared out of the way. The questions of Turkey and Tangier must be settled, France must co-operate in European reconstruction, and she must agree to the summoning of an economic conference at which all the countries of Europe would be represented, including Russia if she accepted certain conditions for the resumption of trade. And if France carried out her submarine programme, the resulting competition would 'react very seriously on British sentiment'.[2]

On 5 January Briand asked for an elucidation of some points of this memorandum, especially Turkey and Tangier. Lloyd George said that they should be discussed with Curzon, and asked what Briand thought about the guarantee. Briand, who had already suggested that the conditions which Russia was to be asked to accept should include an undertaking not to attack her neighbours, said that this undertaking and one by Germany might be included in a general European understanding. Lloyd George asked how a non-aggression undertaking would differ from the Covenant: as soon as Germany and Russia joined the League they would be bound to respect the frontiers laid down by the peace treaties. Briand replied that the

1 See *DBFP*, Ser. I, Vol. XV, No. 111.

2 AJ 311, CAB 29/35. The French wished to assimilate Tangier into Morocco: see *Survey of International Affairs, 1925*, Vol. II, 163-74.

Covenant was not sufficiently binding in form. He undertook to put his views into writing.[1]

The next two days were taken up with the conference. Resolutions were adopted on the summoning of an economic conference and conditions for participation.[2] The French memorandum on an understanding with Britain was given to Lloyd George on 8 January. The main points were, first, that the agreement must express the two countries' will to act together for the maintenance of peace; the guarantee should therefore be reciprocal. Secondly the guarantee should cover violations of the demilitarised zone of the Rhineland as well as attack on French territory; and the two countries should undertake to concert their action in case of violation of the military clauses of the Treaty of Versailles. In order to give effect to these provisions they should also undertake to regulate the strength of their armed forces by agreement. Thirdly, they should agree to act together on any question of a kind likely to endanger the general peace.[3]

When they met the same evening, Lloyd George suggested to Briand that his memorandum tended towards an alliance and said that while Britain was ready to do again what she had done in 1914 and to sign a declaration to that effect, she would not go farther. Briand replied that it was a purely defensive alliance limited to the case of attack by Germany. Lloyd George reiterated that Britain would not guarantee the general peace of Europe since to do so might involve her in enterprises which public opinion would not contemplate. Briand replied that his general understanding would not entail military obligations: he thought the non-aggression undertaking mentioned in the resolution on trading with Russia might be expanded into a general undertaking. Lloyd George said that Britain would work for such an undertaking, but it must include all the countries capable of disturbing peace, particularly Germany, Russia, Poland and Hungary. Briand agreed. He said that he wanted in the first place an 'accord entre deux' and following on that an 'accord générale'. In this way they might build up a powerful system to stop war, one more practical than the League. Lloyd George said that it would at any rate be a powerful system to reduce armaments.[4]

1 *DBFP,* Ser. I, Vol. XIX, No. 3; MAE, Grande Bretagne, Vol. 69; Suarez, *Briand,* Vol. V, 359-61.

2 See *DBFP,* Ser. I, Vol. XIX, No. 6, Appendix.

3 MAE, Grande Bretagne, Vol. 69; *Documents relatifs aux garanties,* No. 21; AJ 318, CAB 29/35; Cmd 2169 of 1924, No. 35.

4 *DBFP,* Ser. I, Vol. XIX, No. 10; MAE, Grande Bretagnè, Vol. 69; Suarez, *Briand,* Vol. V, 380-2.

After this conversation Lloyd George sent to London for the Cabinet a draft treaty and the third version of his memorandum.[1] The draft treaty provided for British assistance in the event of direct and unprovoked German aggression against the soil of France; for the two countries to concert together to protect Belgian neutrality in case of German aggression; and for consultation in case any breach of the demilitarisation of the Rhineland were threatened or Germany took military measures inconsistent with the Treaty of Versailles. The treaty was to last for ten years and was not to bind the Dominions unless they approved it.[2] In the revised memorandum, too, the offer of the guarantee was limited to 'unprovoked aggression against French soil'; and the non-aggression undertaking was mentioned as the possible basis for a wider system of European accord.[3] The Cabinet generally approved the draft treaty and feared that reciprocal guarantees might give France a say in the size of the British armed forces. They informed Lloyd George that they were opposed to the French proposal for extending the agreement but concurred in his proposal subject to the conditions for an understanding being realised: they attached particular importance to the submarine question.[4]

The third version of the British memorandum was given to the French delegation before the Cabinet's comments reached Cannes. At a meeting with Lloyd George in the afternoon of 10 January Briand said that he feared a detailed list of conditions would make a bad impression in France, and asked whether they could be expressed in more general terms. Lloyd George said that he was willing to drop Tangier if Curzon agreed, but British opinion, as the message from London now showed, would be sensitive about submarines. He suggested a sentence recommending joint discussion of naval programmes. He agreed with Briand that greater emphasis might be laid on Britain's vital interest in the safety of France.[5]

As yet Briand had received no answer from Paris about the proposed

1 The second version (AJ 321, CAB 29/35) was drawn up on 8 January, but there is no evidence that it was communicated to the French. In it the forecast of Dominion participation in a guarantee to France was reduced to a forecast that Dominion opinion would 'support that of Great Britain in giving such a guarantee'. This version alone of the four included an offer to co-operate in negotiating an agreement between the powers on lines analogous to those of the Pacific treaty.

2 British delegation, Cannes, to FO, 9 Jan. 1922, W 251/50/17, FO 371/8249.

3 AJ 323, CAB 29/35.

4 C 1 (22), 10 Jan. 1922, CAB 23/29; FO to British delegation, Cannes, 10 Jan., W 251/50/17, FO 371/8249.

5 Grigg to Massigli, 10 Jan. 1922, MAE, Grande Bretagne, Vol. 69; minute by Grigg, 10 Jan., AJ 328, CAB 29/35; *DBFP*, Ser. I, Vol. XIX, No. 17.

temporary moratorium for Germany. Opinion in Paris had become roused by reports of the discussions on reparations, the economic conference, trade with Russia, and the Anglo-French pact; and Briand received telegrams of protest from several political groups. On the morning of 10 January the French Cabinet expressed doubts about Russia being invited to the economic conference, decided not to agree to a moratorium for Germany without adequate guarantees, and agreed that an Anglo-French pact would be unacceptable if it led to other pacts in which Germany might be able to discuss the Treaty of Versailles – in other words Briand's idea of including Germany in a wider grouping. Telegraphing to Briand in the afternoon the President, Millerand, added that ministers realised that these decisions would not make the negotiations with Lloyd George easier, but the two memoranda revealed differences which made a rapid decision unlikely and the questions would have to be discussed in Paris. Briand replied that there had never been any question of his signing a pact without the Government's approval.[1]

On the next day further communications from Paris made Briand decide that he must go back and confront Millerand and his colleagues. He held his own with the Cabinet, but rather than face a crisis with the President with uncertain support he resigned on 12 January without having been defeated in the Chamber. This brought the Cannes conference to an end. It is not certain whether Briand saw the final version of the British memorandum or the revised draft of the treaty.[2] The terms of this were identical with those of 9 January except that Belgium was not mentioned and provision was made for renewal. In the memorandum only the submarine question was now treated as a condition for an understanding, and the proposal for consultation on naval programmes was added. Tangier was not mentioned: the other conditions appeared as wishes.[3]

1 Suarez, *Briand,* Vol. V, 388-90, 393-5. The exchanges between Millerand and Briand printed by Suarez show that they differed primarily on Russia and reparations, and that the Anglo-French pact was a subsidiary issue, Briand was not laying stress on it in order to justify concessions to Lloyd George on other points. A further blow to Briand's already weakened position was the publication in the press of photographs of him, Lloyd George and the Italian Prime Minister, Bonomi, on the golf course at Cannes, in which Briand, who had never played golf, was made to appear in a humiliating position of tutelage: Austen Chamberlain, *Down the Years* (London, 1935), 180-1; Lord Riddell, *Intimate Diary of the Peace Conference and After* (London, 1933), 347.

2 CP 3623, CAB 24/132. In Cmd 2169 of 1924 the draft treaty (No. 38) is said to have been handed to Briand on 12 January; but he had left Cannes on the previous day. The copy in MAE, Grande Bretagne, Vol. 69, is dated 11 January.

3 CP 3622, CAB 24/132; Cmd 2169 of 1924, No. 34, misdated 4 January. The final British memorandum and draft treaty were published in the press on 12 and 14 January.

The reason why Belgium was not mentioned in the second draft of the pact was that it was now proposed to conclude a separate Anglo-Belgian treaty. Britain's policy towards Belgium immediately after the war was uncertain. Her interest was in no way diminished, but her attitude to Belgium's international status was doubtful. Shortly before the armistice, in September 1918, the Belgian Government had announced that their country intended to seek complete independence and sovereignty, free of the restrictions imposed by the treaties of 1839, and the British Government acknowledged this desire.[1] But when it came, in the summer of 1919, to revising the 1839 treaties the Belgian Government were anxious to obtain a new guarantee from France and Britain, or at least an interim one to last until fresh arrangements were made by the League of Nations.[2] In order not to appear the cause of breakdown of these negotiations (which were complicated by Belgian-Dutch disagreement) the Cabinet reluctantly agreed to give a guarantee for not more than five years provided that Belgium would undertake to maintain neutrality.[3]

It was never made clear what this stipulation meant. Curzon told the Belgian Ambassador, Baron Moncheur, that military undertakings would be unpopular with Parliament and would need some return. But as Crowe (who was at the time in charge of the remainder of the British delegation in Paris) pointed out, a neutral Belgium could not take part in the military occupation of the Rhineland and might not be able to carry out obligations under the Covenant; and even voluntary neutrality smacked to the Belgians of 'servitude'.[4] Rather than accept the condition, therefore, the Belgian Government decided to drop the request for an interim guarantee: the British accepted the decision with relief, and did not explain their attitude further.[5]

A possible reason for the desire for Belgian neutrality, and one which could not have been publicly stated, was a fear that Belgium might fall under German influence. Such a fear, expressed in the Political Intelligence Department of the Foreign Office just before the armistice, had led to the conclusion that unless Germany became a willing partner in the new international organisation which it was hoped to set up, it would be too dangerous to allow Belgium to

1 Cf. *DBFP,* Ser. I, Vol. V. No. 302.

2 Op. cit. *passim.*

3 Conference of Ministers, No. 13, 2 Dec. 1919, CAB 23/27; *DBFP,* Ser. I, Vol. V. Nos. 281, 282, 308.

4 Op. cit. Nos. 286, 302, 335

5 Op. cit. No. 343.

decide her own status and choose her own friends.[1] But the British Government made no attempt to influence Belgian policy or secure Belgian good will either by giving the interim guarantee or by joining in military talks. The possibility of joint military plans was first discussed by the French and Belgian Governments in the summer of 1919, and the Belgians enquired whether the British would take part.[2] The matter then hung fire, partly because of the negotiations over the revision of the 1839 treaties and partly because of Franco-Belgian disagreement about Luxembourg. An invitation was delivered in London on 2 February 1920, but the talks were still delayed.[3] On 2 June, the French and Belgian Governments having reached agreement on the Luxembourg railways, the invitation was renewed. Later in the month the Belgian Foreign Minister, Hymans, asked Crowe to impress on Curzon the importance of an Anglo-Belgian understanding but said that there was no intention of asking for a British commitment.[4]

The War Office favoured taking part in the talks and Chamberlain advocated a treaty undertaking to Belgium; but the Cabinet agreed that they were not prepared to contemplate a treaty and that military talks should not take place in advance of agreements between governments. No formal reply was sent, but at the Spa conference in July Lloyd George told the Belgian Prime Minister of the decision.[5] The Franco-Belgian staff talks then took place without British participation and resulted in a military agreement.[6]

Thereafter Belgium did not feature in discussions of a renewed guarantee to France, and appeared merely as an object in the first draft of the Anglo-French treaty at Cannes. When the Foreign Minister, Jaspar, asked Curzon for information about the Anglo-French talks and was shown the draft, he at once asked why no guarantee for his country was envisaged. Curzon replied that this was an Anglo-French treaty, that Belgium had her military agreement with

1 GT 6213, 4 Nov. 1918, CAB 24/69.

2 *DBFP*, Ser. I, Vol. V, Nos. 108, 211.

3 Cambon to Curzon, 2 Feb. 1920, Curzon Papers, MSS. Eur. F.112/243; CID paper 240-B, CAB 4/7; *DBFP*, Ser. I, Vol. XII, Nos. 6, 7, 9, 11; *Documents diplomatiques belges 1920-1940. La Politique de sécurité extérieure,* hereafter cited as *DDB*, Vol. I (Brussels, 1964), No. 141.

4 *DBFP*, Ser. I, Vol. IX, No. 501; Vol. XII, No. 23; *DDB*, Vol. I, Nos. 153, 157-9, 161, 163-5.

5 CID papers 240-B, 244-B, 246-B, CAB 4/7; C 38(20), 30 Jan. 1920, CAB 23/21; *DBFP*, Ser. I, Vol. XII, No. 11, n. 2; *DDB*, Vol. I, Nos. 164-5, 169, 172-3; Jones, *Whitehall Diary*, Vol. I, 115-7. The General Staff again advocated an alliance with Belgium and France in August 1920 as a way of influencing both countries' policy towards Germany: CP 1782, CAB 24/110.

6 *DDB*, Vol. I, No. 175.

France, and Britain had not joined in it because the Belgian Government had been unwilling to undertake to maintain neutrality; and he asked whether Jaspar would prefer that Belgium should not be mentioned.[1]

Curzon concluded from this conversation that if it were desired to extend a guarantee to Belgium a hint to the Belgian Ministers would elicit a request. There does not seem to be any record of the question being discussed by the British delegation at Cannes; but the hint must have been given and the request made, for on 13 January Curzon, with Lloyd George's approval, agreed on a text with Jaspar and his Prime Minister Col. Theunis. The Belgians proposed a guarantee against direct attack by Germany only. The text agreed contained two short articles. The first pledged Britain to come to Belgium's assistance in the event of direct and unprovoked attack on Belgian territory. The second read: 'Belgium will employ all her military and air forces to defend her frontiers in the event of any attack or violation of her territory. She will refrain from concluding agreements or arrangements incompatible with the present engagement'.[2]

Although not forewarned about the idea of guaranteeing Belgium, the Cabinet approved the proposal after Lloyd George and Curzon returned from Cannes, on condition that it was made plain that the guarantee applied only to aggression by Germany and that the Dominions were excluded and the duration of the treaty limited as in the treaty with France.[3] By the time these amendments reached Brussels the Belgian Government had approved the Cannes draft, but they did not like the provision binding Belgium not to make agreements which might be inconsistent with the treaty. It was clearly meant to secure something like a position of neutrality for Belgium, but the kind of arrangement that might be objectionable proved difficult to explain.[4] The Belgians therefore proposed to delete the article and instead state in the preamble that Belgium was determined to resist any German aggression with all the means in her power and not to conclude any agreement conflicting with this determination. By 20 February the pact had been agreed, subject to Cabinet approval and one or two

1 Memorandum by Curzon, 10 Jan. 1922, Curzon Papers, MSS. Eur. F.112/243.

2 Curzon to FO, 14 Jan. 1922; FO to Grahame (Brussels), 20 Jan., W 468, 613/432/4, FO 371/8239; *DDB*, Vol. I, No. 204.

3 C 2(22), 18 Jan. 1922, CAB 23/29; FO to Grahame, 19 Jan., W 543/432/4, FO 371/8239.

4 FO to Grahame, 20 Jan.; 1922; Grahame to FO, 21 Jan., 24 Jan.; FO to Grahame, 27 Jan.; Grahame to FO, 30 Jan.; FO to Grahame, 4 Feb., W 613, 710, 806, 964/432/4, FO 371/8239; *DDB*, Vol. I, Nos. 204, 211, 212, 218, 220.

matters of wording which depended on the final form of the French treaty.[1] But no further progress was made. The Belgian Government certainly wanted the treaty although there was some doubt about Belgian opinion as reflected in the press; but the failure of the Anglo-French negotiations put an end to the Belgian treaty as well.[2]

There was no question of a guarantee for Italy; but the Italian representatives at Cannes were nervous, as always, of any exclusive Anglo-French understanding. In reassuring the Prime Minister Lloyd George belittled the Anglo-French pact and, it appears, indicated that he regarded it as only a stepping-stone to the projected non-aggression undertaking and a means of getting France to the economic conference.[3]

Disagreements over the treaty, January-March 1922

Briand's fall, and its circumstances, was a bad omen for the Genoa conference. President Millerand was strongly opposed to the recognition of Soviet Russia and the new Prime Minister (and former President of the Republic) Poincaré was known both to dislike conferences, where, he considered, it was always France who made sacrifices, and to be wedded to the integral fulfilment of the Treaty of Versailles, the terms of which he had at the time of the peace conference thought inadequate for the protection of France. Poincaré was a Lorrainer and a lawyer, who studied his brief, mastered the legal arguments, and deployed them relentlessly with the object of convincing by forceful repetition rather than by persuasion. When vital matters were at stake he preferred to have everything cut and dried in a contract. He was in practically every respect poles apart from Lloyd George, and from Briand. But the latter at this time, although personally more agreeable to the British, did not display the vision and fertility of imagination that were to be such outstanding features of his tenure of the Quai d'Orsay in the later twenties. Foretastes of his later policy may be discerned, but in 1921 Briand was constrained by public opinion, the temper of the 'bleu horizon' Chamber of Deputies elected in 1919, and Millerand's ambition to be an active President.[4] However on the Anglo-

1 Grahame to FO, 9 Feb. 1922; FO to Grahame, 13 Feb.; Moncheur to Curzon, 20 Feb., W 1325, 1356, 1436, 1671/432/4, FO 371/8239; *DDB,* Vol. I, Nos. 223, 225, 226.

2 Grahame to FO, 7 and 28 Mar. 1922; FO to Grahame, 15 Jun., W 2263, 2795, 4959/432/4, FO 371/8239; *DDB,* Vol. I, Nos. 228-9.

3 *DBFP,* Ser. I, Vol. XIX, Nos. 2, 11, 18; AJ 312, 337, CAB 29/35. See also *I Documenti diplomatici italiani,* 7th series, hereafter cited as *DDI,* Vol. III, No. 70.

4 Suarez's biography *Briand. Sa via, son oeuvre* is indispensable. There is no comparable biography of Poincaré: Jacques Chastenet, *Raymond Poincaré*

French negotiations Poincaré's position, allowing for the difference in tone, was not very different from that of the French memorandum of 8 January. In a long talk with Lloyd George, who stopped in Paris on 14 January on his way home, Poincaré agreed that there ought to be a general liquidation of problems between the two governments, but said that he feared publication of the draft treaty would make things more difficult. He would need time to look into the questions of Turkey and Tangier, and would not commit himself to an early meeting with Curzon and the Italian Foreign Minister Torretta. He would prefer to postpone discussion of the treaty until the other questions were settled, but his preliminary view was that the guarantee must be reciprocal and a military convention was most important.

On this last point there ensued a lengthy and at times evidently rather heated argument. Poincaré said that the treaty would not have much value without a military convention. Lloyd George replied that a convention could only relate to such forces as Britain had actually in being whereas her real strength was millions of trained men who would keep their value for as long as Germany's reserves of trained manpower could be considered dangerous. A guarantee to come to the aid of France with all Britain's forces would serve the most important purpose, which was to deter Germany from thoughts of revenge. Furthermore, although the Dominions might adhere to a guarantee, they would certainly not sign a military agreement or undertake in advance to supply any forces. Poincaré said that all that was necessary was joint plans made and kept under review by the General Staffs, and some reference in the treaty. Where, he asked, would France stand if Britain disarmed altogether? Lloyd George did not answer: he merely asked what difference a mention in the treaty would make. The reserves, their equipment, the pledge, would be there. He would not bind the Government to maintain any particular strength in peacetime. 'If the word of the British people was not sufficient for France, he feared the draft treaty must be withdrawn. The British people would honour their pledge, if France were attacked, with the whole of their strength, but they would never bind themselves by military conventions as to the forces which they would maintain in present conditions during a time of peace'.

Poincaré replied that it was a question of knowing whether the guarantee would be effective. If France had no idea of the strength Britain would maintain, how could she calculate what she

(Paris, 1948), is short. Poincaré's own articles in the *Revue des deux mondes* between March 1920 and September 1921, reprinted in his *Histoire politique, Chroniques de quinzaine,* 2 vols. (Paris, 1920, 1921), illustrate his attitude at the time. Raoul Persil, *Alexandre Millerand* (Paris, 1949), is also brief.

would have to maintain herself? Without a military convention the guarantee would be illusory. If this was Poincaré's view, said Lloyd George, he had only to communicate it officially and there would be no treaty. The French people must judge their own interests, but if they were not satisfied with Britain's pledge there was no possible basis of understanding.

At this Poincaré retreated slightly, saying that France did not doubt Britain's word: she knew that even without a treaty Britain would do all she could. But how could France measure her own forces if she did not know what the situation would be if war broke out? Lloyd George answered that the strength of the British Empire had been demonstrated and it could be deployed more quickly than that of Germany, for the Empire had the equipment and Germany had not. But it seemed preposterous to be talking about military conventions now when Germany was disarmed. If a German revival made a military convention necessary Britain would not hesitate to conclude one, but he could not understand difficulties being made now.

Lloyd George then said that he was particularly anxious to know whether the change of government in France betokened a change of policy. No, said Poincaré, the aims would be the same although some nuances might be different.[1]

A few days later Poincaré repeated to Curzon, who went to Paris to talk about Turkey and Tangier, that the pact could follow and set the seal on the elimination of these questions.[2] However he hoped that the problems could be dealt with quickly, and a new draft of the treaty was sent to St-Aulaire on 23 January. It provided for a reciprocal obligation to give assistance in case of unprovoked aggression against either country; violation of the demilitarisation of the Rhineland was to be considered as an act of aggression; the two countries were to concert together in case of any threat of violation, or breach of the military, naval, or air clauses of the Treaty of Versailles; there would be constant staff contacts; and the two governments would consult on all questions of a nature to endanger peace or jeopardise the order established by the peace treaties, and would examine together measures to ensure a quick, peaceful and equitable solution. The treaty was to last for thirty years and to be renewable.[3]

1 ICP 235A, CAB 29/35; MAE, Grande Bretagne, Vol. 69; *Documents relatifs aux garanties,* No. 23.

2 *DBFP,* Ser. I, Vol. XVII, No. 508.

3 Q d'O to St-Aulaire, 23 Jan. 1922, MAE, Grande Bretagne, Vol. 70; *Documents relatifs aux garanties,* No. 23; W 963/50/17, FO 371/8250; Cmd 2169 of 1924, No. 39.

Handing the draft to Curzon St-Aulaire said that the request for a military convention had been dropped: all that was wanted was regular staff conversations and a mention in the treaty to impress the Germans. Curzon said that the Cabinet might consider a reciprocal guarantee if it were a matter of self-respect for France; but there would be serious objection to treating violations of Articles 42 and 43 of the Treaty of Versailles as aggression, and the clause about consultation on questions of a nature to endanger peace was ambiguous. Asked how Poincaré proposed to discuss the other questions which it had been agreed should be settled, St-Aulaire said that he thought Poincaré hoped the pact could be concluded before the Genoa conference. Curzon said that he doubted whether there would be time: he preferred, as he had thought Poincaré did, to solve the other questions first.[1]

St-Aulaire followed up this conversation with some written explanations. One paper developed the argument for consultation in case of a threat to peace. It was true that Germany was unlikely for many years to be able to attack Britain or France directly; but there was little doubt that she would invade Poland or Czechoslovakia, or absorb Austria, if she thought she could do so with impunity, and success would give her new strength which would be turned against the west later. France did not expect Britain to undertake obligations in the east but peace would remain precarious unless the two countries undertook to facilitate collective action by the League of Nations.[2] Another paper went into some detail about violations of Articles 42 and 43 of the Treaty of Versailles. For example a German request for permission to send troops into the demilitarised zone to deal with disorder would be neither a violation nor a threat of one. But signs of a German intention to send troops in after permission had been refused would be a threat of violation and the two governments would have to consult. And if German forces actually went in, either without asking permission or after it had been refused, it would be a violation and the *casus foederis* would arise. Such a provision was essential if the protection afforded by the demilitarisation of the Rhineland was to be real. In addition St-Aulaire wrote that the French Government were now prepared to transfer the reference to staff talks and the undertaking to consult in case of threats to peace from the treaty to separate notes, and to accept twenty years for the duration of the treaty.[3]

1 FO to Hardinge, 28 Jan. 1922, W 937/50/17, FO 371/8250; Cmd 2169 of 1924. No. 40; St-Aulaire to Q d'O, 27 Jan., MAE, Grande Bretagne, Vol. 70; *Documents relatifs aux garanties,* No. 24.

2 St-Aulaire to Curzon, 28 Jan. 1922, W 963/50/17, FO 371/8250.

3 St-Aulaire to Curzon, 1 Feb. 1922, W 1162, 1695/50/17, FO 371/8250;

The connexion between the west and the east, and violations of the demilitarised zone, were to be the subject of much negotiation in 1925. But at this stage Foreign Office officials showed no inclination to discuss them. The example of Germany sending in troops to quell disorder was not happily chosen if the object of the explanation was to reassure the British. The three stages were almost exactly what had happened over the disorders in the Ruhr in April 1920, when the French retaliatory occupation of Frankfurt and Darmstadt had aroused the sharp disapproval of the British Government. But although Lord Kilmarnock, the High Commissioner in the Rhineland, recognised the validity of the French wish to ensure as far as possible that another war was not fought on French soil, his suggestion of differentiating between petty violations and the beginning of aggression was not followed up; and on the east it was merely noted that Parliamentary and public opinion would not contemplate an Anglo-Polish pact.[1]

In the mean time two of the Dominion Governments had sent their views on the proposed pacts with France and Belgium. As might have been expected after the 1921 Imperial Conference the New Zealand Government favoured them and the South African Government did not. Smuts telegraphed that while he approved the British efforts for European reconstruction he thought an alliance too high a price to pay for French co-operation. The South African Parliament would not approve such treaties and then the problem would arise of some parts of the Empire being bound and others not. He did not believe that France needed a guarantee. Still worse, the efforts at reconstruction might fail and then Britain would be left allied to 'the state whose present reactionary policy fills with alarm both Europe and America and creates special danger for the British Empire'.[2]

Lloyd George's initial expression of confidence that the Dominions would join in a guarantee had quickly been modified into a forecast that they would approve a British guarantee. Even this was now shown to be doubtful. In Parliament too debates in the first week of February not only revealed much objection to anything going beyond the terms of the 1919 guarantee; there were sections

Q d'O to St-Aulaire, 30 Jan., 1 Feb., MAE, Grande Bretagne, Vol. 70; *Documents relatifs aux garanties,* No. 25; Cmd 2169 of 1924, No. 41.

1 Max Muller (Warsaw) to FO, 26 Jan. 1922; Kilmarnock (Coblenz) to FO, 10 Feb., W 1128, 1508/50/17, FO 371/8250.

2 CO 2511, CO 532/244; CO 3077, CO 532/215; CO 2298, 2299, 3568, 4701, CO 532/207. The Australian and Canadian Governments do not seem to have sent any comments.

of opinion, including the chief supporters of the League of Nations like Lord Robert Cecil, who were opposed to any guarantee at all.[1] After these debates Curzon warned St-Aulaire that the Cabinet were very unlikely to wish to go beyond the scope of the 1919 treaty, and in particular the French must expect refusal of their case on violations of the demilitarised zone.[2]

Curzon himself recommended to the Cabinet rejection of almost all the French proposals. The suggestion that the guarantee should apply in case of 'attack on France' (instead of, as in the British draft, 'direct attack on the soil of France') was undesirable because it would widen the obligation and lead to difficulties in deciding what constituted an attack. Curzon thought that British opinion would not be willing to treat the Rhineland as though it were French territory or to be bound to go to war if it were violated, and he disliked the idea of overriding the common obligation of all the signatories of the Treaty of Versailles expressed in Article 44. He was opposed to mentioning staff conversations even in a separate exchange of notes, because it would imply the existence of military commitments. The proposal about consultation was in some ways desirable because it would bind the French, but looked at more closely it seemed to be an attempt to involve Britain all over Europe and indeed to set up a kind of Anglo-French hegemony which Britain did not want and other countries, notably Italy, would resent. The only points on which Curzon recommended meeting French wishes were reciprocity of the guarantee and the duration of the treaty, as to which he admitted that from the French point of view ten years was too short.[3]

Curzon advised keeping the pact in suspense, as a means of pressure on the French Government, until the other problems were nearer solution. Poincaré was indeed anxious to see the pact concluded, and was willing to abandon a good many of his wishes over its terms.[4] But he was not prepared to fall in with British wishes all round for the sake of the pact; and even if he had been willing it would not have been easy to select the best area on which to make concessions, for while Lloyd George's main concern was the Genoa conference Curzon's was Turkey.[5] Progress on both questions was slow. During another

1 See *HC Deb.*, 5th ser., Vol. 150, cols. 8-226. *Parliamentary Debates, House of Lords,* hereafter cited as *HL Deb.*, 5th ser., Vol. 49, cols. 4-122.

2 FO to Hardinge, 9 Feb. 1922, C 2000/458/62, FO 371/7418; Cmd 2169 of 1924, No. 42; *Documents relatifs aux garanties,* No. 26.

3 CP 3760, 17 Feb. 1922, CAB 24/133; part in Cmd 2169 of 1924, No. 44.

4 Q d'O, to St-Aulaire, 23 and 30 Jan. 1922, MAE, Grande Bretagne, Vol. 70; *DDB,* Vol. I, Nos. 216, 217; St-Aulaire, *Confession d'un vieux diplomate,* 609, 616-7.

5 St-Aulaire to Q d'O, 27 Jan., 15 Feb. 1922, MAE, Grande Bretagne, Vol. 70.

wrangle on Turkey at the end of January Hardinge felt it necessary to warn Poincaré that no one in England was more friendly to France than Lloyd George and Curzon, and there was some resentment in London at the French making 'conditions' on the pact instead of accepting Britain's handsome gesture.[1] The next meeting of Foreign Ministers was delayed by an Italian governmental crisis. Poincaré was also doing his best to limit the scope of the Genoa conference by excluding discussion of the peace treaties, reparations, or disarmament, and laying down more conditions for the recognition of Soviet Russia. His desire to do everything by correspondence was eventually overcome, however, and he agreed to meet Lloyd George at Boulogne on 25 February. Here Lloyd George accused Poincaré of trying to wreck the conference and said that if necessary Britain would go ahead without France; but he ended by accepting some of Poincaré's conditions and agreeing that the conference should be postponed until April. The pact was not discussed in detail.[2]

There was no further discussion of the pact in the remaining weeks before the Genoa conference. Although at the end of March British ministers were still thinking of the treaty as a possible means of pressure on France, the objects to be achieved thereby were becoming less rather than more definite and the Cabinet did not consider Curzon's memorandum. On 18 March Curzon made it clear to St-Aulaire that there would be no decision before the summer and the ambassador was left reflecting that if the pact were not rescued before Genoa it was unlikely, whatever the outcome of the conference, to succeed thereafter.[3]

The end of the Anglo-French negotiations, April-August 1922

The Genoa conference did not advance either the reconstruction of Europe or the cause of Anglo-French understanding. Poincaré would not attend and kept the French delegation on a tight telegraphic rein. He had refused to allow discussion of reparations, but there were

1 *DBFP*, Ser. I, Vol. XVII, No. 516.

2 Op. cit., Vol. XIX, No. 34. Anglo-French correspondence, 5-14 Feb., in Cmd 1742 of 1922, *Correspondence between His Majesty's Government and the French Government respecting the Genoa Conference*. Beneš, the Czechoslovak Foreign Minister, acted as an intermediary: S 42, 43, 45, 46, CAB 23/36; Beneš to Lloyd George, 22 Feb., Lloyd George Papers, F/49/9/3; aide-mémoire from Beneš, 22 Feb., C 2931/458/62, FO 371/7421; minute by Grigg, 24 Feb., Lloyd George Papers, F/86/1/19; Piotr S. Wandycz, *France and her Eastern Allies* (Minneapolis, 1962), 257.

3 C 19(22), C 21(22), CAB 23/29; FO to Hardinge, 19 Mar. 1922, W 2448/50/17, FO 371/8251 (part in Cmd 2169 of 1924, No. 45); St-Aulaire to Q d'O, 19 Mar., MAE, Grande Bretagne, Vol. 71 (part in *Documents relatifs aux garanties*, No. 31).

informal talks with German experts. On the central subject of the conference, the western powers failed to reach agreement with the Russians on a settlement by which Soviet Russia would get recognition and help for reconstruction through an international consortium in return for acknowledging Tsarist debts and obligations to former property owners. Instead, in the middle of the conference, the Russian and German delegates signed the Treaty of Rapalle, which was a blow to Lloyd George and greatly angered the French.[1] A minor casualty of the conference was the proposed general non-aggression undertaking. Lloyd George took with him a draft treaty, which was explained to the British Empire delegation as involving no obligations beyond those of the Covenant but as being thought likely to create conditions in which measures for reviving trade would have a chance of success. But even preliminary discussion with representatives of other countries revealed difficulties about unrecognised frontiers and respect for existing treaties; and at the end all that remained was what Hankey described as 'a sort of Truce of Non-Aggression' in the resolutions providing for further negotiations with the Russians at The Hague in the summer.[2]

The outcome of the conference and the prospect of a new crisis over reparations at the end of May impelled fresh consideration in the Foreign Office of Anglo-French relations and the guarantee. In a long paper on the reparation situation S.P. Waterlow, a member of the Central Department, wrote that British policy had been to apply the Treaty of Versailles 'in a spirit at once just and reasonable - to

1 Proceedings of the conference in *DBFP,* Ser. I, Vol. XIX. A contemporary account is J. Saxon Mills, *The Genoa Conference* (London, 1922). On Rapallo see G. Rosenfeld, *Sowjetrussland und Deutschland 1917-22* (Berlin, 1960); K. Rosenbaum, *Community of Fate. German-Soviet Diplomatic Relations 1922-1928* (Syracuse, N.Y., 1965); Theodor Schieder, 'Die Entstehungsgeschichte des Rapallo-Vertrags', *Historische Zeitschrift* 204 (1967), 545-609; H.G. Linke, *Deutsch-sowjetische Beziehungen bis Rapallo* (Cologne, 1970). Some of the papers in *Rapallo und die friedliche Koexistenz,* ed. A. Anderle (Berlin, 1963), give a modern Soviet view. Although Rathenau was stampeded into signing the treaty by reports that the western powers and the Russians were on the point of agreement, this was not the case and recent eastern European works do not claim that it was. Nor do the British files on the conference (principally CAB 29/95, CAB 31, FO 371/8185-98) provide any evidence for the story that Lloyd George either knew of the treaty in advance or approved of it.

2 Memorandum by Hurst, 16 Mar. 1922; Crowe to Hankey, 24 Mar.; Hankey to Crowe, 25 Mar., C 4356, 4543/458/62, FO 371/7423; BED 74th conference, 10 Apr.; BED 285, CAB 31/1; Gregory to Crowe, 23 Apr.; FO to Gregory, 27 Apr., N 3952/646/38, FO 371/8188; S G 17, 23, 25, 27, CAB 31/5; memorandum by Beneš, 26 Apr., C 8025/458/62, FO 371/7423; Lloyd George Papers, F/199/3/5; Wigram to Waterlow, 2 May, C 6652/458/62, FO 371/7431; Hankey to Chamberlain, 11 May, N 4775/646/38, FO 371/8191; *DBFP,* Ser. I, Vol. XIX, No. 138, annex.

permit that economic recovery of Germany which is a necessity for ourselves, and at the same time to secure the disarmament which is equally a necessity if French fears are to be allayed'. The task called for wisdom and patience; there had been many difficulties; but Genoa was meant to resolve them and to be the culmination of the policy of turning the Versailles settlement into a 'real peace'. The Rapallo treaty and the current deadlock over reparations, however, were the negation of the whole of British policy. There was bound to be a strong reaction to Poincaré's recent speech threatening unilateral French action: 'It is intolerable that the intransigence of one Power, whose military strength dominates the Continent, and whose aerial and submarine projects are a potential threat to ourselves, should frustrate our efforts to bring Russia back into the economic orbit of Europe, to restore the general commercial and financial conditions that are vital to the British Empire, and to avoid any return to that European Group system that provided the conditions for the last war'. If Genoa failed, and if Germany were driven to despair of a practical reparation settlement, she and Soviet Russia would be cemented in a union of hostility to western Europe. Perhaps it was time to make it clear to France that if she insisted on her own policy Britain must refuse further responsibility and dissolve the partnership. Yet there were strong objections to a breach with France. It would bring little moral advantage, for Britain was equally responsible for imposing the reparation burden, or even more so, for it was Britain's doing that pensions had been included; and her record over the lapse of the 1919 guarantee was not good. New methods ought to be tried: but all that Waterlow could suggest was the appointment of a politically weightier figure as British representative on the Reparation Commission and a more positive attitude towards the League.

Sir William Tyrrell, the Assistant Under-Secretary of State, had a more sweeping proposal. He was convinced that there would not be peace until they arrived at a comprehensive settlement in which France would undertake to pursue a 'sane' policy in Europe and the Near East in return for security on her eastern frontier. He would begin by concluding a guarantee pact to which Belgium and Italy, and eventually Germany, would be asked to adhere. He would meet French demands about Poland by 'constituting the integrity of the countries and frontiers created by the Treaty of Versailles as a special charge on the functions of the League of Nations, and, in order to enable the latter to discharge such a task, I would, jointly with France, make a declaration that for that purpose the two countries would place at the disposal of the League all their resources for the enforcement of its decisions'.

Curzon liked neither suggestion. Waterlow's proposals he regarded as thin, Tyrrell's as putting the cart before the horse: France was to behave badly everywhere and Britain was to 'run round and conclude our Treaty of Guarantee and all will be well', all the more if the frontiers created by the peace treaties were to be placed under the protection of the League, which had been unable to get the Poles to leave Vilna and was unwilling to take responsibility for protecting Christians in Anatolia. It was no use asking him to put a new policy to the Cabinet unless it was 'practical, practicable (two different things) and coherent'.[1] Revising his paper to meet Curzon's objections, Waterlow strengthened the argument for an Anglo-French pact: if, he now wrote, Britain had stated, when the United States Senate rejected the Treaty of Versailles, that the British guarantee would be maintained, it would have paid a hundred times over. As it was the French had reason to feel that they had been led into a 'characteristic British trap' as regards the security of their eastern frontier. The pact ought to be taken up again and not postponed until a settlement had been reached on other questions: it was putting the cart before the horse to aim at the periphery rather than the central question. Waterlow then combined part of Tyrrell's proposal with his own concern over reparations. Since France could not give up her demand for immediate financial relief he suggested, in addition to renewing the offer of the pact and combining it with a complex of agreements including Belgium and Italy and eventually Germany, offering to write down Britain's reparation claim and perhaps offering to reduce France's debt to Britain in return for a reasonable settlement of the whole reparation problem.[2]

Curzon did not see the revised paper: he was ill for some weeks in May and June and away from the Foreign Office. It would hardly have convinced him, running counter as it did to his own attitude and that of the Cabinet. Here the line still was to keep the pact in reserve, although Lloyd George was no longer confident about its effectiveness as a means of pressure on the French. At the end of a long discussion of reparations on 23 May Churchill asked whether fear of losing it could be used to induce the French to co-operate. Lloyd George replied that he did not think Poincaré set much store by the treaty.[3]

It was Poincaré who took the next step. As Hardinge supposed, he regarded the German-Soviet treaty as an additional reason for concluding the pact, and at the beginning of May he instructed St-Aulaire to take

1 Memorandum by Waterlow, 28 Apr. 1922, with minutes by Tyrrell and Curzon, C 6200/6200/18, FO 371/7567.

2 Memorandum by Waterlow, 9 May 1922, C 6875/6200/18, FO 371/7567.

3 C 29(22), CAB 23/30.

up the negotiations again.[1] The ambassador at first demurred, but on 30 May he called on Balfour, who was acting in Curzon's place, and suggested that the other subjects being discussed between the two countries need not hold up consideration of the treaty.[2] Balfour would not give an immediate answer, but it was soon decided to inform Poincaré that the Government stood by their decision that outstanding questions must be settled before a treaty was concluded. The outstanding questions now included European reconstruction, peace with Turkey, and Tangier. The prospect of an early settlement, Hardinge was told to say, seemed far from hopeful, largely owing to the attitude of the French Government, and no useful purpose would be served by discussing the treaty at present.[3]

On receiving this communication Poincaré told Hardinge that the inclusion of European reconstruction in the list of questions to be settled was a means of escape for Britain from proceeding with the treaty, since the French position on negotiations with Russia was well known. Poincaré also indicated that he would not regard the British terms of the treaty as worth paying for since they added nothing to what Britain would have to do in her own interest.[4] He had by now evidently given up hope of getting what he regarded as suitable terms. He visited London in the middle of June, but the treaty was not mentioned.[5] On 4 July St-Aulaire read to Balfour the French reply. The French Government, it said, were ready to take part in a conference on Tangier and were acting with the British in seeking a settlement with Turkey. But to make the pact conditional on European reconstruction was tantamount to postponing it indefinitely. The original condition, that France should co-operate in calling the economic conference, had been met: the realisation of reconstruction was another matter, and no one could say how and when it might come about.[6]

1 Q d'O to St-Aulaire, 2 May 1922, MAE, Grande Bretagne, Vol. 71; *Documents relatifs aux garanties,* Nos. 32-3; Hardinge to FO, 30 Apr., C 5922/458/62, FO 371/7427.

2 St-Aulaire to Q d'O, 16 and 19 May 1922; Q d'O to St-Aulaire, 19 May; St-Aulaire to Q d'O, 21 and 31 May, MAE, Grande Bretagne, Vol. 71; *Documents relatifs aux garanties,* No. 36; FO to Hardinge, 30 May, W 4880/50/17, FO 371/8251; Cmd 2169 of 1924, No. 46.

3 Crowe to Curzon, 2 Jun. 1922, Curzon Papers, MSS. Eur. F.112/223; FO to Hardinge, 13 Jun., W 4880/50/17, FO 371/8251; Cmd 2169 of 1924, No. 47.

4 Hardinge to FO, 16 Jun. 1922, W 4995/50/17, FO 371/8251; Cmd 2169, No. 48; Q d'O to St-Aulaire, 28 Jun., MAE, Grande Bretagne, Vol. 71.

5 ICP 249C, CAB 29/96.

6 FO to Hardinge, 4 Jul. 1922, W 5657/5657/50, FO 371/8300; Cmd 2169, Nos. 49, 50; St-Aulaire to Q d'O, 5 Jul., MAE, Grande Bretagne, Vol. 71; *Documents relatifs aux garanties,* No. 38.

With this reply the negotiations over the Anglo-French treaty simply faded out. Technically it was for the British Government to answer the French proposals of 1 February, but Lloyd George's wider plan having failed few people seem to have been interested in pursuing the pact on its own. The summer saw worsening disagreement over reparations - which is presumably what the British now meant by reconstruction, the hope of a settlement with Russia having evaporated at the Hague talks. In the Balfour note of 1 August the British Government offered to reduce their reparation claim on Germany and ask for repayment of war debts only to the amount needed to pay Britain's debt to the United States.[1] But this apparently generous offer did not encourage the French to agree to a moderate reparation settlement, since under it the less France took from Germany the more she would have to pay Britain herself. After another conference in London in August had failed to produce agreement it seemed only a question of time before the French would embark on taking 'productive pledges'. The time when a Turkish settlement would be possible drew nearer with the Greek defeat in Anatolia but the immediate consequence, the Chanak crisis in September, was one of the worst Anglo-French breaches since the armistice.

The negotiations for an Anglo-French treaty failed in 1922 over a basic difference of aim. The French desired a definite assurance of military support in case of German attack and a commitment to maintain the European order set up by the peace treaties. The request for a convention specifying numbers of forces, like the one attached to the Franco-Polish treaty of 1921, was an unrealistic demand to make of any British Government and was quickly dropped; but on the need for some kind of military co-operation Briand and Poincaré were at one.[2] Although they probably envisaged the wider undertaking on Europe in different ways, the desire for a link between Britain's commitment to France and France's commitment to Poland was common to both, and must have been felt by any French Government. To some extent the Franco-Polish alliance lessened the immediate French need for a British guarantee; but while it was on the whole an asset to France in respect of Germany it might be a burden, and a source of trouble for her in eastern Europe. Henceforth the demilitarised Rhineland and the Rhine bridgeheads had the function not only of

1 *DBFP.*, Ser. I, Vol. XX, No. 45; Cmd 1737 of 1922, *Despatch to the Representatives of France, Italy, Serb-Croat-Slovene State, Roumania, Portugal and Greece at London respecting war debts;* C 35(22), C 36(22), C 40(22), C 42(22), CAB 23/50. Britain concluded a debt-funding agreement with the United States in January 1923.

2 Cf. *Journal officiel, Chambre des députés, Compte-rendu*, 3 Nov. 1923.

protecting the French frontier but also of enabling France to bring assistance to Poland, and from 1924 Czechoslovakia.

On the British side, while there was some acknowledgement of a moral obligation to make up for the failure of the 1919 guarantee and of Britain's own interest in the security of France, renewal of the guarantee was conceived as part of a new bargain over European recovery, and was not meant to involve wider responsibilities or military commitments. No government would have agreed to subject the level of British armaments to the influence of another country; and even though Poincaré dropped the demand for a military convention the outcome of the staff conversations with France before 1914 was sufficiently fresh in the mind for Liberal ministers, in particular, to be loath to repeat the experience.

A feature of the story of these negotiations is the absence, on the British side, of any consideration of the proposed pact from the military point of view. It was never discussed by the Committee of Imperial Defence. Early in April 1922 the War Office sent some comments to the Foreign Office. The General Staff favoured accepting several of the French proposals for the treaty since in military terms the French were right in wishing to forestall violation of their frontier and if British forces were to co-operate usefully they must do so from the outset. But by this time the negotiations were already more or less at a standstill: the comments received little attention in the Foreign Office and none elsewhere.[1] It is hard to say how seriously Lloyd George took the argument which he used to Poincaré about the real strength of the British Empire - that it had enormous manpower. One would suppose that he realised that millions of once-trained men were a wasting asset unless they were periodically retrained or renewed in some way such as, the French maintained, their German counterparts were being trained and recruited in police and paramilitary forces. Lloyd George ought to have remembered that however much better than her word Britain had been in 1914, it had taken two years of war before her contribution in manpower on the western front had been substantial. The conclusion must be that the British Government never intended the guarantee to be militarily meaningful. It was conceived as a political gesture, partly to pay an obligation outstanding since 1919 but chiefly to induce France to fall in with British policy elsewhere.

The attempts of both sides to bargain with the pact failed. Poincaré could not use Lloyd George's desire for the Genoa conference to secure it because he was not in a position to commit France to full

1 War Office to FO, 3 Apr. 1922; FO to War Office, 18 Apr., W 2996/50/17, FO 371/8251.

co-operation in a settlement with the Soviet Union or a moderate reparation policy. The British could not use it to secure concessions elsewhere because the pact offered was not sufficiently attractive to induce the French to change their policies: as Poincaré pointed out, treaty or no treaty Britain would be bound in her own interest to come to the help of France in case of renewed German attack. The threats which Lloyd George was fond of making about ending the Entente were largely meaningless since, unless Britain were to withdraw even more completely than the United States had done from all the organs set up to execute the peace treaties, she was inextricably tied to France in carrying them out. Although at times there would have been a good deal of public support for withdrawal of the occupation forces from the Rhineland or withdrawal from the Rhineland High Commission, there was never any suggestion of withdrawing from the control commissions or the Reparation Commission, in whose activities Britain had an important stake.[1]

The Foreign Office appear to have given little sustained attention to the pact proposals. They were not asked to do so; Curzon was not greatly interested in Europe and was not inclined to challenge Lloyd George's control of policy in this area; economic policy and reparations were outside their field of responsibility. Lloyd George thought of the guarantee as part of a wider plan, and when that failed he lost interest. Even if the British Government had declared the 1919 guarantee to be in force despite the American rejection of the Treaty of Versailles, or had agreed in 1922 to a real defensive alliance, French policy towards Germany might not have become more flexible: the Chamber of Deputies and French opinion believed until the end of 1923 that, if pressed hard enough, Germany could pay. On the other hand the number of occasions, in 1919, in 1924, and in 1925, when French Governments of different complexions, faced with the choice between gaining British support and pursuing French interests single-handed, chose Britain, suggests that the same might have been the case in 1922.

1 Hardinge wrote later that when on one occasion of tension he asked Lloyd George and Curzon what their phrase 'rupture with the French' meant, neither was able to say: Lord Hardinge of Penshurst, *Old Diplomacy* (London, 1947), 260.

2

GENERAL SECURITY AND WESTERN EUROPE 1923-24

After the negotiations for an Anglo-French treaty came to an end in the summer of 1922, the question of regional security in western Europe was not discussed in London for about a year. In the mean time the first proposals for general security additional to the Covenant, and linked with the reduction of armaments, were produced at Geneva. They confronted the British Government with the equivocal position of Great Britain, left by the abstention of the United States as the chief producer of security and with a public which believed in the League but ignored the implied obligations. Their position was the more delicate because the chief author of the proposals was British, a leading figure in the League movement, and a passionate believer in disarmament as a preventive of war, Lord Robert Cecil.

The Treaty of Mutual Assistance, 1922-24

Cecil's proposals grew out of the discussions in the League of Nations from 1920 about the application of Article 8 of the Covenant, which stated that the maintenance of peace required 'the reduction of national armaments to the lowest point consistent with national safety and the enforcement by common action of international obligations', and laid on the Council the duty of formulating plans for such reduction. A commission to advise the Council on the execution of Article 8 and on military, naval and air questions generally was set up as soon as the League was constituted. This Permanent Advisory Committee was composed of professional service advisers to the governments of countries represented on the Council. Alongside it in 1921 was created a Temporary Mixed Commission consisting of individuals chosen for their expertise and of representatives of the Permanent Advisory Committee, the League's Economic and Financial Committee, and the International Labour Office. These two bodies began by considering the private manufacture of arms and the exchange of information on existing armaments, and the Assembly passed resolutions inviting member countries not to increase their military, naval and air expenditure.[1]

The first proposal for a general reduction of armaments was put forward by Lord Esher, a British member of the Temporary Mixed

1 See Walters, *History of the League of Nations,* Vol. I, 219-23; *Survey of International Affairs, 1924,* 17-21.

Commission. He suggested a numerical ratio for land forces, on an analogy with the ratio for capital ships adopted at the Washington conference, and on a scale which would have required substantial reductions by several countries; but the proposal was criticised for taking no account of varying needs for security and Esher withdrew it. Thereupon Cecil, also a member of the Commission, took the initiative in trying to link limitation of armaments with general guarantees of security.

Cecil submitted propositions to the Temporary Mixed Commission in July 1922. They were put before the Assembly in September and were commended by it in a resolution stating that (1) no scheme for the reduction of armaments could be fully effective unless it were general; (2) many countries could not significantly reduce their armaments unless they received a satisfactory guarantee of their safety; (3) such a guarantee could be found in a defensive agreement, open to all countries, binding signatories to render immediate and effective assistance according to a prearranged plan, provided that the obligation to give assistance were limited in principle to countries situated in the same part of the world; (4) prior consent to the reduction of armaments was the first condition of the treaty. The Council was asked to send the proposals to individual governments for observations, and the Temporary Mixed Commission was asked to prepare a draft Treaty of Mutual Guarantee.[1]

Cecil showed his proposals informally to members of the Government in London. Both Balfour and Worthington-Evans, the Secretary of State for War, criticised the limitation of the obligation to give assistance to countries situated in the same part of the world. This attempt to forestall the reluctance to undertake general obligations of countries far from likely scenes of trouble was to prove one of the main objections to the proposed treaty so far as Britain and the Dominions were concerned, for the world-wide spread of the Empire seemed to indicate that Britain would be involved practically everywhere while other countries were not; yet one part of the Empire might be theoretically involved while others were not. Balfour and Worthington-Evans were also doubtful about the efficacy of prearranged plans for military co-operation, and Balfour doubted whether France would ever be satisfied with anything that the British Empire would be willing to offer.[2]

1 League of Nations, *Resolutions and Recommendations adopted by the Assembly during its Third Session* (Geneva, 1922), 24-7.

2 Worthington-Evans to Cecil, 11 Aug. 1922; Cecil to Worthington-Evans, 14 Aug.; Balfour to Cecil, 15 Sep., Cecil Papers, British Library Add. MS 51095. At some stage Cecil saw Lord Cavan, the Chief of the Imperial General Staff, and

The procedure of collecting the views of government departments for the Committee of Imperial Defence was slow, and nothing that could be called an official opinion was forthcoming in time for the next meeting of the Permanent Advisory Committee or the Temporary Mixed Commission. In an attempt to hasten matters Cecil told Hankey that the French Government were taking the scheme seriously but were going to press for specific pacts between groups of countries rather than a general treaty, a method which would give France security but would not lead to disarmament. He was hoping to present in January an elaborated scheme for a general treaty; but he would immediately be asked what the Government thought, and at present he would have to reply that 'the British Government do not think'.[1] Cecil pointed out that his proposal was for a general treaty with supplementary conventions relating to countries which believed themselves to be in particular danger. He believed that if the treaty were universal it would certainly prevent aggression. If it were accepted by a majority of states aggression would be prevented and disarmament secured provided that the majority included the great powers. If the great powers (among them Germany and Russia or at least one of the two) did not co-operate, the plan would fail.[2]

The service departments all criticised the scheme. The General Staff and the Air Staff considered that it would not provide effective assistance and therefore would not lead to a reduction of armaments. The Admiralty feared that such a treaty would involve Britain in commitments of unknown magnitude which might mean expansion of her forces, and thought that it would be dangerous for a signatory state to reduce its armaments in reliance on assistance from others while non-signatories were free to develop their strength as they chose.[3]

The Foreign Office were asked for advice on guarantees in general. Discussing what was wanted Hankey pointed out that the existing guarantee in Article 10 of the Covenant had not brought any help to Poland in 1920. He thought it necessary to consider how far it would be possible to fulfil such guarantees without increasing forces. At present if Britain earmarked, say, a quarter of her forces for League

asked him to have the plan studied, but he was given no encouragement: Cecil to P. Noel Baker, 22 Mar. 1924, BL Add. MS 51106.

1 Cecil to Hankey, 15 Dec. 1922, BL Add. MS 51088. The Committee of Imperial Defence had the previous day decided to ask the service departments for papers on the scheme: 168th meeting, CAB 2/3. Cecil also sounded the views of Ramsay MacDonald, without finding support: MacDonald to Cecil, 22 Feb. 1923, BL Add. MS 51081.

2 CID paper 383-B, CAB 4/8.

3 CID papers 381-B, 387-B, CAB 4/8; CID papers 395-B, 405-B, CAB 4/9.

of Nations purposes the whole army would be immobilised.[1] In reply the Foreign Office stated the existing position: unless Article 10 were given a peremptory interpretation, which seemed unlikely in view of the attempts which had been made to abrogate it, the Covenant imposed on Britain no obligation to take military action without the consent of her representative on the Council. As to whether guarantees could be effective, the Historical Adviser to the Foreign Office pointed out that in the past general guarantees had not prevented war but they had never contained military commitments. Alliances, which did contain such commitments, often had prevented war. Cecil's proposal amounted to a general defensive alliance of unlimited duration. Headlam-Morley agreed that the main burden of enforcement would probably fall on Britain, and considered that the question whether treaties of guarantee could be depended on was one of political will. 'If any British Government, after full and mature consideration, after debate in Parliament and general public discussion, feel themselves authorised to become parties to a treaty of guarantee and to make the maintenance of this a permanent part of British policy; if this is publicly proclaimed; if in presenting the estimates for naval and military defence, the importance of providing for liabilities under this treaty is shown; then I believe that in the long run the treaty will become effective'. But if the Government were half-hearted, then any such treaty would break down.[2]

Meanwhile Cecil was amending his draft. To meet the criticism that assistance could be paralysed by lack of unanimity on the Council, he proposed that it should decide on the identity of an aggressor by a three-quarters majority, a change which immediately brought the new criticism that British forces might be committed against the vote of the British Government's representative.[3] The Committee of Imperial Defence decided on 11 April that until the treaty had been considered by the Cabinet the British representatives on the Permanent Advisory

1 Hankey to Crowe, 7 Feb. 1923 and minutes, W 1075/30/98, FO 371/9418.

2 CID paper 416-B, CAB 4/9. Ever since 1920 Canada had been trying to delete Article 10 from the Covenant. At the Assembly of 1923 a resolution was passed by a majority stating that the Council should take into account the special circumstances and geographical position of each member when recommending military measures, and that it should be for the constitutional authorities of each state to decide in what degree it was bound to use its military forces. The resolution received one adverse vote and therefore did not become binding; but it carried much weight. In 1921 the Assembly resolved that the Council might, in the case of individual members, postpone the coming into force of economic measures decided on, if postponement would help attainment of the object of the measures or was necessary to minimise loss and hardship to such members: League of Nations, *Monthly Summary,* 1923, 198; *Resolutions and Recommendations adopted by the Assembly during its Second Session* (Geneva, 1921).

3 CID papers 406-B, 408-B, 412-B, CAB 4/9.

Committee might discuss technical problems but not political questions such as whether mutual guarantees should be given, whether they could be considered effective, whether the Council should decide by a majority vote, whether member countries should provide a fixed portion of their effectives, and whether there should be a general treaty with special conventions or partial treaties leading to a general one.[1]

On technical grounds alone the Permanent Advisory Committee decided at their April meeting that Cecil's plan was unworkable and would involve an increase rather than a reduction in armaments. But the French in particular were anxious to keep the idea of mutual guarantees alive, and the Temporary Mixed Commission set to work again. In the interval before the 1923 Assembly the whole idea was subjected to further criticism in London. At a meeting of the Committee of Imperial Defence on 29 June Amery, the First Lord of the Admiralty, and Curzon questioned the whole concept; and the argument continued in writing. Hankey questioned whether the peoples and parliaments of democratic countries could be relied on to fulfil a general guarantee at any moment, and reissued a paper of 1906 to the same effect by his predecessor as secretary to the Committee.[2] Cecil, who had recently joined the Government, pointed out that his scheme would only come into force after a general reduction of armaments had taken place, and asserted that the guarantee would probably never need to be acted upon.[3] Amery again criticised the idea of general guarantees and doubted whether they would conduce to the reduction of armaments. He denied the contention, so frequently advanced at the time, that armaments were a cause of war; and argued that where there was no real conflict of interests competition could be reduced by frank discussion as at Washington over capital ships, while where fundamental differences existed disarmament either was impossible or, if achieved, would not lead to peace. Amery also maintained that British commitments under such a treaty would far outweigh any advantages gained, and saw no reason why Britain need become involved in European conflicts. The continental limitation, he said, if carried to its logical conclusion would mean the end of the British Empire.[4]

Crowe was sceptical whether any general scheme for the reduction of armaments was possible. He doubted whether the Washington naval treaty would ever have been negotiated had not Britain been 'inspired

1 CID 171st. meeting, CAB 2/3; CO 18855/23, CO 532/241.

2 CID 173rd meeting, CAB 2/3; CID papers 415-B, 420-B, CAB 4/9.

3 CID paper 431-B, CAB 4/10.

4 CP 311(23), CAB 24/161.

by a wish to save money and by a suspicion that capital ships might be, under conditions of modern warfare, a bad investment'. He doubted too whether France would agree to any substantial reduction in her forces even in return for a guarantee: 'Do we expect her to diminish the number of her divisions, or the strength of her artillery or air squadrons in reliance on a powerful British expeditionary force coming to her assistance? Can we honestly ask her to do so?' He doubted further whether disarmament, if achieved, could be maintained: 'Germany is "disarmed" owing to the operation of the Treaty of Versailles. Yet it is the recorded opinion of all the allied authorities that it is in practice quite impossible to prevent her from reconstituting a formidable force, more or less surreptitiously, and that preparations for doing so are undoubtedly in existence'. In the second place Crowe questioned the effectiveness of general guarantees. Headlam-Morley had written that guarantee alliances had been effective in the past: in so far as this was true, Crowe argued, it was because such treaties had contained very precise conditions for their operation. The proposed treaty contained only general stipulations: if threatened states were to be induced to cut down their armaments the guarantee would have to go beyond what was contemplated in Articles 10 and 16 of the Covenant, but even in their present form these had caused objections. Finally Crowe put his finger on one of the fundamental points that divided, and was to continue to divide, the spokesmen for collective security from those whom Cecil called the 'reactionary elements': 'Lord R. Cecil endeavours to meet the objections raised in respect of the serious burden thrown upon this country in particular in virtue of the far-reaching nature of the commitments involved in the draft treaty, by arguing that these are not in fact likely to arise, and need not therefore be seriously considered. But this argument is hardly calculated to inspire the absolute confidence that if a situation did arise which brought the commitments into play, we should unhesitatingly stand by them'. Without such confidence nations would not reduce their armaments. Crowe thought that they were unlikely to do so in any case, that the Covenant did not bind them to do so, and that Britain ought not to go on taking the initiative on disarmament.[1]

In August the Temporary Mixed Commission approved a new version of the scheme, now renamed the Treaty of Mutual Assistance, which was a compromise between Cecil's draft and one by the French Colonel Réquin. Compared with the first version, the Treaty of Mutual Assistance laid greater weight on the supplementary agreements which two or more states might conclude for their mutual defence, and which they might

1 Memorandum by Crowe, 24 Jun. 1923, W 5047/30/98, FO 371/9419.

put into immediate affect in advance of a decision by the League Council. The text was put before the League Assembly in September: it passed through a committee without substantial amendment; but the Assembly was not prepared either to approve or disapprove it, and it was sent to the governments without comment.[1] Among the countries which had by now sent comments on the 1922 resolution was Canada, who stated briefly that she could not take part in a treaty of mutual guarantee. None of the other Dominions had replied, nor the British Government; but at the same time as the new treaty was before the Assembly the British were expressing, in connexion with the Corfu crisis, alarm at the consequences of a literal application of Article 16.[2]

Cecil's position was anomalous. In 1921 and 1922 he was not a member of the Government, nor even a British representative at the Assembly - he represented South Africa - and he was a member of the Temporary Mixed Commission as an individual. Cecil became Lord Privy Seal in May 1923, charged with League of Nations affairs. His relations with Curzon were awkward. Cecil complained of Curzon's refusal to give him a room in the Foreign Office and of lack of consultation on League matters; Curzon complained about Cecil talking to foreigners about British policy in general and sending papers on League matters to the Cabinet without consulting the Foreign Office.[3] Curzon was certainly jealous of his authority and not much interested in the League, having been content with the previous arrangement whereby Balfour and Fisher represented Britain at Council and Assembly meetings without any continuing responsibility. But it is also clear that Cecil was demanding, and pursued his conception of a League policy without taking much account of other aspects of foreign policy. Cecil's personal prestige in League circles was great, and he could not but appear at Geneva as speaking for Britain. It was therefore, as a Foreign Office official remarked, 'undoubtedly awkward that the originator and prime mover of a scheme which is violently opposed by every Dept. of H.M. Govt should be the principal representative

1 The text is printed in Cmd 2200 of 1924, *Correspondence between His Majesty's Government and the League of Nations respecting the proposed Treaty of Mutual Assistance*, and is summarised in *Survey of International Affairs, 1924*, 22-5.

2 Treasury to Foreign Office, 4 Sep. 1923, C 15356/15065/62, FO 371/8615.

3 See their correspondence of June 1923 in FO 800/149 and Cecil Papers, BL Add. MS 51077; Cecil to Baldwin, 20 Jun., BL Add. MS 51077, Baldwin Papers, University Library, Cambridge, F.2 (Vol. 114): also Viscount Cecil, *A Great Experiment* (London, 1941), 145-6, and *All the Way* (London, 1949), 178. Until October 1922 League of Nations work was channelled through the Cabinet secretariat; thereafter it was transferred to the Foreign Office.

of H.M.G. at Geneva'.[1] Matters become even more difficult when Cecil, without instructions, voted at the Assembly of 1923 in favour of resolutions on budgetary limitation and the manufacture of arms several of which were disapproved of by the service departments so that Cecil would probably have to voice the Government's objection when the resolutions came before the Council. It was now suggested that Cecil could hardly remain both a member of the Temporary Mixed Commission and British representative on the Council.[2]

When Curzon asked for his comments Cecil replied that the difficulty was real but he did not think it would be cured by dissolving the Temporary Mixed Commission. It might be that his views on the Treaty of Mutual Assistance were so different from those of the rest of the Government that he would have to resign, but that point had not been reached since the Cabinet had not yet considered the treaty. Cecil took the opportunity of stressing his belief that members of the League were bound to reduce their armaments, so that it was no use the services taking a purely negative view.[3]

It might be expected that the Treaty of Mutual Assistance would have been discussed at the Imperial Conference of 1923, which met shortly after the League Assembly. But the British Cabinet had not considered the treaty, and everyone seems to have avoided the subject. When Cecil gave an account of League matters to the conference he did not at first mention the treaty. Only when the Australian Prime Minister, Bruce, said that his country would be very much afraid of it did Cecil reply briefly that participation would be voluntary.[4] After that governmental discussion was overtaken by the general election.[5]

Under the Labour Government the Committee of Imperial Defence

1 Minute by Villiers, 14 Sep. 1923, W 7127/30/98, FO 371/9420. Amery also expressed anxiety at Cecil going ahead with the Treaty of Mutual Assistance and practically forcing on the Government the odium of rejecting a scheme of which their representative had been the chief architect. He was the more opposed to the scheme now that Canada had rejected it; Amery to Curzon, 21 Sep., Curzon Papers, MSS. Eur. F 112/224.

2 Memorandum by R.H. Campbell, 26 Nov. 1923, W 9218/30/98, FO 371/9421; Cecil Papers, BL Add. MS 51077.

3 Cecil to Curzon, 28 Nov. 1923, W 9336/30/98, FO 371/9421; BL Add. MS 51077.

4 CID 176th meeting, CAB 2/4; Hankey to Cecil, 3 and 5 Oct. 1923, BL Add. MS 51088; Salisbury to Baldwin, 7 Oct., Baldwin Papers, F.4.1 (Vol. 129): E 6th and 7th meetings, CAB 32/9.

5 Unfavourable comments were recorded by the service departments, the Government of India, and the Foreign Office: CID papers 464-B, 465-B, 484-B, CAB 4/10-11; minute by Curzon, 7 Oct. 1923; memorandum by Orde, 18 Oct.; India Office to FO, 28 Dec., W 7982, 8091, 10050/30/98, FO 371/9421.

did not discuss the treaty until 3 April 1924 but then, in view of the unanimous departmental opposition, decided that they could not recommend it to the Cabinet. The main objections were the familiar ones of the unlimited nature of the obligations, the difficulty of the continental limitation, the difficulty of defining an aggressor, the impossibility of preparing all plans in advance, the probable formation of new alliances, and the extension of the powers of the Council.[1] The decision was not announced at once because MacDonald wanted to deal with reparations first and an early British rejection of the treaty might make Anglo-French relations more difficult, and possibly to allow time for other countries to reject the treaty too.[2] The draft reply to the League was not sent to the Dominions for comment until the end of May; the rejection was finally sent to Geneva in July.[3]

The Treaty of Mutual Assistance brought into the open the difficulties about general security guarantees implicit in the League of Nations Covenant. The first fundamental problem was the will of governments and peoples not only to undertake general obligations but to remain able and willing to fulfil them in any circumstances and at any time. When the attempt was made to provide machinery for supplying assistance, it came up against the second problem, that such assistance, to be effective, must involve a sacrifice of national decision such as no power that could provide the assistance was willing to make. Compared with these difficulties most of the other points criticised in the treaty were, though important, secondary.

For Britain the position of the Dominions was of great military and political importance. The continental limitation could not satisfy her on either count. Imperial defence was treated in London as a whole: it could not be organised in separate geographical compartments; in the navy Britain in fact supplied all but the minimum local defence of the Dominions as well as of the colonies for which she was directly responsible; but in some cases the Dominions and India might provide

1 CID 183rd meeting, CAB 2/4; CP 311(24), CAB 24/167.

2 Drummond to Parmoor, 1 Apr. 1924; Parmoor to MacDonald, 3 Apr.; Hankey to Gower, 10 Apr., MacDonald Papers, PRO 30/69/1/21; Hankey to Crowe, 28 Apr., W 3539/134/98, FO 371/10568; Jones, *Whitehall Diary,* Vol. I, 272-3. The United States Government, to which, like those of other countries not members of the League, the treaty was sent, rejected it in June 1924: League of Nations, *Official Journal,* Aug. 1924, 1035-6; *Papers relating to the Foreign Relations of the United States,* hereafter cited as *FRUS, 1924,* Vol. I, 79-83. See also *Survey of International Affairs, 1924,* 25-6.

3 W 3539, 4368, 4857, 5558/134/98, FO 371/10568-9; CO 20417/24, CO 532/186; CO 28235/24, CO 532/274; CP 309(24), CAB 24/167; C 34(24), C 35(24), CAB 23/48, Cmd 2200 of 1924; League of Nations, *Official Journal,* Aug. 1924, 1036-9.

reinforcements for Britain.[1] In political terms the treaty raised the still unsettled problem of imperial foreign policy and the constitutional status of the Dominions. It had been possible since 1919 to envisage a commitment to France that did not necessarily involve them, but it was inconceivable that Britain would undertake commitments outside Europe that they would not consider. Cecil might protest that while the Dominions must be consulted they could not be given a *liberum veto* over British policy:[2] in cases such as the Treaty of Mutual Assistance and, later, the Geneva Protocol, their objections were bound to weigh very heavily with any British Government.

French security, 1923

As the French Government, from the London Conference of August 1922 onwards, insisted increasingly upon 'productive pledges', such as taking over German state mines and forests, as a condition for granting Germany a breathing space in which to re-establish her currency, the possible connexion between reparations and French security was in the minds of many people. If, it was thought, the Allies were to make the concessions necessary for German financial and economic health they would need to be convinced of Germany's sincerity and will for peace. The German Government sent to the Reparation Commission on 14 November 1922 a note outlining a plan for stabilising the mark with the help of foreign loans and asking for a moratorium on reparation payments of three or four years and the fixing of the liabilities at a sum which Germany could pay out of budget surpluses. They substantially repeated these proposals in a note to a conference in London in the middle of December. Here Poincaré refused to agree to any reduction of the German liability greater than the amount of the French debt which might be remitted by Britain, and insisted on the necessity of productive pledges. No agreement was reached, but it was decided to meet again in Paris in the New Year.

The United States Administration had been considering participating in an attempt to tackle the problem from the point of view of Germany's capacity; but the Secretary of State, Hughes, was not able to get France to take the initiative, nor could he undertake that war debts would be considered. On the eve of the Paris meeting Hughes decided to take an initiative himself, by publicly offering American participation in an enquiry into the amounts to be paid by Germany and a plan for working out the payments. The proposal bore fruit nearly a year later,

1 For imperial defence see Chapter 6.

2 Cecil to MacDonald, 25 Jun. 1924, BL Add. MS 51081; *HL Deb.*, 5th ser. Vol. 58, cols. 994-5.

but it could not affect the immediate course of events. Nor could the German Chancellor, Cuno, stave off French action by making a security offer.[1] His proposal, that the powers interested in the Rhine should solemnly agree among themselves, and promise to the United States as trustee, that they would not go to war with one another for a generation unless authorised to do so by plebiscites of their peoples, was made to Hughes on 15 December with the intention that the United States Government should put it forward as their own. On learning that Poincaré would not accept the proposal Hughes told the German Ambassador that there was no object in pursuing it.[2] News of the proposal leaked to the press in Paris and Cuno therefore referred to it in a speech at Hamburg on 29 December, without mentioning the United States by name.

Poincaré reported the Cuno offer to the Allied conference in Paris on 2 January, stressing that there had been no formal proposal to or rejection by France. The British reaction was not very different from Poincaré's. Although Lord D'Abernon, the British Ambassador in Berlin, later became enamoured of the proposal he had nothing to do with its origins, hearing of it for the first time in Cuno's speech. He recommended that it should be considered, but Curzon described it as a 'piece of impertinence' and refused to encourage its revival.[3] The conference in Paris ended in total disagreement on reparations and productive pledges, a new British proposal coming too late to alter the French determination.[4] The Reparation Commission had already by a majority found Germany in default on timber deliveries, and on 9

1 For the origins of the Cuno offer and of Hughes's speech at New Haven on 29 Dec. 1922 see D.B. Gescher, *Die Vereinigten Staaten von Nordamerika und die Reparationen 1920-1924* (Bonn, 1956), 114-35; *FRUS, 1922,* Vol. II, 163-203; L. Zimmermann, *Deutsche Aussenpolitik in der Ära der Weimarer Republik,* (Göttingen, 1958), 138-42, Stephen A. Schuker, *The End of French Predominance in Europe, The Financial Crisis of 1924* and the *Adoption of the Dawes Plan* (Chapel Hill, N.C. 1976), 24, n. 32.

2 *FRUS, 1922,* Vol. II, 203-11; German Foreign Ministry archives, Auwärtiges Amt (hereafter AA) to Wiedfeldt (Washington), 13, 20, 27 Dec. 1922; Wiedfeldt to AA, 15, 19, 28 Dec., 3243/D718462-64, D718494, D718553-54, D718641, D718684-85 (documents from the files of the German Foreign Ministry cited here and subsequently are identified by the serial and frame numbers of the collection of microfilm copies in the Public Record Office); MAE, Allemagne, Vol. 477.

3 D'Abernon to FO, 2, 3, 4 Jan. 1923; Dormer (Vatican) to FO, 13 Jan.; FO to Dormer, 17 Jan., C 178, 186, 432, 721/178/18, FO 371/8696; memorandum by Rosenberg, 4 Jan., 3243/D718858-59.

4 See Cmd 1812 of 1923, *Inter-Allied Conferences on Reparations and Inter-Allied Debts held in London and Paris, December 1922 and January 1923;* France, *Documents diplomatiques, Demande de moratorium du gouvernement allemand à la Commission des Réparations (14 novembre 1922), Conférence de Londres (9-12 décembre 1922), Conférence de Paris (2-4 janvier 1923)* (Paris, 1923).

January did the same on coal. On 11 January the Franco-Belgian occupation of the Ruhr began.

However much the occupation was deplored in London, since the Government believed that it would neither help to solve the reparation problem nor produce much money, there was no desire for a breach with France and no intention of undertaking mediation.[1] Measures taken by the French in the Allied-occupied Rhineland caused difficulties throughout the year, but the Cabinet decided that the British forces should remain and every effort be made to avoid incidents that might rouse public opinion to demand their withdrawal.[2]

For the first few weeks little was done to try to elucidate the French and Belgian motives. The Belgians disclaimed any political motive for the occupation; but to judge by the Paris press the French motives were more mixed: terms like a permanent international control of the Rhineland featured in discussion of a possible outcome, and French correspondents in London believed that an Anglo-French pact was being considered again.[3] In fact different French personalities seem to have had different expectations of the occupation. President Millerand hoped for advantages in both security and reparations; but Poincaré was primarily concerned with reparations, in the sense less of expecting to obtain large sums (although he did expect some) than of wishing to force Germany to acknowledge defeat and to put pressure on Britain and the United States to do something to give France what she needed.[4] Officially Poincaré denied any security motive. In preparation for an impending debate in Parliament Curzon on 21 March asked the French Ambassador for a statement on France's aim in the Ruhr. The French reply stated that the aim was reparation, and confirmed earlier statements that France would only withdraw as

1 C 1(23), CAB 23/45; FO to D'Abernon, 8 Jan. 1923, C 499/1/18, FO 371/8626; *DDI,* Vol. I, No. 344.

2 Meeting of Ministers, 24 Jan. 1923, CAB 21/70; C 3(23), CAB 23/45; FO to Kilmarnock, D'Abernon, and Crewe (Paris), 24 Jan., C 1301/313/18, FO 371/8706.

3 Grahame to FO, 24 Feb. 1923; FO to Grahame, 26 Feb., C 3472, 3626/313/18, FO 371/8716; *Echo de Paris,* 1 and 2 Mar.; *Europe nouvelle,* 3 and 10 Mar.; Phipps (Paris) to FO, 18 Mar., W 2080, 2261, 2338/1585/17, FO 371/9394; Phipps to FO, 28 Mar., C 5825/313/18, FO 371/8723; Phipps to FO, 2 Apr., C 6110/313/18, FO 371/8726.

4 See Chastenet, *Raymond Poincaré,* 240-6; Persil, *Alexandre Millerand,* 150-1; Denise Artaud, 'A propos de l'occupation de la Ruhr', *Revue d'histoire moderne et contemporaine,* 17 (1970), 1-21. Wider ambitions entertained in some French circles are discussed by Ludwig Zimmermann, *Frankreichs Ruhrpolitik. Von Versailles bis zum Dawesplan* (Göttingen, 1971), esp. Ch. 3.

Germany carried out her obligations.[1] Poincaré made another statement to this effect on 27 March and again denied any annexationist aims in a speech in the Chamber two days later.[2]

The German Government, however, with D'Abernon's encouragement, had been considering repeating the Cuno offer. They did not mention security in their approach to the British and United States Governments on 16 March,[3] but on 22 and 29 March the German Ambassador, Sthamer, told Curzon that his Government would be willing to renew the Cuno offer and to declare themselves prepared to submit all political disputes with France to an international conciliation body. Curzon merely said that the German Government should make proposals on reparations without attaching impossible conditions.[4]

In the first week of April Loucheur, who was out of office, came to London with the knowledge and probably with the approval of Poincaré and Millerand. He put to Bonar Law proposals for a reparation settlement, a series of international loans, and evacuation of the Ruhr by stages related to German payments; and further suggested that the Rhineland should be separated from Prussia and completely demilitarised, with an international gendarmerie under League of Nations supervision; that the railways in the Rhineland should be managed by an international board under the League; and that the Saar should become a special state under League control but with the mines remaining French property.[5] Loucheur was not given much encouragement but returned to Paris hopeful that the British and French positions were getting closer. However he was soon disavowed by the French Government. Semi-official statements issued on 17 April were

1 FO to Phipps, 21 Mar., 1923; St-Aulaire to Curzon, 23 Mar., C 5302, 5783/313/18, FO 371/8724-5. On 26 March Curzon turned down a suggestion by Crowe that it might be worth enquiring whether the French Government would see a way out of the Ruhr if Britain renewed the offer of a pact: W 2261/1585/17, FO 371/9394.

2 Phipps to FO, 28 Mar. 1923, C 5824/313/18, FO 371/8725; *Journal officiel, Chambre des députés,* 29 Mar.

3 Viscount D'Abernon, *An Ambassador of Peace* (London, 1929-30), Vol. II, 157, 184-5, 186, 190, 200-1, 203-4; D'Abernon to Crowe, 11 Mar. 1923, D'Abernon Papers, BL Add. MS 48926; FO to D'Abernon, 14 Mar., C 4876/1/18, FO 371/8632; Sthamer (London) to AA, 16 Mar.; AA to Sthamer, 18 Mar., 3116/D639167-73; Earl of Ronaldshay, *The Life of Lord Curzon,* (London, 1926), Vol. III, 347; Gescher, *Die Vereinigton Staaten und die Reparationen,* 168-9.

4 FO to Head (Berlin), 22 and 29 Mar. 1923, C 5439, 5906/313/18, FO 371/8724-5; AA to Sthamer, 20 Mar., 2406/D501196-97; Sthamer to AA, 22 Mar.; AA to Sthamer, 25 Mar., 3116/D639181-82, D639184-90.

5 FO memoranda, 7, 13 and 17 Apr. 1923, C 6300/1/18, FO 371/8632; C 6338/129/18, FO 371/8660; C 8383/313/18, FO 371/8730; Curzon Papers, MSS. Eur. F. 112/247; Loucheur, *Carnets secrets,* 117-21.

uncompromising on reparations and said that no fresh agreement on the Rhineland would be needed until the end of the period of Allied occupation, which in the French view had not yet begun to run.[1]

Despite the lack of interest shown by Curzon the German Foreign Ministry gave considerable attention to security when preparing a new note on reparations towards the end of April. They were encouraged by D'Abernon, who advised returning to the Cuno offer and stating that Germany was ready for any agreement based on reciprocity and German sovereignty.[2] The Germans considered other suggestions as well, including one which foreshadowed the proposals of January 1925 in suggesting that (1) the western powers (Germany, France, Great Britain, Belgium, the Netherlands, Switzerland, and Luxembourg) should undertake to respect the integrity of their present frontiers and mutually and severally guarantee to fulfil this undertaking; (2) in the same sense the powers would guarantee the fulfilment of the obligations laid on Germany in the Treaty of Versailles in respect of the demilitarisation of the Rhineland; (3) Germany and France would undertake, under the guarantee of the other powers, to deal with any disputes between them which could not be settled by diplomacy according to an international procedure of arbitration for juridical disputes and conciliation for other disputes; (4) the pact would have a duration of 99 years.[3]

Neither this proposal nor a repetition of the Cuno offer was spelt out in the German reparation note of 2 May. A detailed offer at this stage would not have achieved any result. After the French semi-official statement of 17 April the German Chargé d'Affaires in Paris reported that security had retreated into the background; and Curzon stated in the House of Lords on 20 April that it was not immediately relevant to the reparation question.[4] The German note contained only a brief

1 Phipps to FO, 10 Apr. 1923, C 6482/1/18, FO 371/8633; memoranda by Tyrrell, 12 and 13 Apr.; Phipps to FO, 17 Apr., C 6697, 6913, 8323/313/18, FO 371/8727, 8730. According to a French interpretation of the Treaty of Versailles the fifteen-year period of the occupation would only begin with fulfilment of the peace terms. The British view was that it had begun with the entry of the treaty into force on 10 January 1920.

2 Memorandum by Rosenberg, 8 Apr. 1923, 3243/D719345-47; D'Abernon to FO, 11 and 17 Apr., C 6880, 7315/313/18, FO 371/8727, 8729; D'Abernon to Phipps, 16 Apr.; Phipps to D'Abernon, 24 Apr., BL Add. MS 48926.

3 Undated drafts of reparation note; memorandum by Schubert, 25 Apr. 1923, 3243/D719150, D719162, D719170-80. The proposal was included in some of the drafts of the note, and one version included the further proposal that alongside this pact Germany would be ready to conclude a general treaty of arbitration with her other neighbours.

4 *HLDeb.*, 5th ser., Vol. 53, col. 794; Hoesch (Paris) to AA, 24 Apr. 1923, 3243/D719469-78.

statement that the Government were ready for any agreement calculated to secure peace which was based on reciprocity. More especially they were ready for an agreement binding Germany and France to an international procedure for settling disputes.[1] So far as the main subject-matter, reparations, was concerned, the note seemed inadequate to all the Allies, but the action of the French and Belgian Governments in rejecting it without consulting Britain not merely caused annoyance in London but raised doubts whether Poincaré wanted a settlement at all.[2] The British reply was a rejection too, but it ended with an invitation to the German Government to make a better offer.[3]

Although D'Abernon denied press reports that the Germans were consulting him on what to do next, he suggested to the Foreign Minister, Rosenberg, that before sending another note they should make soundings in London to find out what would be acceptable, and gave advice on what should be said.[4] On 29 May the Germans asked the British and Italian Governments for advice on the likely acceptability of a new communication on reparations. Sthamer was instructed to add that Germany was ready to give France and Belgium any political guarantees which were based on reciprocity and did not affect the freedom of the Rhineland.[5]

Curzon refused to give advice to the Germans, but he was being driven to the conclusion that Britain would have to do something if the next proposals were reasonable and were rejected by France.[6] The next German note, presented to the Allied and the United States Governments on 7 June, represented something of an advance. It declared willingness to accept the decision of an international tribunal on the amount and the method of Germany's payments and to provide financial guarantees, and asked for a conference. When delivering the note Sthamer said that his Government would offer any guarantees on

1 France, *Documents diplomatiques, Documents relatifs aux notes allemandes des 2 mai et 5 juin 1923 sur les réparations, 2 mai-3 août 1923* (Paris, 1923), No. 1; Belgium, *Documents diplomatiques relatifs aux réparations, du 26 décembre 1922 au 27 août 1923* (Brussels, 1923); FO to D'Abernon, 2 May; Sthamer to Curzon, 2 May, C 7832, 7896/1/18, FO 371/8633.

2 FO to Crewe, 3 and 5 May, 1923; FO to Grahame, 5 May, C 7837, 8072/1/18, FO 371/8633-4.

3 Curzon to Sthamer, 13 May 1923, C 8311/1/18, FO 371/8635.

4 Memorandum by Rosenberg, 14 May 1923, 3116/D638581; D'Abernon to FO, 25 May, C 9274/1/18, FO 371/8637.

5 AA to Sthamer, 27 May 1923, 3243/D720185-89; FO to D'Abernon, 29 May, C 9451/1/18, FO 371/8637; *DDI*, Vol. II, No. 62.

6 FO to Graham (Rome), 31 May 1923, C 9592/1/18, FO 371/8638; *DDI*, Vol. II, No. 65.

security that were consistent with German sovereignty.[1] In the discussion of the answer to be sent the crucial questions were the demand of the French and Belgian Governments for the abandonment of passive resistance in the Ruhr before reparations could be discussed, and their unwillingness or inability to state either what they would accept on reparations or what would happen to the occupation if passive resistance ceased. Attempts to clarify these points were unsuccessful. Finally on 6 July Curzon told the French Ambassador that he would draft a joint reply to the German note: if the Allied Governments could not agree to it he would send it from the British Government alone.[2] A few days later he offered to discuss security; but although there had been some more comments on the subject in the press the official French reply still was that the Ruhr issue was in no way connected with security.[3]

The note to the Allied Governments, accompanied by a draft reply to the Germans, was sent on 20 July. It proposed the end of passive resistance, progressive evacuation of the Ruhr, an independent enquiry into Germany's capacity to pay and the nature of suitable guarantees of payment, and inter-Allied discussions on a comprehensive financial settlement. The note ended with a statement that Britain was ready to discuss security.[4] The French and Belgian replies were both unfavourable. The French one, which Curzon described as a rebuff, restated the previous French position and said that the French Government would be glad to discuss security but it had nothing to do with the Ruhr. The Belgian note welcomed the offer of a discussion on security but was no more satisfactory about reparations. The Italian Government, after some hesitation, replied favourably.[5]

1 FO to D'Abernon, 7 Jun. 1923, C 9940/1/18, FO 371/8638; Cmd 1943 of 1923, *Correspondence with the Allied Governments respecting Reparation Payments by Germany,* No. 1; France, *Documents relatifs aux notes allemandes des 2 mai et 5 juin,* No. 17; Belgium, *Documents diplomatiques relatifs aux réparations,* No. 27.

2 Correspondence, 8 Jun.-6 Jul. 1923, printed in Cmd 1943; France, *Documents relatifs aux notes allemandes des 2 mai et 5 juin;* Belgium, *Documents diplomatiques relatifs aux réparations.* Also FO to Crewe, 11 and 15 Jun., 2, 3 and 6 Jul.; FO to Grahame, 3 and 6 Jul., C 10185, 10512, 11506, 11638, 11639, 11802, 11803/1/18, FO 371/8639-42.

3 Crewe to FO, 6 Jun. 1923; memorandum by Crowe, 9 Jun., C 9872, 10092/1/18, FO 371/8638-9; Crewe to Curzon, 21 and 23 Jun., 7 Jul., Curzon Papers, MSS. Eur. F.112/201; Crewe Papers, University Library, Cambridge, C/12; *DDI,* Vol. II, Nos. 110-12; FO to Grahame, 6 Jul.; FO to Crewe, 10 Jul., C 11801, 12052/1/18, FO 371/8642.

4 C 12540/1/18, FO 371/8644; Cmd 1943 of 1923, No. 5.

5 Cmd 1943, Nos. 6-9; France, *Documents relatifs aux notes allemandes des 2 mai et 5 juin,* No. 35; Belgium, *Documents diplomatiques relatifs aux réparations,* Nos. 43-4; *DDI,* Vol. II, Nos. 146-8; FO to Grahame and Crewe, 30 Jul., C 13160, 13162/1/18, FO 371/8645.

The possibility of independent action such as setting up an enquiry into Germany's capacity without France and Belgium had been discussed in London and discarded as impracticable, as had the possibility of putting pressure on France by creating difficulties for French borrowers on the London money market.[1] The Cabinet now decided not to pursue the correspondence with the German Government but to publish what had already passed, with a final note in the nature of an appeal to world opinion.[2] The note sent to the French and Belgian Governments on 11 August was Curzon at his most magisterial. It deplored the rejection of the proposal for an enquiry into Germany's capacity, contested the legality of the Ruhr occupation, and stated that since according to the French Government the occupation had nothing to do with security the British Government would not pursue the question.[3]

Entering on a discussion with Poincaré by published note was not likely to advance a settlement. Curzon himself did not like proceeding in this way;[4] Poincaré's powers as a draftsman were certainly not inferior to his; and the public argument did little but harden opinion on both sides. The French reply of 20 August was long and contentious. After justifying the Ruhr occupation at length it declared that France was ready to examine security at any time, but even effective guarantees (and those offered in 1922 had not been effective) could not deprive France of her right to reparation. The Belgian reply was less argumentative and contained a hint that an agreement on security would make Belgium more forthcoming on other matters, but it too offered little hope of progress.[5]

There now seemed to be nothing that the British Government could do except wait for passive resistance to break down in Germany.

1 Minutes by Crowe, 15, 17, 31 May 1923, C 8895, 10294/1/18, FO 371/8636, 8639; Baldwin Papers, F.3.1(Vol. 125); FO memorandum, 29 Jun., C 11456/1/18, FO 371/8641; Curzon to Crowe, 17 Jul.; memorandum by Cadogan, 19 Jul., Curzon Papers, MSS Eur. F.112/241; memorandum by Crowe, 31 Jul., C 13652/1/18, FO 371/8648.

2 C 44(23), C 46(23), CAB 23/46. There was some disagreement about the nature of the final note: CP 376(23), CAB 24/161; Randolph S. Churchill, *Lord Derby, 'King of Lancashire'* (London, 1959), 512-7. Cecil was rebuked by Baldwin and Curzon for speaking to Millerand on 4 August about a new distribution of reparation receipts: Curzon to Baldwin, 7 Aug., Baldwin Papers, F.2 (Vol. 114): Curzon to Cecil, 7 Aug.; Cecil to Baldwin, 7 Aug., C 13536, 13547/1/18, FO 371/8647; Cecil to Baldwin, 9 Aug., BL Add. MS 51080, 51096.

3 Cmd 1943 of 1923, No. 10.

4 Minute by Curzon, 23 Aug. 1923, C 14380/1/18, FO 371/8650; Curzon to Baldwin, 27 Aug., Baldwin Papers, F.2 (Vol. 114).

5 France, *Réponse du gouvernement français à la lettre du gouvernement britannique sur les réparations, 20 août 1923* (Paris, 1923); Belgium, *Documents diplomatiques relatifs aux réparations,* No. 54.

Hints came from Paris that Poincaré was anxious for agreement with Britain, and the Belgians were said to desire talks.[1] But when Baldwin stopped in Paris on 19 September on his way home from a holiday at Aix-les-Bains his conversation with Poincaré did not produce anything definite. Baldwin talked of public opinion in Britain, the fear that delay would make a settlement more difficult, and the doubt whether present methods would produce the desired German payments. Poincaré claimed to be supported by 99 per cent of French opinion, and said that the lack of understanding between France and Britain was due not so much to the failure of the pact negotiations the previous year - for French opinion was well aware that the proposed pact was valueless without a military convention - as to the fact that at every inter-Allied conference France had made sacrifices and Britain had not supported her. Poincare said that he would welcome consultations when passive resistance ceased, but Baldwin concluded that he had no plan.[2]

The meeting may have done some good in showing that both Prime Ministers wanted to prevent a breach, but it advanced matters not at all.[3] However the sands were running out for Germany. Cuno resigned on 11 August and was succeeded by Stresemann, who took over the Foreign Ministry as well. Stresemann's aim was to rescue Germany from collapse and disintegration. In a speech at Stuttgart on 2 September he stated that Germany would accept the policy outlined in the British note of 20 July; and he appealed through D'Abernon for British help in averting a complete collapse. He also tried to secure from the French and Belgian Governments some promise of better conditions in the Ruhr for the time when passive resistance was called off. In his Stuttgart speech and these approaches Stresemann expressed German willingness to join in a pact of powers interested in the Rhine to guarantee the *status quo* in the area.[4]

British intervention in the Franco-German exchanges was not thought possible, despite anxiety over the possibility of exclusive economic

1 Phipps to FO, 23, 28, 30 Aug. 1923; Grahame to FO, 31 Aug., C 14484, 14752, 14872, 14950/1/18, FO 371/8650, 8652, 8654.

2 Notes of conversation, CAB 21/271. Baldwin Papers, F.1.1 (Vol. 108).

3 British observers in Paris thought that it had done some good: Crewe to Curzon, 21 Sep., 1923, Crewe Papers, C/12; Malcolm to Baldwin, 3 Oct., Baldwin Papers, F.2.1 (Vol. 114). Keith Middlemas and John Barnes, in their biography *Baldwin* (London, 1969), Ch. 9, treat it as of great importance.

4 D'Abernon to FO, 30 Aug. 1923, C 14921/313/18, FO 371/8740; D'Abernon to FO, 4, 6, 11, 14 Sep.; Grahame to FO, 5 Sep., C 15320, 15335, 15404, 15714, 15459, 15797, 16013, 16179/1/18, FO 371/8654-5; MAE, Ruhr, Vols. 28-9, *passim.* Extracts from the Stuttgart speech in Gustav Stresemann, *Vermächtnis, Der Nachlass in drei Bänden,* ed. Henry Bernhard (Berlin, 1932-3), Vol. I, 100, 104.

arrangements; but finally, when passive resistance ended unconditionally on 26 September and it became clear that the French had no plan other than local industrial arrangements, Curzon told St-Aulaire that the French Government must take an initiative in restarting conversations on reparations and he was going to say so publicly.[1] The occasion was provided by the Imperial Conference. The Dominion Prime Ministers, with the exception of Smuts, expressed sympathy for France and anxiety for an early settlement, Smuts, as expected, was anti-French and called for a conference.[2] Curzon had already spoken to the Cabinet about trying to get the United States to help by rejoining the Reparation Commission;[3] but it does not appear that he had taken any steps before President Coolidge announced that his Government stood by Hughes's speech of December 1922, a statement which led by the end of the year to the setting up of two expert committees to enquire into Germany's finances.[4]

During these weeks there was no discussion of security. When in December the German Government decided to approach the French and Belgian Governments about an administrative *modus vivendi* for the occupied territory D'Abernon heard that they were prepared to offer security guarantees if the French mentioned the matter.[5] But having informed Stresemann in September that he did not wish to mix up security with reparation pledges, Poincaré did not change his mind.

MacDonald and Herriot, 1924

The French encouragement of separatist movements in the Rhineland and the Palatinate at the end of 1923[6] strengthened D'Abernon's conviction that the urgent question was security, not for France against Germany but for Germany against France. D'Abernon was in an unusual position in Berlin. He was not a professional diplomat: the first part of his career had been spent in the Ottoman Debt, as financial adviser to the Egyptian Government, and as Governor of the Imperial

1 FO to Crewe, 3 Oct. 1923, C 17141/313/18, FO 371/8743.

2 E 3rd, 4th, 5th meetings, CAB 32/9. Smuts had been demanding independent British action and support of Germany since March: telegrams exchanged by him and Bonar Law and Baldwin are in CO 532/238. For his efforts for a conference and American support see W.K. Hancock, *Smuts,* Vol. II, *The Field of Force* (London, 1968), 132-9.

3 C 47(23), CAB 23/46.

4 For these negotiations see *Survey and International Affairs, 1924,* 340-8.

5 D'Abernon to FO, 10 Dec. 1923, C 21359/313/18, FO 371/8751.

6 See *Survey of International Affairs, 1924,* 300-20; J.A. Dorten, *La Tragédie rhénane* (Paris, 1945).

Ottoman Bank. He then sat as a Conservative in the House of Commons from 1899 to 1906, was chairman of a Royal Commission on imperial trade in 1912, and during the war was chairman of the liquor control board. Lloyd George appointed him to Berlin in 1920 because of his financial expertise. Of all the foreign representatives in Germany at the time he was the most active and the most trusted in government circles, becoming known as the 'Lord Protector'. He was a friend of Stresemann before the latter held office, and was close to von Schubert, who headed the department of the Foreign Ministry dealing with western Europe until he became State Secretary at the end of 1924. D'Abernon was lavish with ideas and advice, to the Germans and his own government. He often thought German policy, particularly on finance, foolish; but he was convinced that Germany must be restored and trusted, and this theme runs through the diary which was later published under the title *An Ambassador of Peace.* For many years this work held the field as an authoritative account not only of D'Abernon's views but of British policy. But in reality his influence was less great than appears. He was not so well informed as he thought; and his reporting and advice were frequently marred by over-optimism and haste. In London his advice did not carry much weight: in Berlin it often led to disappointment when the British support which he forecast did not materialise. The Germans could not ignore D'Abernon, but at least by the later years of his mission they had learned not to rely on him completely. The position was not made easier by the fact that D'Abernon's opposite number in London, Sthamer, never won the confidence of the Foreign Office. Sthamer too was not a professional diplomat: he was a Hamburg senator appointed to meet a British wish not to have as the first postwar German representative a prewar career diplomat or Prussian aristocrat. Sthamer was personally respected, but he never became skilled at representing the views of either government to the other and generally avoided giving advice or taking initiatives. The most energetic member of the German Embassy staff was the counsellor, Dufour von Feronce.[1]

In the circumstances of the winter of 1923-4 it was natural that D'Abernon's thoughts on security were concentrated on the Rhineland and the Ruhr. The Germans themselves, after the negative result of their approach to Poincaré for a *modus vivendi,* were thinking of trying to get negotiations on a broader basis. They were the more anxious to do

1 D'Abernon's French colleague, de Margerie, characterised him as 'à la fois imaginatif, assez superficiel et très indépendant' (Margerie to Q d'O, 8 Jun. 1925, MAE, Autriche, Vol. 75). His diary was not a private document: he used to send passages from it at the time to personages in England. See also Werner Weidenfeld, *Die Englandpolitik Gustav Stresemanns* (Mainz, 1972), 130-4, 150-3; H.G. Sasse, *100 Jahre Botschaft in London* (Bonn, 1963), 47-55.

so because, even though the threat of separatism collapsed, the French press were again discussing neutralisation of the Rhineland and control over the railways. The Germans did not approach the French Government directly: when von Hoesch returned to Paris at the beginning of February to take up the post of ambassador and make a new attempt at a *modus vivendi,* his instructions did not mention security.[1] The Auswärtiges Amt were preparing to try to enlist British help when D'Abernon raised the security question himself. On 2 February he suggested to Schubert that it might be possible to find a régime for the Rhineland that would make it a barrier to aggression from either side and still preserve German sovereignty.[2] D'Abernon reported to London that he believed the German Government were prepared to make an offer for the demilitarisation of the Rhineland going beyond Articles 42-44 of the Treaty of Versailles, provided that German sovereignty were not impaired and the security protected both sides. The Cuno offer could perhaps be revived and combined with some scheme involving the League of Nations.[3] A few days later D'Abernon talked with Stresemann, and recorded him as saying that he saw no difficulty in declaring the Rhineland and the Palatinate demilitarised under German sovereignty; but it would have to be neutralisation, prohibiting use of the territory for military purposes in peace and in war by France as well as Germany.[4]

By this time Sthamer had received instructions to tell MacDonald that although the German Government considered the guarantees for France in the Treaty of Versailles were ample, they were prepared for

1 K936/K239303-09. Hoesch had done so well as chargé d'affaires in 1923 (the ambassador having been withdrawn when the Ruhr occupation began) that at Poincaré's request he was appointed ambassador in February 1924.

2 Memorandum, 2 Feb. 1924, D'Abernon Papers, BL Add. MS 48927; memorandum by Schubert, 2 Feb., 2368/490724-28.

3 D'Abernon to FO, 5 Feb. 1924, C 2048/2048/18, FO 371/9818; memorandum by Schubert, 5 Feb., 2368/490734-37. It should be noted that Schubert, according to his record of 2 February (see n. 2), was non-committal about any offer that the German Government might be prepared to make.

4 Diary entry, 7 Feb. 1924, BL Add. MS 48927, not in *Ambassador of Peace.* On 11 February D'Abernon reported a conversation with Stresemann that day (C 2564/737/18, FO 371/9801). In view of the apparent lack of a German record of this conversation and the existence of a record of one between Schubert and D'Abernon on 11 February (2368/490748-56), F.G. Stambrook (' "Das Kind" - Lord D'Abernon and the origins of the Locarno pact', *Central European History* 1 (1968), 233-63) is in doubt whether D'Abernon did see Stresemann. According to his diary D'Abernon had tea with the Stresemanns on 7 February and the social nature of the occasion may account for the lack of a German record. In his despatch of 11 February D'Abernon reported Stresemann as saying that he was anxious to meet MacDonald, a statement unlikely to be made by Schubert. It seems probable that D'Abernon did see Stresemann about this time, but whether once or twice, and on which day or days, is not clear.

an agreement on the lines of the Cuno offer or Stresemann's Stuttgart speech, or indeed any safeguards conceivable between independent and equal states so long as they did not diminish Reich sovereignty over the Rhineland. The French talk of a demilitarised Rhineland under the League of Nations, however, was clearly meant as a first step towards its separation from Germany, and no German Government could lend themselves to that. Infringements of German sovereignty going beyond the Treaty of Versailles could only be discussed if France accepted the same conditions for herself.[1] Sthamer left a memorandum to this effect at the Foreign Office, but he did not have an opportunity to discuss it with MacDonald. On the same day Schubert gave D'Abernon a similar paper, which said in addition that a proposal on the Rhineland should preferably come from France.[2]

With the setting up of the Dawes Committee and the advent of the Labour Government in Britain the French too began new approaches. On taking office MacDonald exchanged civil letters with Poincaré, which included some general references to security.[3] Poincaré's language in public was as intransigent as ever, but the British Embassy in Paris were told that he was anxious for an agreement with Britain about security and reparations and that St-Aulaire was going to approach the Foreign Office.[4] As for possible terms, the Embassy thought the French were unlikely to favour neutralisation of the Rhineland and would probably insist on the continuance of control over the line of the Rhine, which was vital for France even if she had a pact with Britain.[5] The French themselves were pointing out that the line of the Rhine was vital for France's allies.[6] When St-Aulaire saw MacDonald he said, in contrast with the previous year, that it was the view of the French Government that security and reparations were bound up together. They had no definite proposals but were willing to take a wider view of security

1 AA to Sthamer, 4 Feb. 1924, K126/K102934-46.

2 Memorandum from Sthamer, 11 Feb. 1924, C 2602/2048/18, FO 371/9818; K126/K103012-16; memorandum by Schubert, 11 Feb., 2368/490748-56; D'Abernon to FO, 19 Feb., C 2842/2048/18, FO 371/9818.

3 *The Times,* 4 Feb. and 3 Mar. 1924.

4 Phipps to FO, 17 and 18 Mar, 1924, C 4545, 4546, 4604/1288/18, FO 371/9813.

5 Phipps to FO, 14 and 16 Mar. 1924, C 4393, 4411/2048/18, FO 371/9818.

6 Hoesch to AA, 12 Feb. and 4 Mar. 1924; memorandum by Stresemann, 12 Feb., 3243/D722655-61, D722671-75; K1885/K474497-99; Stresemann, *Vermächtnis,* Vol. I, 295-8. In view of this consideration Stresemann at the beginning of March consulted Hoesch and the Minister in Warsaw, Rauscher, about the advisability of taking pre-emptive action by offering Poland a conciliation or arbitration treaty without recognition of the frontier. Rauscher was discouraging and the idea was not pursued: 4356/E148361-68, E148359, E148354-57, E148345-46.

than just an Anglo-French arrangement, and to bring in the League.[1]

MacDonald, however, was not willing to discuss security until agreement had been reached about reparations, and his views on security were different from those of either the French or the Germans. Before taking office he had written: 'The policy of a Labour Government would proceed on lines very different from those hitherto pursued in search of national security and confidence. . .We have to abandon every vestige of trust in military equipment', and during a transition period when purely defensive forces might be necessary, 'work sleeplessly to place national security on a totally different foundation'. As to what that foundation might be: 'We must find in the League of Nations the focus of our contacts with Europe. We must have no sectional alliances. We must give no guarantees of a special kind. . .We can keep the initiative. . .by patiently building up Councils and Courts that would be more judicial than legislative,. . .that would afford general guarantees of safety and establish that calm and confident mind which must precede, or at any rate accompany, any general scheme of disarmament'.[2] MacDonald allowed the Foreign Office to collect advice about the future of the Rhineland and the implications for Britain of permanent French control;[3] but he sent instructions that Stresemann should be told that a solution of the security problem should be aimed at 'not through regional combinations of individual States, which might savour of the old system of alliances, but through general and more universal arrangements for neutralisation and non-aggression'. He spoke only in very general terms to Sthamer on 17 March; and he indicated to St-Aulaire a week later that he thought a satisfactory reparation settlement which Germany could accept would go far towards solving the security problem as well.[4]

After the publication and acceptance, in April, of the Dawes Report the security question was therefore in suspense while the Allies discussed putting the plan into effect. One problem was the French and Belgian desire for guarantees of joint action in case of future German default. When the Belgian Prime Minister and Foreign Minister, Theunis and

1 FO to Crewe, 24 Mar. 1924, C 4992/32/18, FO 371/9730; St-Aulaire to Q d'O, 24 Mar., MAE, Grande Bretagne, Vol. 71.

2 Ramsay MacDonald, *The Foreign Policy of the Labour Party* (London, 1923), 19-24.

3 Memorandum by Sterndale-Bennett, 5 Feb. 1924, Phipps to Nicolson, 20 Feb.; Addison (Berlin) to Nicolson, 1 Mar.; Board of Trade, Air Ministry, Admiralty, War Office to FO, 12, 18, 22, 28 Mar., C 2028, 2946, 3814, 4218, 4640, 4893, 5185/1346/18, FO 371/9813.

4 FO to Addison, 26 Feb. 1924, C 2564/737/18, FO 371/9801; Sthamer to AA, 17 Mar., K126/K013037-40; FO to Phipps, 24 Mar., C 4992/32/18, FO 371/9730.

Hymans, visited him at Chequers on 2 and 3 May, MacDonald said that he would be willing to declare that a wilful German default would automatically bring the Allies together to take common action; but he would hold out no hope of going farther. Security was not discussed.[1]

The Belgian visit was to have been followed by one from Poincaré, but this had to be cancelled when, as a result of the general election victory of the Cartel des Gauches, he announced his government's intention to resign. A visit by the new President of the Council, Herriot, was fixed for June. Before leaving for England Herriot, in a statement to the Chamber of Deputies, drew a distinction between guarantees for the execution of the Dawes Plan which he intended to discuss with MacDonald, and guarantees for security which he implied would not be discussed now. But to Hymans Herriot stressed the need for some arrangement about security.[2]

The greater part of the conversations at Chequers on 21 and 22 June was about putting the Dawes Plan into effect. Herriot accepted MacDonald's promise to declare publicly that a wilful German default would bring the Allies together to take common action, rather than decide on sanctions in advance. He also gave way to some extent on the question of negotiating with the Germans about applying the Dawes Plan in so far as it went beyond the terms of the Treaty of Versailles. Then at the end Herriot asked whether, once reparations had been settled, Britain would join in studying a pact of mutual guarantee within the framework of the League of Nations and including Germany. He proposed an agreement about the guarantees provided by the Treaty of Versailles and an Anglo-French pact on the lines of the recent Franco-Czechoslovak treaty.[3] Then a non-aggression pact with Germany could be considered, and finally the two pacts could be included as regional arrangements in the Treaty of Mutual Assistance. MacDonald replied that he was very desirous of going deeply into the whole question of security but he must mention various difficulties. The Dominions were one, Lloyd George another. The Treaty of Mutual Assistance was not likely to be accepted. His own view was opposed to a pact, but he would agree to a full examination of the whole question and he threw out an idea of widening it by bringing in the United States in connexion with disarmament. Herriot replied with a

1 Record of conversation, 2-3 May 1924, C 7427/70/18, FO 371/9743.

2 *Journal officiel, Chambre des députés,* 19 Jun. 1924; Grahame to FO, 20 Jun., C 9842/70/18, FO 371/9748.

3 This treaty provided for consultations and concerted action in case of threats to the two countries' security or to the situation created by the peace treaties. There was no military convention. See Wandycz, *France and her Eastern Allies,* 297-301.

speech about the danger to France if one day Germany refused to pay reparations and expelled the control organs. France, he said, could not rely on a conference alone and the United States was far away. France could not face a new war: could they not try to find a formula of guarantee against a danger of a kind that would make the Dawes Plan useless?

MacDonald said that he would do all in his power to avoid a new war and would join in a study of the question, but he could not offer France a military guarantee. He was ready to visit Paris, once the Dawes Report was out of the way, and discuss debts and security and other matters. He had no complete plan in mind but he had a profound conviction, which, he indicated, mainly had to do with enlightening public opinion. MacDonald spoke of a 'vast conception of broad policy and continuous collaboration', and Herriot summed up the result of their meeting as 'a sort of moral pact of continuous collaboration'. On that note the talks ended.[1]

A certain confusion was caused a few days later by a Belgian newspaper report of an interview in which Herriot appeared to have said that MacDonald had promised solidarity in case of German aggression, and MacDonald denied it in the House of Commons.[2] Worse agitation was caused in France by the publication of a British memorandum sent to the Italian Government with the invitation to the conference on the Dawes Plan, because it seemed to ignore French views about negotiating with the Germans, defaults, and the relationship between the plan and the Treaty of Versailles.[3] MacDonald therefore went over to Paris. Besides dealing with these matters, the French again raised the question of security. Their draft proposals concerning the London conference ended by saying that reparations and security were connected, and

1 Record of conversations, 21-22 Jun. 1924, C 10427, 11976/70/18, FO 371/9749, 9751. The British record is a translation of the French interpreter's notes, largely printed in Georges Suarez, *Herriot 1924-32* (Paris, 1932), 55-148. The accounts in Edouard Herriot, *Jadis*, Vol. II (Paris, 1952), 139-45, and Michel Soulié, *La Vie politique d'Edouard Herriot* (Paris, 1962), 159-61, are based on this record. See also Schuker, *The End of French Predominance in Europe*, 237-44.

2 Soulié, *Vie politique d'Edouard Herriot*, 162-3; *HC Deb.*, 5th ser., Vol. 175, cols. 593-6. Since the French record of the conversation is clear on this point it seems more likely that the *Indépendance Belge* misconstrued Herriot's references to MacDonald's promise of solidarity in case of German default than that, as Snowden suggested (*Autobiography* (London, 1934), Vol. II, 667-9), Herriot misunderstood MacDonald. Hymans at any rate was clear that Herriot told him that MacDonald had refused a new guarantee: Grahame to FO, 23 Jun., C 10151/70/18, FO 371/9748.

3 Cmd 2184 of 1924, *Correspondence concerning the Conference which it is proposed to hold in London on July 16, 1924 to consider the measures necessary to bring the Dawes Plan into operation.*

that none of France's problems could be regarded as completely solved until a satisfactory solution had been found on security. As Herriot put it: 'On the day that Germany finds herself strong enough to refuse to pay us she would inevitably bring about a new war'.

MacDonald said that the danger was possible, but all that they were discussing at present was the wording of a paragraph in a joint memorandum on the London conference. The other was a difficult problem to be solved between their two countries. He had already said that when the question was dealt with two considerations should be borne in mind. First, the greatest security was that it was a question of honour; secondly, in his view the only guarantee lay not in armaments or alliances but in an entente between France and Britain, general security, and the establishment of peace in Europe. It would be really unfortunate if they could not find a way of bringing about a complete entente between them: they must begin to work out a common policy by educating public opinion in both countries. He knew the French difficulties, but if they would help him they would together succeed in 'establishing psychological conditions which will permit us to dissipate the reasonable fears of your country in regard to security. This security will be achieved to the greatest possible extent if we succeed in obtaining disarmament'.

After dinner MacDonald asked Herriot what would satisfy the Chamber without contradicting his own statements. Herriot said that French opinion remained wedded to the idea of a pact with Britain, but he had suggested at Chequers a non-aggression pact into which Germany could be introduced. The fact must be faced that when the guarantees on the left bank of the Rhine expired France would be exposed: if there were no defensive system he would be unable to ask the Assembly for military reorganisation and reduction of the period of conscription.

MacDonald said that the next President of the United States was certain to call a disarmament conference, and if he were still in office he would do his utmost to have general security discussed. The question must be put broadly, for a number of people in Britain regarded French armaments as a threat to British security. But he and Herriot had agreed to go to Geneva in September. This would make it clear that they were taking more than an exclusively national view of security. If he were a French minister he would explain that the two governments wished to create a general system and that each country would benefit itself by contributing. Herriot said that he shared these views: such a programme could be stated as: 'The security of each nation is a particular instance of the general security of the world'. But before they arrived at that ideal state there would be a period when France would be unprotected; and he pressed for an assurance that this problem would be considered. MacDonald refused. He would prefer, he said, to go on talking in that 'moral collaboration' of which he had spoken at Chequers, with frequent meetings which might sometimes include other countries. But Herriot might send him a note, and could tell the Chamber that the two governments agreed to take up the security problem again at an early meeting.[1]

All questions other than that of putting the Dawes Plan into operation were excluded from the agenda of the London conference of July-August 1924. The British, having taken no part in the occupation of the Ruhr, tried to mediate in the Franco-German negotiations over evacuation. The Germans seem to have hoped for British support; and it appears that MacDonald pressed for early evacuation but was alone in doing so because the United States representative, Kellogg, supported the French view that a period of one year was reasonable.[2] There is only scant evidence of security being discussed. The Germans were particularly anxious to provide against any possible repetition of the occupation. Some weeks before the conference D'Abernon suggested to the State Secretary in the Auswärtiges Amt that they should offer an agreement combining a neutralised strip on both sides of the frontier with the evacuation of all Allied troops from Germany and the withdrawal of the Control Commission; but his idea does not seem to have been pursued.[3] During the conference German officials dropped hints that the French should be content with security on their own

1 Record of conversations, 8 Jul. 1924, C 12031, 11468/10794/18, FO 371/9849. The memorandum published at the end of the meeting, embodying an agreed approach to the London conference, ended with a statement that the two governments intended to co-operate in devising means of securing the complete pacification demanded by public opinion, and to continue the consideration of the question until the problem of general security could be finally solved: Cmd 2191 of 1924, *Franco-British Memorandum of July 9, 1924, concerning the application of the Dawes Scheme.*

2 File C 11495/18, FO 371/9855-8; CP 441(24), CAB 23/168; MacDonald Papers, PRO 30/69/1/167; 3398/D739833-740585; 4492/E099507-100401, *passim.* The British records of the conference are not nearly so full as those of other conferences of the early 1920s, and no record was made of meetings of heads of the Allied delegations or of private conversations of British ministers, The *procès-verbaux* of plenary meetings were published in Cmd 2270 of 1924, *Proceedings of the London Reparation Conference, July and August 1924.* Published accounts include Herriot, *Jadis,* Vol. II, 152-67; Soulié, *Vie politique d'Edouard Herriot,* 170-2; Stresemann, *Vermächtnis,* Vol. II, 469-98; Paul Otto Schmidt, *Statist auf diplomatischer Bühne* (Bonn, 1949), 49-63; David Marquand, *Ramsay MacDonald* (London, 1977), 342-50. Schuker, *The End of French Predominance in Europe,* 295-382, uses important banking material.

3 Memorandum by Maltzan, 7 Jun. 1924, 4492/E098727-30.

frontier and stop worrying about Poland: if they did so it should not be difficult to conclude a pact, since Germany had every reason to seek security against French action.[1]

Security was, however, a factor in the minds of the French in discussing the evacuation of the Ruhr, and was the reason why Herriot consulted Marshal Foch as well as the Cabinet when he returned to Paris in the middle of the conference. Afterwards he sent MacDonald the suggested note on French security. It elaborated the proposal which Herriot had outlined at Chequers and set out the French position as based firstly on the guarantees provided in the Treaty of Versailles. On these the French Government asked for 'strict, complete and effective execution', by the completion of German disarmament, by the organisation of the right of investigation of the demilitarised condition of the Rhineland under Article 213, and by the maintenance of the occupation under the conditions provided in the Treaty - i.e. as long as the guarantees resulting from the Treaty were not organised. Then there was the question of supplementary guarantees to replace the Anglo-American treaties of 1919. Here the French asked for: '(a) Conclusion between France and England of a defensive pact destined to replace that concluded in 1919; this pact, an essential factor in the maintenance of peace in Europe, would be completed by similar defensive pacts concluded between the Allies neighbouring on Germany; (b) Conclusion between the signatories of the above-mentioned pacts and Germany of a reciprocal undertaking of non-aggression, this undertaking and those pacts being placed under the safeguard of the League of Nations; (c) Reinforcement of the effective authority of the League of Nations by the efficacious organisation of mutual assistance against States guilty of aggression'. The French Government, the note concluded, were ready to examine any proposals made to them, but if French opinion were to be pacified the guarantees offered must be effective. The framers of the Treaty of Versailles had understood that necessity when they provided in Article 429 that if at the moment fixed for the end of the occupation of the Rhineland the guarantees against German aggression were not considered sufficient, evacuation might be delayed. The French Government hoped that it

1 Memorandum by Schubert, 11 Aug. 1924, 4492/E100325-29; AA to Stresemann, 12 Aug., 3398/D740365-67; D'Abernon, *Ambassador of Peace,* Vol. III, 87-8; Wandycz, *France and her Eastern Allies,* 313. According to Henry L. Bretton, *Stresemann and the Revision of Versailles* (Stanford, 1953), 81, there is evidence that while in London Stresemann offered to revive the Cuno offer; but Bretton does not cite it, and it has not proved possible to confirm his statement. Stresemann himself reported a French expression of interest in a pact: 3398/D740267-69.

would never be necessary to apply that clause, but they must seek really effective guarantees in agreement with their Allies.[1]

The anxieties expressed by the French about the completion of German disarmament arose out of a long argument during 1924 about a general inspection by the Military Control Commission. During 1922 the Aeronautical Control Commission had been withdrawn and replaced by a committee of guarantees, and the naval commission had almost completed its work. In the autumn the Ambassadors' Conference proposed to the Germans, on certain conditions, the restriction of military control to five aspects of disarmament - reorganisation of the police, adaptation of factories, surrender of war material, provision of figures of war material existing at the time of the armistice and of production before and since, and promulgation of legislation on trade in war material and on recruiting and army organisation. The occupation of the Ruhr interrupted negotiations on this offer and the activities of the Control Commission had to be suspended because of the risk of incidents; but there were numerous reports during 1923 of illegal expansion of the Reichswehr. On 5 March 1924 a note was sent to the German Government proposing a general inspection to find out whether the position was the same as that at the end of 1922, after which, if the result was satisfactory, control would be limited to the five points. The Germans, who maintained that disarmament had been completed, did not at first agree. After their meeting at Chequers MacDonald and Herriot appealed to the German Chancellor, Marx, not to reject the latest note from the Ambassadors' Conference and warned him that a new failure on disarmament would seriously affect the international situation just at the moment when there was a real hope of improvement. The German Government then agreed to the general inspection and it was fixed to begin in September. At the London conference the French tried to get MacDonald to agree to a declaration about it. MacDonald, having already written to Marx about the importance of allowing the inspection to be carried out without obstruction, refused; but he agreed that if it later transpired that obstruction was occurring the matter should be taken up by the Ambassadors' Conference.[2]

1 Herriot to MacDonald, 11 Aug. 1924, C 12870/2048/18, FO 371/9819; MAE, Grande Bretagne, Vol. 71.

2 Conversation between MacDonald and Marx, 12 Aug. 1924, 4492/E099932-40, 3398/D740363; MacDonald to Marx, Herriot, Theunis, De Stefani, and Hayashi, 13 Aug.; Herriot to MacDonald, 14 Aug.; Marx to MacDonald, 16 Aug.; Lampson to Hankey, 19 Aug.; FO to D'Abernon, 25 Aug.; Schubert to Lampson, 25 Aug.; C 12850, 13070, 13247, 13346, 13724/9/18, FO 371/9727-8. For the negotiations of 1924 see *Survey of International Affairs, 1925,* Vol. III, 172-9. A full account of the whole subject from the German side is Michael Salewski, *Entwaffnung und Militärkontrolle in Deutschland 1919-1927,* (Munich, 1966).

After the London conference MacDonald went on holiday before going to Geneva for the League Assembly meeting. Herriot's note was sent to the Committee of Imperial Defence and the comments of the service departments were invited. The General Staff sent in a long paper supporting a pact with France on the ground that 'under conditions as they now are and are likely to be for many years to come German aggression is the greatest danger that faces us, and French security is our security'. They had concluded earlier in the year [1] that there were only two directions in which to look for security, a strong and effective League of Nations or a defensive alliance with France. The first was still too remote for present French needs; the second had twice failed but was now proposed again. The General Staff believed that a pact would have definite advantages for Britain as well as France. It would in one sense be no more than a formal recognition of the fact that Britain would inevitably be involved on the side of France in the case of renewed aggression; but it would allow the French to reckon on Britain being with them at the earliest and most critical moment; it would open the way for closer staff contacts and freer exchange of military information; and it would give Britain the great advantage of having definitely enlisted the most powerful army and air force in Europe as a screen between herself and Germany.

There was, the General Staff agreed, little chance of German aggression in the immediate future: at present Germany could not defend herself against the Allies. Her future capacity to engage in war depended on manpower and armaments. German fit manpower [2] greatly exceeded that of France and Belgium combined (by about 5 million in 1924 according to French calculations) and would do so even more in the 1930s. Germany had ample industrial capacity to rearm. She must therefore not be allowed to do so in peacetime: 'In no circumstances must the Allies be so supine as to sacrifice the initiative in a future war'. This implied a policy of keeping a firm hold on Lorraine and, for the time being, the Saar, and maintaining the demilitarisation of the Rhineland. To implement this purely defensive policy France and Belgium needed the moral and material support of Britain.

1 War Office to FO, 28 Mar. 1924, C 5185/1346/18, FO 371/9813; War Office to FO, 24 Jun., C 10067/2048/18, FO 371/9818.

2 I.e. men between the ages of 20 and 36 physically fit for battle service. In view of doubts about the accuracy of the figures in this paper, the estimates were recalculated by the Government Actuary and the Registrar-General. The revised figures showed that the General Staff had made insufficient allowance for the effects of the war and had overestimated both French and German fit manpower for the next five years; but that the German fit male population aged between 20 and 35 would exceed the French by 1.6 million in 1924, 2.5 million in 1929, 3.3 million in 1934, 2.8 million in 1939, and 2.6 million in 1944: CID paper 654-B, CAB 4/14.

On the terms of the alliance thus advocated, the General Staff recommended that Britain should not undertake obligations beyond the defence of France and Belgium, even if other pacts were concluded by the Allies bordering on Germany. As to carrying out these obligations, she could not state even approximately the size of the land forces that she could contribute; but she must be prepared to contribute with all three services and meanwhile must not weaken her home defences. The General Staff welcomed the idea of non-aggression undertakings with Germany. They also welcomed the idea of strengthening the League, but considered that it would be many years before regional pacts would be unnecessary.[1]

[1] CID paper 516-B, CAB 4/11. Air and Naval Staff comments, CID papers 518-B, 545-B, CAB 4/11, 4/12.

3

THE GENEVA PROTOCOL AND THE ORIGINS OF LOCARNO

The Protocol for the Pacific Settlement of International Disputes arose out of the moral collaboration of Herriot and MacDonald and out of the Assembly's determination to pursue the cause of disarmament and security despite the rejection of the Treaty of Mutual Assistance. In less than a month from the adoption of a resolution inviting two of its committees to consider security, disarmament, the obligations of the Covenant, and the settlement of disputes, the Assembly received the complete Protocol and unanimously recommended it to member governments.

The main features of the Protocol were, first, an undertaking by signatories that they would in no case go to war except with the consent or at the behest of the Council of the League. This provision was supposed to stop the 'gap' in the Covenant, under which members recovered freedom of action in the event of the Council failing to reach a recommendation. To reduce the chances of such failure the second feature was elaborated provision for the settlement of all disputes. Signatories were to accept the compulsory jurisdiction of the Permanant Court of International Justice for the four categories of dispute listed in the optional clause of its statute. For non-juridical disputes further stages of arbitration were added to the procedures laid down in the Covenant. In each case signatories undertook to accept the award made, and not to increase their armaments or effectives while a dispute to which they were party was pending. Thirdly, the Protocol provided a more automatic definition of an aggressor than any found hitherto: namely that a state which resorted to war in defiance of the obligations of the Covenant or of the Protocol, that is which refused to comply with an award, or which violated measures enjoined by the Council for the period while proceedings were under way, was presumed to be an aggressor unless the Council unanimously declared otherwise. Fourthly, if aggression took place the Council would call upon signatories to apply the sanctions provided for in Article 16 of the Covenant. Their obligation to do so became operative at once, and each was bound to co-operate loyally and effectively so far as its geographical position and its military situation allowed. General plans of economic action were to be drawn up. Signatories might make promises to the Council about contributing forces: existing military agreements were to stand provided that they were opened to accession by other countries and would not come into operation until the Council called on signatories to apply military sanctions. Finally a disarmament conference was to meet in July 1925, and the Protocol was not to come into effect until a plan for the reduction of armaments had been accepted and carried out.[1]

None of this had been prepared or studied in Whitehall in advance. MacDonald had sought some information from Geneva, but does not appear to have consulted his colleagues.[2] The British delegates, Parmoor and Henderson, acted very much on their own in helping to draft the Protocol. The service representatives at Geneva were not consulted, and raised the alarm in London. The Dominion delegates complained of being rushed.[3] MacDonald reassured the Dominion Governments that they had not been committed, and on 22 September told a meeting of ministers that the obligations of the Protocol did not exceed those of the Covenant; but still a week later the Cabinet expressed concern lest the Protocol be signed before they had had a chance to consider it.[4] Parmoor therefore, to his regret, was instructed not to sign, but to emphasis that the Protocol would have to be examined by governments and parliaments.

Examination had barely begun in London before the Government were defeated in the House of Commons and Parliament was dissolved. Despite the lack of discussion, the evidence of Dominion and departmental objections and of differences of approach within their own ranks is strong enough to make it appear extremely unlikely that the Labour Government, had they remained in office, would have been able to sign the Protocol without amendments so far-reaching as to ensure its eventual failure.[5] They might have been more willing than

1 The text of the Protocol and the Assembly resolutions is in Cmd 2273 of 1924, *League of Nations, Fifth Assembly, Arbitration, Security and Reduction of Armaments. Protocol and Resolutions adopted by the Assembly, and Report by the First and Third Committees of the Assembly.* A full contemporary commentary is P.J. Noel Baker, *The Geneva Protocol* (London, 1925).

2 Salter to Selby, 11 Aug. 1924; Drummond to Selby, 22 Aug., W 7259/134/98, FO 371/10569; Sir Frederick Maurice, *Haldane,* Vol. II (London, 1939), 167. The basis for the Protocol was provided mainly by the replies of governments on the Treaty of Mutual Assistance and the work of an American committee: Noel Baker, *The Geneva Protocol,* 18-19; Walters, *History of the League of Nations,* Vol. I, 269-70.

3 CP 456(24), CAB 24/168; summary of BED meetings, W 8073/134/98, FO 371/10570.

4 Colonial Office to FO, 23 Sep. 1924, W 8226/134/98, FO 371/10570; C 51(24), CAB 23/48.

5 MacDonald, on returning from Geneva before the Protocol was completed, expressed to Herriot the hope that the work would not be regarded as 'unalterable gospel' since it would have to be the subject of further negotiations. Herriot in reply indicated that France would need more than the Protocol before she could disarm: Herriot, *Jadis,* Vol. II, 174-5, 177-8. See also Marquand, *Ramsay MacDonald,* 351-6; MacDonald, 'Protocol or Pact', *International Conciliation*

their immediate successors to accept compulsory arbitration;[1] but it is most improbable that they would have been more ready to accept automatic sanctions. Without these, however, agreement on disarmament was virtually inconceivable, and so an amended Protocol would not have come into force. But then the failure would have appeared to be less Britain's responsibility than that of militaristic European governments.

Examination of the Protocol and an alternative policy, November 1924 - February 1925

When serious discussion of the Protocol started in London it soon became apparent that it would not be accepted as it stood, but also that it could hardly be simply rejected. The consequences of doing either seemed likely to be serious. The extension of the provisions for compulsory arbitration beyond even the juridical types of dispute listed in the optional clause of the statute of the Permanent Court of International Justice carried the risk that in case of an adverse award on a matter felt to be of vital interest a government might feel bound to repudiate 'the most solemn engagement entered into with the League, if this offers the only means of resistance to a political engagement which a free country will not accept at foreign dictation'.[2] The provision on sanctions introduced not only a form of commitment which British governments and opinion particularly disliked - the obligation to use force in circumstances which could not be foreseen - but also that of setting up the complicated machinery of blockade for purposes in which the chief sufferers might have little interest, which could not be effective unless universally applied, and which would involve Britain in disputes with non-signatory countries. Admittedly if Britain accepted the Protocol other major powers would be more likely to do so; but the United States was likely to be further deterred from joining the League, and the war had shown the danger of conflict with her: 'there is no exaggeration in saying that this country, if a signatory of the Protocol, may easily find itself placed in a position of having to choose between abandoning the fulfilment of its

No. 212, Sep. 1925; Lord Parmoor, *A Retrospect* (London, 1936), 234-41; Mary Agnes Hamilton, *Arthur Henderson* (London, 1938), 247-50. Further evidence of service objections expressed before polling day is in CP 478(24), CAB 24/168; CID paper 527-B, CAB 4/11.

1 The Labour Party favoured British signature of the optional clause of the statute of the Permanent Court of International Justice. The Lord Chancellor, Haldane, advised against acceptance in July 1924 but the matter was not discussed by the Cabinet: file W 338/98, FO 371/10573. The second Labour Government signed the clause in 1929.

2 Crowe in CID paper 538-B, CAB 4/12.

obligation under the Protocol or either having to pay blackmail to, or actually going to war with, the United States'.[1] Finally the attitude of the Dominions, although not yet known, might well be hostile to the Protocol. If Britain decided to accept it for the sake of Europe, and failed to persuade the Dominions to do so too, the Empire would be dangerously divided.

On the other hand the consequences of rejection would be serious at once. The argument of the Protocol's supporters - that it provided the only possible basis for the reduction of armaments and strengthened the League - could be contested. But that the Protocol gave France new guarantees of security could not be denied, even though there was some doubt whether she would want a supplementary pact with Britain as well. British defection from a scheme of Anglo-French origin would produce a strong reaction in France, and hence affect a whole range of European problems. The only thing that would compensate France for the loss of the guarantee in the Protocol was a British guarantee of assistance.

When the Committee of Imperial Defence began their discussion of the Protocol in December all these considerations had been put to them.[2] At first little progress was made and it seemed doubtful whether the task could be completed before the March meeting of the League Council.[3] On 16 December the new Foreign Secretary Austen Chamberlain, who had been attending the December Council meeting in Rome, reported on his conversations and impressions. Chamberlain had accepted the Foreign Office in Baldwin's Cabinet determined to have a policy and to take responsibility for foreign affairs as a whole. He saw close Anglo-French relations as the key to the solution of European problems.[4] Behind his monocle and glacially English-gentleman exterior Chamberlain was a man of strong feelings and of complete honesty, who put loyalty above his personal advancement. He was

1 Ibid.

2 CID papers 527-B, 536-B, 537-B, 538-B, 539-B, 540-B, 542-B, CAB 4/11-12; CP 481(24), CAB 24/168.

3 CID 190th, 191st meetings, CAB 2/4.

4 For Chamberlain's appointment, his intentions and his relations with Cecil see Douglas Johnson, 'Austen Chamberlain and the Locarno Agreements', *University of Birmingham Historical Journal* 7 (1961), No. 1, 62-8. Cecil was not asking, as Johnson states, to see all Foreign Office papers (which not even the Secretary of State necessarily saw), but for all the confidential print, the more important correspondence printed and circulated in the Foreign Office and to missions abroad. Even this was more than any other minister received and Crowe feared that granting his request would create an undesirable precedent and cause trouble in the Cabinet: memorandum by Crowe, 20 Nov. 1924; Chamberlain to Cecil, 21 Nov.; Cecil to Chamberlain, 22 Nov., Chamberlain Papers, AC 51/83, 43, 46; Cecil Papers, BL Add. MS 41078.

particularly touchy when others failed to keep their word to him. As the son of Joseph Chamberlain he believed in the British Empire, but he understood Europe (or at least western Europe) better than many other British politicians. Passing through Paris on 5 December Chamberlain tried to find out from Herriot whether the Protocol would satisfy the French desire for security. He got the impression that France would want a pact as well, an impression confirmed by Briand, who was the French delegate to the Council. Hymans, too, left Chamberlain sure that Belgium would ask for a pact. Even Beneš, who regarded the Protocol as satisfactory from a European point of view, said that what chiefly mattered to his country was that Germany should not go to war, and she would not do so if France and Britain were united in an alliance. Mussolini, on the other hand, seemed likely to reject the Protocol.[1]

His journey, Chamberlain told the Committee, had left him with a profound sense of the importance of the decision facing them. The dominant feeling in Europe was fear. Unless British policy - the policy of the Empire - were made such as to give Europe a sense of security there would be another war. It would be easy to turn down the Protocol, but to do nothing more would be a disaster. Cecil suggested that they should try to revise the Protocol rather than substitute something different. He believed that great difficulties would arise from a pact with France and Belgium, because European peace could not be secured without Germany. Chamberlain replied that a pact with Germany might follow but the French would not have such an arrangement in the initial document. He undertook to explore the position of the United States, and urged that a conclusion should be reached by March. It was decided to set up a sub-committee to report on the Protocol, and to ask the Dominions to send their Prime Ministers to London for discussions.[2]

The first replies from the Dominions made it clear that it would be impossible to organise a conference.[3] Three of them sent their views

1 Records of conversations, 5-11 Dec. 1924, C 18401/1288/18, FO 371/9813; W 10620, 10747, 10867, 10868/134/98, FO 371/10572; W 10865/9992/4, FO 371/10531; Chamberlain to Crowe, 6 Dec., W 11388/631/17, FO 371/10540; CID 192nd meeting, CAB 2/4. The Conseil Supérieur de la Défense Nationale had sent Herriot on 3 December a draft of a pact with Britain within the framework of the Protocol: MAE, Grande Bretagne, Vol. 71.

2 CID 192nd meeting, CAB 2/4.

3 CO 59996/24, CO 532/283. Most of the correspondence was published in Cmd 2458 of 1925, *Protocol for the Pacific Settlement of International Disputes. Correspondence relating to the Position of the Dominions,* and some in Cmd 2301 of 1925, *Consultation on matters of foreign policy and general Imperial interest. Correspondence with the Governments of the self-governing Dominions.*

on the Protocol in January. The New Zealand, Australian and South African Governments all said that they could not accept it, for various reasons including the extension of compulsory arbitration and the probable effect on the United States. The Canadian Government did not reply until March. They were ready to go farther on arbitration but would not undertake any obligation to apply sanctions, and were particularly concerned about the United States. The Irish Free State Government did not reply until June. None made any positive proposals.[1]

Enquiries in Washington elicited an expression of hostility to the Protocol from Hughes, who said that if it went through the United States would hardly be able to avoid regarding the League as a 'potential enemy', although he thought that sanctions would be impossible to apply in practice. The British Ambassador, Sir Esmé Howard, suggested to Chamberlain that if the Protocol were accepted the British and Dominion Governments should acknowledge the status of the United States by declaring that they would not be bound to apply sanctions until they had reached agreement with her.[2]

The CID sub-committee, composed of senior officials,[3] soon decided that it was virtually impossible to amend the Protocol since the whole structure depended on compulsory arbitration and Chamberlain had encouraged them to assume that the Government would rule out both it and automatic sanctions. They also agreed that if the Dominions did not accept the Protocol Britain could not do so.[4] After Christmas Hankey raised the question of France's desire for a pact in addition to the Protocol; and Crowe said that he thought they could point out the possibility of a pact as an alternative.[5] Examination of the Protocol was changing Hankey's view of a pact with France. He had been opposed to one in 1922, believing that it would bring more difficulties than advantages although he had not doubted that if France were again threatened by Germany Britain would go to her assistance. He now

1 Cmd 2458 of 1925; W 335/9/98, FO 371/11064; CO 48495/24, CO 532/283; CO 2897/25, CO 532/316.

2 Chamberlain to Howard, 22 Dec. 1924, W 11199/134/98, FO 371/10572; Howard to Chamberlain, 9 Jan. 1925, W 1174/9/98, FO 371/11064; Chamberlain to Howard, 28 Jan.; Howard to Chamberlain, 13 Feb., Chamberlain Papers, AC 52/479, 482; *FRUS, 1925,* Vol. I, 16-18.

3 Hankey (chairman), Crowe, Sir Arthur Hirtzel (Under-Secretary of State for India), and Sir Henry Lambert (Acting Permanent Under-Secretary of State for the Colonies). The Legal Adviser to the Foreign Office, Hurst, attended several of the meetings, and representatives of the Treasury, the Board of Trade, and the Chiefs of Staff were called in for advice.

4 Sub-committee, 1st-4th meetings, CAB 16/56.

5 Sub-committee, 6th meeting, loc. cit.

accepted that Britain would be in a difficult position if she were at loggerheads with France and there was a real risk of being at loggerheads if the Protocol were rejected and nothing put in its place; and Crowe had a proposal for a declaration which removed some of the dangers which he had seen in a pact. Hankey considered a pact, which would be geographically limited, precise, and within British control, preferable to the Protocol, which was vague, unlimited, and applicable either automatically or by a majority vote of the Council.[1]

Crowe's new proposal was embodied in the sub-committee's report, which began by saying that the Protocol tended to emphasise and extend the provisions of the Covenant relating to the use of force in preventing war, provisions which were originally accepted with hesitation and had been viewed with misgivings by government departments ever since the United States had decided not to become a member of the League. It therefore represented a parting of the ways for the League. The Government, the sub-committee assumed, would prefer the League to go on developing on the lines of achieving pacification by conciliation and discussion, with moral force as the principal weapon and material force in the background. In case it was decided to try amending the Protocol they produced a new draft, omitting compulsory arbitration and the ban on defensive measures during proceedings for the settlement of a dispute, and qualifying the obligation to take particular measures in support of the Covenant. On military sanctions members of the League might, they suggested, inform the Council of specific cases in which they would be prepared to make their maximum effort.

These recommendations, however, changed the character of the Protocol so fundamentally that France was no longer likely to regard it as any use from the point of view of security. The only alternative was some kind of pact of guarantee, which was less objectionable than the Protocol from the British point of view. A draft declaration was submitted, in which the British, French and Belgian Governments would announce that the maintenance of the independence and integrity of their territories bordering on the North Sea and the Channel constituted a vital interest of their respective countries, and would undertake to notify the Council of the League that they would regard any unprovoked aggression threatening the said independence and integrity as one of the contingencies in which they were prepared to make the maximum military effort.

1 CID paper 571-B, 23 Jan. 1925, CAB 4/12. Stephen Roskill's account of Hankey's views at this juncture (*Hankey, Man of Secrets*, Vol. II (London, 1972), 393-6) does not seem to be entirely well founded. Hankey did sign the report.

The sub-committee thought that France and Belgium might accept such a declaration as a sufficient British guarantee, and that it was as far as the Dominions could be asked to go. They had considered whether such a pact could be so framed as to include Germany, but had decided that it could not, because the French would wish to include Germany's eastern neighbours whom Britain would not undertake to defend. However the form could be used for declarations by other groups of states, so that Germany could be brought into a more general system. On procedure the sub-committee recommended that when an understanding had been reached with the Dominions, the Government should try to come to terms with France and Belgium and other members of the Council before replying to the League on the Protocol. Since there would not be time for all this before the March Council meeting, they suggested an interim reply, saying that Britain could not accept the Protocol as it stood but would make further proposals.[1]

At the same time Chamberlain had initiated within the Foreign Office a discussion of Britain's policy in Europe. To begin with he asked for a clear statement of the problem. The first two elements were obvious: a statement of the present position and an historical background. 'But then there remains Chapter III which should be The Solution, and here I am frankly at a loss. Can we propose an Anglo-Franco-Belgian pact of guarantee to be followed by a Quadruple Pact embracing Germany? Or ought we to propose a unilateral declaration of British interests and of what we should regard as a casus belli? Or again is there some third course? And how in any case are we going to defend our vital interests in the West whilst safeguarding ourselves against being dragged into a quarrel over Lithuania or Latvia or Poland or Bessarabia? And what is or ought to be our policy in relation to these countries?'[2]

A statement of the present position was provided by Harold Nicolson, who started by acknowledging that the peoples of the Empire would not accept the task of guaranteeing the complete security desired by the European nations. In his analysis Nicolson left Russia out of account not because she was not important - she was indeed 'the most menacing of all our uncertainties' - but because she was at present an Asian rather than a European problem and her future was so obscure that a policy of security must be framed 'in spite of Russia, perhaps

1 CID paper 559-B, 23 Jan. 1925, CAB 4/12. Crowe also tried his hand at a Franco-Belgian-German declaration, guaranteeing the Franco-German and Belgian-German frontiers and the sanctity of the demilitarised zone but saying nothing about Germany's eastern frontiers, but it was not included in the report: C 6882/459/18, FO 371/10731.

2 Minute, 4 Jan. 1925, W 362/9/98, FO 371/11064.

even because of Russia'. For the rest, briefly, 'all our late enemies desire to recover what they lost; and all our late allies are fearful of losing what they won'. Austria was only a problem in so far as she desired fusion with Germany but in terms of French security this was sufficiently disturbing, for it would be hazardous to suppose that in fifteen years' time the Allies would be able to prevent 'so logical and so inevitable a union'. Hungary and Bulgaria were nuclei of insecurity in central and south-east Europe. But the essential cause of insecurity was the fact that, although the lesser peace treaties were secured by a preponderance of manpower on the side of the victors, in the case of the Treaty of Versailles the preponderance told against the *status quo.*

It might be taken as axiomatic that the majority of the German people did not accept the Treaty of Versailles as permanent. Germany hoped to be one day in a position to reverse the verdict: she would doubtless prefer to do so by agreement, but failing agreement she would use force. She would try to avoid being faced again by an alliance between France, Britain and Russia. France on her own could be defeated; Russia could be won as a friend; Britain must not be driven again into hostility. For this reason, and because Germany's principal grievance related to her eastern frontier, her attack, when it came in fifteen to twenty years, would be aimed not at Britain nor directly at France, but at Poland. France's attitude was one of fear, based on the experience of invasion and her declining birthrate. One result of this fear, the network of alliances to the east of Germany, compromised rather than enhanced French security for it drained French resources, increased French commitments, and heightened German resentment without being strong enough to contain it. If France could not be solaced and controlled she would provoke the menace of which she stood in terror. Some fear of Germany was inevitable, but some was due to causes for which Britain was partly responsible and which she might therefore be able to remove. While the League of Nations might one day be able to deal with deep-seated rivalries, at present in any vital matter security could not come from Geneva.

In such an uncertain situation the only line for Britain to follow was that of British interests. Isolation was no longer possible. Britain's primary interests were the defence of the Empire (which was not here in question) and of Great Britain itself. This required that a hostile power should not be in a position to dominate the North Sea and Channel coasts. A secondary interest was the stability of Europe. To some extent this could be fostered by support of the League, but in the short term something must be done to diminish Franco-German hostility without over-burdening imperial resources. Both interests indicated the formation of a new entente with France, and a supplementary policy was needed to keep Germany and Russia apart. Germany might accept a series of non-aggression pacts, which would have some value although they would not carry permanent conviction until 'the dangerous injustices of the Silesian settlement, and the Polish Corridor have been, by mutual agreement, revised'. In the present mood of Europe it would be fatal even to mention treaty revision: gradually, however, the Concert of Europe would be recreated provided France were quietened; but she would only be quietened if Britain could speak to her as an ally. The first hope of European stability therefore lay in a new entente with France.[1]

The historical paper came from Headlam-Morley, who pointed out that one of the difficulties about the Geneva Protocol, and the League, was that they universalised problems that might be better dealt with by something like the Concert of Europe. He demonstrated that Britain had always been part of Europe and that the Concert had worked best when Britain took an active part. She was particularly interested in northern France and the Low Countries, and it was generally agreed that she could not in any circumstances allow that area to fall under German influence. It was much better to say this clearly, and the obligation to defend Belgium and northern France necessarily implied an obligation to prevent a violation of the demilitarised Rhineland.

Beyond this Headlam-Morley saw a more direct British interest in central and eastern Europe than was common. It was a real British interest, he wrote, to prevent Germany breaking through in the east and acquiring new territory and strength which would inevitably be brought to bear in the west. Some details of the existing frontiers could be improved without vital injury to the countries affected, but:

> Has anyone attempted to realise what would happen if there were to be a new partition of Poland, or if the Czechoslovak State were to be so curtailed and dismembered that in fact it disappeared from the map of Europe? The whole of Europe would at once be in chaos. There would no longer be any principle, meaning or sense in the territorial arrangements of the continent. Imagine, for instance, that under some improbable condition Austria rejoined Germany, that Germany, using the discontented minority in Bohemia, demanded a new frontier far over the mountains. . .and at the same time, in alliance with Germany, the Hungarians recovered the southern slope of the Carpathians. This would be catastrophic, and even if we neglected to interfere to prevent it happening, we should be driven to interfere, probably too late.

1 Memorandum by Nicolson, 23 Jan. 1925, W 2035/9/98, FO 371/11065. A shortened version was circulated to the Cabinet by Chamberlain on 19 February: CP 106(25), CAB 24/172. It was not sent to the Dominions nor to any foreign government, but it appeared in some American newspapers in May 1925. See below, p.127.

What the smaller countries of Europe wanted was confidence that in a serious crisis they could count on effective support. It was not enough for Britain to say that she would carry out her obligations under the Covenant. She should state clearly that she was interested in the maintenance of the new system in Europe and could not regard with equanimity the forcible overthrow of any of the new states. Headlam-Morley did not, however, recommend alliances with these states: he proposed a statement of British policy linked with a protocol for dealing with European matters, which must include Germany. Most of the foreseeable European conflicts would probably be minor: only if Germany or Russia were involved would a major war follow. Germany could at present be dealt with, but Russia must not be ignored for she could become a great danger and as long as she remained in her present condition there could be no firm security for her neighbours. [1]

Chamberlain was probably not greatly influenced by any of this advice. He did not agree with Headlam-Morley about Britain's interest in central and eastern Europe, nor with Nicolson about treaty revision. He already favoured a new entente with France, and later pursued something like the recreation of the Concert of Europe. But at this stage his policy was determined largely by circumstance.

The Committee of Imperial Defence began discussion of the report on the Geneva Protocol on 13 February and concluded it six days later. None of the members favoured accepting the Protocol but there agreement ended. The issues, left for the Cabinet to resolve, were: (1) should a simple rejection be sent to the League, or a provisional reply indicating that another policy was being discussed with the Dominions, or a reasoned reply indicating an alternative policy for western Europe? (2) if the last, should Britain take part in a regional arrangement? (3) could the Dominions be brought to agree to a positive British policy at all, and at best would the question have to await a conference with them? (4) should amendments to the Covenant be proposed? The very full records of the meetings reveal that a majority of the members would have preferred to do nothing, but for different reasons. Eleven ministers [2] took part in at least three of the four meetings at which the Protocol was discussed at length. The views that they expressed may be summarised as follows.

1 Memorandum by Headlam-Morley, 12 Feb. 1925, W 1252/9/98, FO 371/11064, published in Headlam-Morley's *Studies in Diplomatic History* (London, 1930), 173 ff. It was not circulated to the Cabinet or the CID.

2 Including Balfour, who held no office at that moment and attended rather in the role of elder statesman. In addition Baldwin presided over the first two meetings, but he expressed no opinion.

Curzon as chairman did not express an opinion on some of the issues. He was in favour of proceeding cautiously, but in the end sufficiently impressed by Chamberlain's plea of urgency to hope that something could be done with the Dominions without waiting a year for a conference. He favoured a reasoned reply to the League and was against trying to amend the Covenant. He was opposed to an Anglo-French pact but favoured Britain joining something that included Germany.

Balfour was in favour of a reasoned reply, against trying to amend the Covenant, in favour of regional arrangements but against British participation beyond a promise to France to consult if danger arose. Churchill was in favour of a reasoned reply but against British action other than blessing a 'real' Franco-German peace giving Germany 'the immediate evacuation of territories which are being held' and a 'substantial rectification of her eastern frontiers'. Amery wished to take the opportunity of depriving the Covenant of all its coercive features. In so far as he, as Colonial Secretary, spoke for the Dominions, he thought that they neither would nor should agree to any positive policy and for himself wished to go no farther than a statement of British interest in the independence of Belgium.[1]

Birkenhead, Secretary of State for India, who admitted that he knew very little about Europe, contributed little to the discussion but favoured a reasoned reply to the League. Cunliffe-Lister, President of the Board of Trade, only voiced his department's dislike of economic sanctions. The service ministers too reflected the views of their staffs. Worthington-Evans and the General Staff supported an Anglo-French pact but hoped that Germany might adhere to it later. Bridgeman and the Naval Staff saw an advantage in the prospect that a pact would safeguard the British position in the western Mediterranean. Hoare and the Air Staff were doubtful. They agreed that Britain would go to the help of France if she were attacked by Germany, but they feared that a

1 For Churchill's attitude see also Martin Gilbert, *Winston S. Churchill,* Vol. V (London, 1976), Ch. 8. Amery's recollection seems to have been at fault when he wrote in his memoirs that 'some of us' urged 'a third course. . .meeting the objections both to the Protocol and to Austen's proposed treaty of guarantee. That was to limit the general obligation to intervene against aggression to the particular danger zone of the French frontier, but to do so impartially as between France and Germany. . .Our argument received an unexpected reinforcement when in February 1925 the German Foreign Minister, Stresemann, himself suggested a pact of mutual security with France' (*My Political Life,* Vol. II (London, 1953), 301-2). This account not only misrepresents Amery's own position if he included himself in 'some of us', but also suggests that some ministers were thinking of a mutual guarantee arrangement before the arrival of the German proposals. It is evident from the records that, with the possible exception of Churchill, they were not. Chamberlain mentioned the German proposals at the meeting of 13 February as a possible basis for a policy of regional arrangements, but they were not discussed.

guarantee would increase German hostility. They were worried about Britain's security against France and at the same time thought that France was going downhill so that in fifteen or twenty years' time it would be dangerous to be tied to her. Hoare was against a reasoned reply to the League and would personally have preferred to do nothing.

Cecil approached the problem from his own individual angle. He wanted above all things disarmament, to which none of the others paid more than lip service except in so far as it was a matter of saving money. To that end, although he did not care much for the Protocol, Cecil did want some general security arrangement with obligations. A western European arrangement could form part of this, but he did not favour a regional pact outside a general framework. He supported Chamberlain on some points, but the impression emerges that his support was something of an embarrassment.[1]

Chamberlain was against all general arrangements but in favour of a pact with France first and the inclusion of Germany later. He had become convinced that a positive British policy was required and its announcement urgently necessary.[2]

German disarmament, November 1924 - February 1925

A complication to the discussion of British policy, but also a spur to decision, was the question of the evacuation of the first zone of the Allied-occupied Rhineland. According to the Treaty of Versailles the fifteen-year occupation was a guarantee for the execution of the treaty as a whole. Provided that its terms were carried out, part of the territory would be evacuated after five years and a second part after ten. After the signature of the London agreement on reparations in August 1924 the evacuation of the first zone on 10 January 1925[3] depended in fact on German fulfilment of the military clauses of the treaty,

1 It is not clear from his own writings what Cecil thought would constitute effective automatic obligations. In a letter to Churchill of 16 January asking for support on the Protocol Cecil urged that a general plan ought to be tried, and maintained that it need not involve burdensome obligations. Would, he asked, an obligation to 'break off relations' (the kind unspecified) and then consult on what to do next, be burdensome? He thought not (Churchill Papers, C 18/8: I am indebted for this reference to Mr Martin Gilbert, Churchill's biographer). In view of his wartime experience as Minister of Blockade Cecil ought to have been aware of the complexity as well as of the ultimate power of economic measures.

2 CID 195th, 196th meetings, CAB 2/4. Hoare had put his views in writing and Balfour had drafted a reply to the League: CID papers 575-B, 581-B, CAB 4/12. After the meetings Chamberlain, Cecil, Churchill, Worthington-Evans and Hoare sent further memoranda to the Cabinet: CP 106(25), 116(25), 118(25), 121(25), 122(25), CAB 24/172.

3 Five years after the entry into force of the treaty. The French had now

although the possibility of bringing in other matters remained. The Allied Military Control Commission began its general inspection in September: by the end of November it was apparent that its report would not be completed by the New Year and that the German position was not satisfactory. After receiving an interim report the Ambassadors' Conference informed the German Government on 5 January that in view of their failure to carry out the military clauses of the treaty the evacuation of the Cologne zone could not take place.

Although the Germans had been warned that evacuation depended on the advice of the military authorities, there was a public outcry at the decision. In London, although the official line was to stand firmly by the terms of the treaty, there was by the end of 1924 a fairly general feeling in the Foreign Office that political considerations ought to take precedence over the remnants of enforcement. Only by political means, it was held, could Germany be prevented from making war in the future. She was admittedly disarmed in the sense that she could not go to war with an advanced country; and since effective control was impossible the attempt should be abandoned as soon as was possibly consistent with the treaty. Hence there was a note of irritation in comments on the interim report of the Control Commission and the General Staff's recommendation that developments in Germany must be watched. The political consequences of condoning breaches of the treaty were not discussed.[1]

The French were less complaisant: disagreement with them about the significance of the German defaults could be foreseen. In addition the French position in the Ruhr, which Herriot had undertaken to evacuate in August 1925, would be militarily untenable if the Allied forces left the Cologne zone before that date. There was in Britain a widespread suspicion (and in Germany a conviction) that the French would seek reasons for maintaining the occupation at least until Britain made an acceptable offer on security, and possibly indefinitely. On past French form and considering the utterances of certain French politicians and newspapers, the suspicion was not far-fetched. Since there were respects, such as the surrender of war criminals, in which the Treaty of Versailles was no longer capable of fulfilment, the British insistence on confining the discussion to disarmament and to major defaults at that, was directed as much towards preventing the French from extending the area of disagreement as to keeping the Germans to the point.

dropped the argument, used in 1923 (see p. 50, n. 1) that the period did not begin to run until the treaty terms had been fulfilled.

1 Minutes on C 18122/9/18, FO 371/9729; C 18874/2048/18, FO 371/9820; C 21, 112/21/18, FO 371/10707; C 248/30/18, FO 371/10711.

The line that Chamberlain wished to take was to negotiate with the French and Belgian Governments to reduce the list of defaults to a minimum, and then to hold a conference with the Germans.[1] The latter did not help matters by demanding early discussions and chapter and verse on the defaults; and fears about the French and Belgian attitudes were reinforced by reports that the Belgian Government meant to use the issue to put pressure on Britain on security, and by Herriot's declaration in the Chamber of Deputies on 28 January that the question was dominated by security.[2] Chamberlain felt it necessary to warn Herriot that the disarmament question must be dealt with strictly in accordance with the peace treaty and that any attempt to use it to force Britain's hand over security would produce the opposite effect to the one desired.[3] But although the questions were distinct technically,[4] there was, as Herriot said, a connexion of fact. Herriot told Crewe that while he would not mix up the two questions he saw great difficulty in Chamberlain's proposed conference settling the details of evacuation without talking about security.[5] There was also the consideration that if Herriot could not satisfy French opinion his government might fall: as Hymans pointed out, many people in France and Belgium genuinely believed that it would be unwise to give up the existing guarantees on the Rhine unless an equally weighty substitute were forthcoming.[6]

The French were also averse to discussions with the Germans because they feared being led into concessions on the substance of the treaty; and it was doubtful whether Herriot could leave Paris before Easter. Chamberlain, who wanted the conversations to be held in

1 Chamberlain to D'Abernon, 9 Jan. 1925, Chamberlain Papers, AC 52/252; Chamberlain to D'Abernon, 12 Jan., C 369/2/18, FO 371/10702; Chamberlain to Crewe, 25 Jan., C 677/21/18, FO 371/10707.

2 Grahame to FO, 18 Jan. 1925, W 528/21/4, FO 371/11041; Grahame to Chamberlain, 19 and 20 Jan., Chamberlain Papers, AC 52/416, 417; Q d'O to Fleuriau, 15 Jan., MAE, Papiers Herriot, dossier 5; *Journal officiel, Chambre des députés,* 28 Jan.

3 FO to Crewe, 2 Feb. 1925, C 1552/21/18, FO 371/10707; FO to Crewe, 6 Feb., C 1849/2/18, FO 371/10703; Chamberlain to Crewe, 6 Feb., Chamberlain Papers, AC 52/186; Crewe Papers, C/8; Fleuriau to Q d'O, 6 Feb., MAE, Grande Bretagne, Vol. 72.

4 In the British view the last paragraph of Article 429 of the Treaty of Versailles (which said that if the guarantees against German aggression were not considered sufficient evacuation might be delayed) referred only to the end of the fifteen-year period.

5 Crewe to FO, 4 Feb. 1925, C 1082/21/18, FO 371/10707; Crewe to Chamberlain, 5 Feb., Chamberlain Papers, AC 52/184; Crewe Papers, C/8; Q d'O to Fleuriau, 10 Feb.; memorandum by Herriot, 11 Feb., MAE, Rive gauche du Rhin, Vol. 80.

6 Wingfield (Brussels) to FO, 7 Feb. 1925, C 1963/21/18, FO 371/10708; Crewe to FO, 7 Feb., C 2085/459/18, FO 371/10727; *DDB,* Vol. II, No. 14.

London and was in the thick of the argument over policy in the Committee of Imperial Defence, became agitated at the prospect of delay and wrote to Crewe that he feared a divergence similar to that over the Ruhr occupation, which would undo all the work of the past year.[1] Eventually he agreed that the question of a conference with the Germans could be left until the Allies met, and that meanwhile the Control Commission report could be discussed through diplomatic channels.[2] The report, received in the middle of February, stated that apart from some reductions in factories the position was very much as it had been in 1922. All the infractions noted then were still unrectified and there had been some increase in effectives, in recruitment and training, in armaments, and in fortifications.[3] Ten days later Crowe still envisaged a meeting of Allied ministers followed by discussions with the Germans, at which views could be exchanged about the problem of a four-power pact.[4] But over the next weeks the discussion of German disarmament was relegated to a subordinate level while that of security took the front of the stage.

The German security proposals, December 1924 - February 1925

The German proposals of 20 January initially cut across the policy which Chamberlain was trying to get his colleagues to adopt, but in the end provided a way out of the impasse. It is tempting to suppose that D'Abernon promoted them for this purpose; but in fact he was proceeding independently of London and the timing of the German move had nothing to do with the state of the discussion there. D'Abernon spent the last part of November and the first half of December 1924 in England; and it was common knowledge that the new Government were examining the Geneva Protocol, that they were unlikely to accept it as it stood, and that French security was in the air again. The Embassy in Berlin would have received copies of Foreign Office papers on the Protocol and records of Chamberlain's conversations in Paris and Rome; but they would not have received Committee of Imperial Defence minutes, or papers emanating from other government departments, and there is no evidence that D'Abernon was told details orally. In any case the full extent of the division within the

1 FO to Crewe, 9 and 13 Feb. 1925, C 1969, 2169/2/18, FO 371/10703; Crewe to Chamberlain, 17 Feb.; Chamberlain to Crewe, 20 Feb., Chamberlain Papers, AC 52/190, 191; Crewe Papers, C/8; FO to Crewe, 21 Feb.; Crewe to FO, 22 Feb., C 2557, 2578/21/18, FO 371/10708; Q d'O to Fleuriau, MAE, Papiers Herriot, dossier 5; memorandum by Massigli, 18 Feb.; Q d'O to Fleuriau, 20 Feb., Rive gauche du Rhin, Vol. 81.

2 FO to Crewe, 24 Feb. 1925, C 2746/21/18, FO 371/10708.

3 CID papers 603-B, 604-B, CAB 4/13.

4 C 2641/21/18, FO 371/10708.

Government was not revealed until after the German proposals had been made.

D'Abernon's motive was at least partly to forestall an Anglo-French pact, to which he was strongly opposed. He was convinced that the European balance was threatened by France and her eastern allies, so that if Britain were to follow her traditional policy of throwing her weight against the strongest continental power she ought to supplement any agreement to defend France by measures to defend Germany. D'Abernon had been corresponding with Headlam-Morley in London and Grahame in Brussels about these ideas and possible solutions, and had come back to thinking of the Cuno offer.[1] On the German side the reasons for taking the initiative, or the decision to take up D'Abernon's initiative, were fear of an Anglo-French alliance, the need to find some way forward from the setback over the Cologne zone, and fear of League of Nations supervision over German disarmament.[2] The timing of the approach owed a good deal to D'Abernon's initiative in raising the security question with Schubert on 29 December.[3] The method owed a good deal to D'Abernon's advice, which the Germans followed with misgivings that were fully justified by the initial reception. The content of the proposal, however, was largely derived from Gaus's and Schubert's suggestion of April 1923.[4]

The German memorandum was handed to D'Abernon on the morning of 20 January. The German Government, it stated, were ready to discuss a treaty arrangement to secure peace with France, and suggested various possible bases - the Cuno proposal for a pact renounc-

1 D'Abernon to Headlam-Morley, 13 Nov. 1924; D'Abernon to Grahame, 10 Dec., D'Abernon Papers, BL Add. MS 48927, 48928. D'Abernon to Chamberlain, 7 Jan. 1925, C 459/459/18, FO 371/10726.

2 Under Article 213 of the Treaty of Versailles Germany was to facilitate any investigation which the Council of the League might consider necessary. In September 1924 the Council accepted a scheme for investigation drawn up by the Permanent Advisory Committee; in December it instructed the Committee to work out its application to the demilitarised zone. These proposals, produced on 5 February, included the establishment of a permanent organ resident in the demilitarised zone. In the British view Article 213 did not cover such bodies, so that German consent to its establishment would be necessary. The British generally supposed that this was the only point of difficulty, but the Germans actually objected to the whole investigation scheme: Salewski, *Entwaffnung und Militärkontrolle,* 268-70.

3 Memorandum by Schubert, 29 Dec. 1924, 4509/E124822-23. References in correspondence during January show that the Germans regarded D'Abernon's initiative (which they thought had probably been taken on instructions from London) as the real starting-point of their proposals.

4 See Gaus to Bülow, 12 Jan. 1925; Dufour to Schubert, 13 Jan.; memorandum by Schubert, 14 Jan., 4509/E124815-19, E124791-93, E124805-09. For the suggestion of 1923 see p. 50.

ing war between the powers interested in the Rhine, a comprehensive arbitration treaty (which Germany was prepared to conclude with all countries) or a pact guaranteeing the existing territorial status on the Rhine and the fulfilment of Articles 42 and 43 of the Treaty of Versailles. These suggestions could be combined in different ways, and were sufficient to show that if all the countries concerned desired guarantees for peaceful evolution it would not be difficult to work out a treaty.[1] D'Abernon wrote at once that the new German Government's attitude was of 'vast importance', and that even if these proposals were not immediately practical it was important to discuss them.[2] On 23 January he reported Schubert's additional explanation, that the Germans thought the model for the arbitration treaties should be the German-Swiss and German-Swedish arbitration treaties of 1921 and 1924. Under these treaties all disputes which were not settled within a reasonable time by diplomatic means were to be submitted to tribunals of arbitration or conciliation - juridical disputes to an arbitration tribunal whose awards would be binding on the two governments, and political disputes to a conciliation tribunal whose recommendations would not be binding. Schubert said that the German Government did not propose to 'eliminate conciliation' in political disputes, but this was a 'detail' which could be discussed. He confirmed that Germany's willingness to conclude arbitration treaties extended to all countries, including those on her eastern frontier. He also said that the expression 'gegenwärtigen Besitzstand am Rhein' meant the territorial status under the peace treaty, i.e. Germany would accept a pact expressly guaranteeing the *status quo* on her western frontier.[3]

The immediate reaction in the Foreign Office was that the German proposal was premature and could not be discussed until the disarmament question had been disposed of and the Allies had agreed among themselves on security. But the idea ought not to be discouraged, and Chamberlain said that he would see Sthamer.[4] There was some doubt

1 D'Abernon to FO, 20 Jan. 1925, C 946, 980/459/18, FO 371/10726; memoranda by Schubert, 20 Jan., 4509/E124770-79. The memorandum is printed in Germany, D.D.R., Ministerium für auswärtigen Angelegenheiten, *Locarno-Konferenz 1925* (Berlin, 1962), No. 2; a translation in D'Abernon, *Ambassador of Peace,* Vol. III, 276-9.

2 D'Abernon to FO, 21 Jan. 1925, C 1133/459/18, FO 371/10726; D'Abernon to Chamberlain, 21 Jan., BL Add. MS 48928. The new German Government, formed on 13 January under Dr Hans Luther, included for the first time since 1918 members of the German Nationalist Party (D.N.V.P.). Stresemann remained Foreign Minister.

3 D'Abernon to FO, 23 Jan. 1925, C 1143/459/18, FO 371/10727; Schubert to D'Abernon, 22 Jan.; memorandum by Schubert, 23 Jan., 4509/E124759-61, E124746-52.

4 Minutes on C 980, 1143/459/18, FO 371/10726, 10727.

about the German intention in making the proposal to the British alone and under the seal of secrecy. The reason was partly German uncertainty whether D'Abernon had acted on his own initiative and doubt about his discretion, partly a wish to prepare the ground without publicity, partly uncertainty of touch. When Sthamer was sent a copy of the proposals he was told not to mention D'Abernon but merely to sound the British Government's views. The tactical problems, real and imagined, were explained. D'Abernon had advised approaching London alone, but the real negotiating partner was France. Britain's interests were not identical with those of either France or Germany, and D'Abernon's advice simply to repeat the Cuno offer, if it did come from London, might have been meant to steer Germany away from making to France the kind of proposal that might involve a British commitment. But his advice could not be ignored, and it was not at all certain how an offer would be received in France. The answer seemed to be to explore the ground in London and approach Paris rather later. A couple of days later Hoesch was instructed to start preparing the ground in Paris but was told that it had not been decided whether to make the content of the offer depend on British approval.[1] D'Abernon reported that the German Government wanted British views on the proposal and advice on the best way of approaching the other Allies; but to Crowe Sthamer said that he had no instructions but would be ready to talk about security if Chamberlain wished. And when he saw Chamberlain Sthamer did not ask for advice on the best way of approaching the French: on the contrary he allowed Chamberlain to conclude that there was no immediate intention of communicating with them, and consequently to suspect the German motives.[2]

By the time that Sthamer saw Chamberlain not only had he been instructed to 'develop a certain activity behind the scenes in London', but Hoesch had begun to prepare the ground in Paris and Schubert had spoken in general terms to the French and United States Ambassadors. Not surprisingly, therefore, the press began talking of a security proposal.[3] But Stresemann appeared to be having second

1 AA to Sthamer, 19 Jan. 1925, 4509/E124780-86; *Locarno-Konferenz*, No. 1; AA to Hoesch, 21 Jan., 4509/E124765-69.

2 D'Abernon to FO, 20 and 23 Jan. 1925, C 946, 980, 1143/459/18, FO 371/10726, 10727; Sthamer to AA, 26 and 30 Jan., 4509/E124725; 3123/D642141-43; FO to D'Abernon, 30 Jan., C 1454/459/18, FO 371/10727. See also Chamberlain to D'Abernon, 11 Sep. 1930; Selby to Chamberlain, 29 Sep. 1930, Chamberlain Papers, AC 39/118.

3 Memorandum by Schubert, 23 Jan. 1925; AA to Sthamer, 24 Jan.; Hoesch to AA, 24 Jan.; Schubert to Sthamer, 26 Jan.; AA to Hoesch, 27 Jan.; memorandum by Schubert, 28 Jan.; 4509/E124701-05, E124730-33, E124726-29, E124716-19, E124710-12, E124693-97. There was an article on security in the *Germania*, the organ of the Centre Party, on 25 January.

thoughts. On 29 January, after Herriot's speech in the Chamber, he told D'Abernon that he gathered that an initiative on security might be regarded in Paris as a device to evade discussion on disarmament. It was most undesirable that an important proposal for the peace of Europe should be seen in a wrong context, and it was essential for Germany's dignity that she should not make proposals at a moment when they would not be properly appreciated. He was inclined to postpone or abandon the whole idea. D'Abernon, naturally in view of his share in the proceedings, urged the Foreign Office that it would be a 'vast pity' to let the Germans recede; but in London it was not thought possible to encourage them, because the proposal was considered premature and because doubts about the French reaction were shared there.[1]

Chamberlain's attitude, therefore, in his conversation with Sthamer on 30 January was extremely cautious. He said that while he welcomed the evidence that the German Government were considering what they could do to allay French fears, he did not think it possible to discuss their proposal until the British attitude to the Geneva Protocol and French security had been defined. Pressed for his opinion on the principle of the proposal, Chamberlain said that he 'did not exclude the idea at the proper time of an agreement between Germany and France or Germany and the Allies, giving a mutual guarantee to the situation established by the peace treaties on their common frontiers, and. . .the British Government would at all times be glad if it could help to promote a better state of feeling between Germany and France'. And he asked why Germany did not at once join the League.[2] Chamberlain wrote to D'Abernon that France might later be willing to consider something like the German proposal, but not until the British attitude to French security was more clearly defined, and not at all if the proposal depended on the complete evacuation of the Rhineland. To this D'Abernon replied: 'I have ascertained that the evacuation of the

1 D'Abernon to FO, 29 Jan. 1925, C 1372, 1416/459/18, FO 371/10727; memorandum by Stresemann, 29 Jan., 4509/E124683-87; D'Abernon to Chamberlain, 31 Jan., Chamberlain Papers, AC 52/255; D'Abernon Papers, BL Add. MS 48928. Cf. D'Abernon, *Ambassador of Peace,* Vol. III, 132-4.

2 FO to D'Abernon, 30 Jan. 1925, C 1455/459/18, FO 371/10727; Sthamer to AA, 30 Jan., 3123/D642141-43. At the Assembly in 1924 MacDonald had tried to promote German entry into the League. The German Government then sent notes to the members of the Council stating conditions for entry - a permanent seat on the Council, release from any obligations arising from Article 16, no reaffirmation of war guilt, and participation in mandates. After the various governments had replied that the matter was one for the League itself, the German Government sent on 12 December a letter to the Secretary-General repeating the objections to Article 16. See Jürgen Spenz, *Die diplomatische Vorgeschichte des Beitritts Deutschlands zum Völkerbund 1924-1926* (Göttingen, 1966), 23-57.

whole of the occupied territory was not contemplated as part of the German proposal'.[1]

Chamberlain's statement to Sthamer that he would not negotiate behind France's back (which implied that he was going to inform the French)[2] and the press rumours (which increased after a speech by Luther on 30 January) decided Stresemann that the approach to Paris must be made even though the tone of the French press was not favourable. Instructions were therefore sent to Hoesch on 5 February, in a despatch setting out the German motives. The French, Stresemann wrote, would certainly insist on the strict fulfilment of German disarmament but there was no doubt that they would use the issue primarily for the pursuit of far-reaching political aims. The arrival of the treaty date for the evacuation of the Cologne zone confronted them with the choice between pursuing in some form the permanent position on the Rhine demanded at the peace conference, and finally accepting the solution in the Treaty of Versailles. Herriot had perhaps not yet made up his mind, but in all probability the second alternative could only be carried through if he could show French opinion a security settlement equal in value to the guarantee treaties of 1919. The Geneva Protocol could hardly be considered an adequate substitute, but together with the guarantee treaties it gave France a means of putting pressure on Britain. Stresemann believed that the British intended to treat the evacuation of the Cologne zone purely as a matter of disarmament, but he was doubtful whether they could make their view prevail with the French. The history of the security question so far gave grounds for a fear that Britain would in the end give France assurances that would be intolerable for Germany, either (and more probably) the so-called physical guarantees in the Rhineland or a pact. The German Government must therefore take the initiative. They must work against the establishment of dangerous guarantees and try to prevent those mentioned in the League's investigation scheme from being put into effect. If they waited for projects from the other side their own proposals would look like a mere defensive reaction. The proposals were meant seriously, but if they failed they would at least have strengthened the German position for combatting dangerous designs from the other side.[3]

1 Chamberlain to D'Abernon, 3 Feb. 1925; D'Abernon to Chamberlain, 7 Feb., Chamberlain Papers, AC 52/256-7; D'Abernon Papers, BL Add. MS 48928. Chamberlain passed this assurance on to Crewe on 16 February: C 2450/459/18, FO 371/10727.

2 On 30 January he informed the French Ambassador of his conversation with Sthamer and of the German proposal, but without saying that it had been made in writing: C 1455/459/18, FO 371/10727.

3 Schubert to Hoesch, 5 Feb. 1925, 4509/E124610-13; AA to Hoesch, 5 Feb.,

The memorandum was given to Herriot on 9 February, still under the seal of secrecy. But the existence, and even the nature of the proposals were becoming common knowledge; and once they had been communicated to the Belgian and Italian Governments on 21 February there was no further pretence. The initial reception in Paris was cautious: the reply given to Hoesch on 20 February said that the French Government were determined not to neglect anything that could contribute to peace, but would consult their Allies. In conversation Herriot was still worried about the evacuation of Cologne, and French officials were anxious about the implications for the League and France's eastern allies.[1]

But the crucial point for the French was what the British Government would decide about security, and this was still uncertain. Chamberlain set out his own view to Crewe on 16 February. He was now inclined to think that a British guarantee of the eastern frontiers of France and Belgium would be a more practical proposition if Germany were associated with it. He regarded a general guarantee as unconvincing and useless, and admitted that public opinion, the Labour and Liberal parties, and the League of Nations Union, would be hostile to partial arrangements. He knew what he wanted to do but could not forecast the Cabinet's decision. Crewe (and D'Abernon, to whom a copy of the letter was sent) must therefore not go farther for the present than to let it be known that he attached great importance to the German approach and considered that it would be a great mistake for the Germans to withdraw it or the French not to take it seriously.[2]

Chamberlain and the Cabinet, March 1925

Chamberlain was determined to get the Cabinet to agree on a policy before he went to the March meeting of the League Council. There was to be a debate in the House of Commons on 5 March, and he hoped to be able to outline the policy then. Although as recently as 26 February Chamberlain had put forward the case for an agreement

3123/D642172-85; *Locarno-Konferenz,* Nos. 4-5. The memorandum to the French Government, a translation of which was printed in Cmd 2435 of 1925, *Papers respecting the proposals for a Pact of Security made by the German Government on February 9, 1925,* was identical with that given to D'Abernon on 20 January, save that the first paragraph of the latter was omitted and a final sentence added referring to the possibility of a general security convention.

1 French reply in *Locarno-Konferenz,* No. 8; Cmd 2435 of 1925. Crewe to FO, 12 Feb. 1925, C 2085/458/18, FO 371/10727; Crewe to FO, 22 Feb.; FO to Crewe, 24 Feb., C 2557, 2746/21/18, FO 371/10708; Hoesch to AA, 17 and 20 Feb., 4509/E124982-87, E124947-51.

2 C 2450/459/18, FO 371/10727, printed in Sir Charles Petrie, *The Life and Letters of the Right Hon. Sir Austen Chamberlain* (hereafter cited as *Life and Letters),* Vol. II (London, 1940), 258-60.

with France prior to the inclusion of Germany, when the Cabinet met on 2 March he argued for a four-power pact including Germany from the start.[1] At this meeting the Cabinet agreed that it was their policy to allay the state of insecurity in Europe, so that although the Geneva Protocol could not be accepted something else must be done: an alternative would be considered two days later. During the meeting a formula was drafted which Chamberlain could use with Herriot. This read: 'His Majesty's Government do not feel able to enter into a dual pact with France with or without Belgium. The question of a quadrilateral agreement between France, Germany, Great Britain, Belgium, and, if possible, with the accord of Italy, for mutual security [and for guaranteeing each other's frontiers in the west of Europe][2] stands on a different footing and might become a great assurance to the peace of Europe and lead to a rapid reduction of armaments. His Majesty's Government have, of course, in these matters to carry with them the assent, or at least the goodwill, of the various self-governing Dominions of the British Empire. If the French Government share the views of His Majesty's Government and will regulate their action towards Germany accordingly, His Majesty's Government will, for their part, begin the necessary discussions with the Dominions, and in all their policy will endeavour to further the common cause'.[3]

Chamberlain later wrote: 'I carried the Cabinet that day for the mutual pact'.[4] Although it is clear, from the mention in the minutes of a further meeting, that the alternative policy was not fully settled, Chamberlain felt able to show to Crewe some confidence about the way things were going.[5] That evening, however, according to his later account, Curzon came to see him, bringing Balfour and saying that he thought the Cabinet's decision had been too hasty. Balfour contributed little to the ensuing argument except the remark that a mutual guarantee involved larger commitments than an alliance with France. Chamberlain

1 See CP 122(25), CAB 24/172. In a letter to D'Abernon in 1930 (AC 39/118), when *An Ambassador of Peace,* Vol. III, was published, Chamberlain wrote that he had hoped to conclude a defensive alliance with France first and only later turn it into a reciprocal arrangement with Germany. He was sure that if he had not continued to press for the former he would not have won consent to the latter. But he was not precise about the date of such change as there was in his own approach. Some discrepancies between this account, written from memory, and the record are noted below.

2 Square brackets in pencil in the original, presumably added on 4 March: see below.

3 C 12(25), CAB 23/49.

4 Chamberlain to D'Abernon, 11 Sep. 1930, AC 39/118.

5 Chamberlain to Crewe, 2 Mar. 1925, AC 52/193; Crewe Papers, C/8.

wrote that he ended the conversation by saying that they must have another Cabinet so that he might know where he stood.[1]

The Cabinet met twice on 4 March. Baldwin was absent (his mother was seriously ill) and Chamberlain himself took the chair. At the outset it became clear that the formula drafted two days earlier did not commend itself: in particular it was feared that to talk of guaranteeing frontiers - not only France and Belgium against Germany but Germany against France - was much more than the public at home and in the Dominions would accept. Chamberlain was authorised to reject the Geneva Protocol and the reply to the League was approved. Chamberlain's summing up of the discussion was approved as the line he was to take with Herriot, namely that the Government attached the highest importance to the German proposal, which seemed to offer the best chance of security for France and peace for the world. To reject it would be to thrust Germany into the arms of Russia. The Government would consult the Dominions. Chamberlain was to explain the difficulty about public opinion but say that he hoped it could be overcome if Germany were included in the proposed arrangement: it could not be overcome if she were not included. If British participation were desired, Chamberlain would not agree to any formula nor pledge the Dominions, but his colleagues had authorised him to say that they would do their best to see that such a project should not fail for want of British concurrence.[2]

This was an exiguous policy for Chamberlain to take abroad. It is not surprising that his statement in the foreign affairs debate was vague and struck at least one observer as barren, nor that just before leaving he wrote to his wife: 'My task is indeed a difficult one'.[3] But he had secured an undertaking that the Government would do their best to co-operate and to convince the Dominions, and he proceeded to act on it.

Chamberlain arrived in Paris on 6 March and had two long conversations with Herriot. He reported the Government's decision not to sign the Geneva Protocol nor attempt to amend it, and then

1 Chamberlain to D'Abernon, 11 Sep. 1930, AC 39/118; also Chamberlain to Nicolson, 28 May 1934, AC 40/123. Writing from memory Chamberlain put the two Cabinet meetings on successive days instead of two days apart. Hankey was active in lobbying against the mutual pact: Roskill, *Hankey,* Vol. II, 396-7.

2 C 13 and 14(25), CAB 23/49. The reply on the Protocol was the statement made to the League Council on 12 March: Cmd 2368 of 1925, *Statement by the Right Hon. Austen Chamberlain, M.P., on behalf of His Majesty's Government to the Council of the League of Nations, respecting the Protocol for the Pacific Settlement of International Disputes, Geneva, March 12, 1925.*

3 *HC Deb.,* 5th ser., Vol. 181, cols. 700-16; Harry, Graf Kessler, *Tagebücher 1918-1937* (Frankfurt, 1961), 420-3; Chamberlain to Mrs Chamberlain, 6 Mar. 1925, AC 6/1/600.

said that, to his regret, the state of public opinion would not allow the Government to enter into an Anglo-French or Anglo-Franco-Belgian pact. But the German proposals seemed to offer the hope of a solution in which Britain could co-operate, and he begged Herriot to consider how they could be made acceptable to France and a real guarantee of French security.

Herriot was not surprised at the British decision on the Protocol, but the refusal to pursue an Anglo-French pact was a severe blow: Chamberlain thought it an unexpected one, even though the new French Ambassador in London, Fleuriau, had been reporting division and indecision in the Cabinet.[1] Herriot was doubtful about the German proposals, while recognising that they were better than anything offered before and were especially important as coming from Luther's government. There were, however, some important omissions (such as a mention of Belgium) and problems (such as the distinction between Germany's eastern and western frontiers). He spoke of Germany's recovery and preaching of revenge while France was struggling with financial difficulties, and said: 'From my heart I tell you I look forward with terror to her making war on us again in ten years'. Finally Herriot asked what became of the League and the Covenant. Chamberlain replied that Britain's obligations under the Covenant remained the same, but Herriot himself had admitted that neither the Covenant nor the Geneva Protocol gave France the necessary security. It was for this reason that he had sought the pact which Chamberlain had to tell him no British Government could give, and for this reason he asked Herriot to consider the German proposals.[2]

Next afternoon Herriot asked whether Britain, France and Belgium might agree among themselves on the terms which they could propose to Germany. Chamberlain, fearing that this was a return to the idea of two pacts, one between the Allies and a second between them and Germany, scotched it while saying that of course the Allies could confer among themselves. Herriot then came back to the subject of Poland. The more the Germans renounced their hopes in the west, he said, the more certainly would they nourish them in the east; and France could not purchase her own security at the expense of her ally. Chamberlain replied that the German undertaking to avoid recourse to war even in the east was a new security for Poland and - an argument that he was to use often in the summer - the general appeasement that

1 Fleuriau to Q d'O, 25 Feb. 1925, MAE, Grande Bretagne, Vol. 73; Fleuriau to Laroche, 2 Mar. Rive gauche du Rhin, Vol. 81; Fleuriau to Laroche, 4 Mar., Grande Bretagne, Vol. 73.

2 Chamberlain to Crowe, 7 Mar. 1925, C 3367/459/18, FO 371/10728.

would follow an agreement in the west would tend to make the situation more secure everywhere.

Turning to the evacuation of the Cologne zone, Chamberlain stressed the importance of concluding the question quickly and on its own. From what Herriot said Chamberlain's earlier fear that the French might insist on staying was revived, and he warned Herriot that such insistence would have a disastrous effect on British opinion. He recalled the existing guarantees and said that he could not share French apprehensions for the immediate future. Germany could not be held down for ever and their object should be to bring about such a change in the situation that by the time Germany could be dangerous again she would no longer wish to gamble on recovering what she had lost.[1]

From Geneva Chamberlain wrote to Crowe that he did not know how far Herriot would be able to bring his colleagues to consider the British offer by the time he passed through Paris again. Meanwhile he was very much afraid of the effect that his statement might have on the discussion of the evacuation. 'I am really oppressed', he wrote, 'by the danger that the French will insist on remaining in Cologne, *for reasons which are within the terms of the Treaty,* but which will be held as insufficient to justify a prolongation of the occupation by all those sections of British opinion which are opposed to a pact'. On the other hand a unilateral British withdrawal would mean the end of any real understanding between the Allies: the issues were thus serious. 'Am I justified in pressing upon M. Herriot the possibility of our having to take this course, or would the consequences of it be so grave in other respects that, in the last resort, the Cabinet would decide to retain our troops just as we maintained them through all the difficulties brought about by the occupation of the Ruhr?' Chamberlain asked Crowe to get an indication of the Cabinet's view, and an indication of how they regarded his conversations with Herriot.[2]

The evidence of what followed in London is largely provided by

1 Chamberlain to Crowe, 7 Mar. 1925, C 3368/459/18, FO 371/10728. The German proposal did not contain an undertaking to avoid recourse to war in the east. Chamberlain seems to have convinced himself that the offer to conclude arbitration treaties amounted to this: each time he mentioned the point his language on it become more categorical, but he should not have been so definite if he had studied the German-Swiss treaty which Schubert indicated as a model. This was the point of the incident with Sthamer on 24 March: see pp. 100-1.

2 Chamberlain to Crowe, 8 Mar. 1925, C 3569/459/18, FO 371/10728, words italicised underlined in the original. Johnson's wording (*University of Birmingham Historical Journal* 7 (1961), No. 1, 74) in summarising this letter might suggest that Chamberlain hoped to be authorised to make a more favourable offer to Herriot. Crowe certainly used the letter as a request for greater latitude, but did so on his own initiative: see below.

Crowe's letters to Chamberlain. On receiving Chamberlain's letter on the morning of 11 March, Crowe sent Baldwin a copy and asked to be present at the Cabinet discussion. He saw Baldwin after that day's Cabinet meeting, to which he was not summoned and at which the matter was not discussed, and said that Chamberlain felt himself to be in a very difficult position with Herriot and feared a breach with France. Crowe said that he did not favour threatening a British withdrawal from the Rhineland but recommended that Chamberlain be authorised to tell Herriot that the Government would contemplate a 'bundle' of pacts, so long as Germany was included and they all came into force simultaneously - a procedure which he had always thought would have advantages for Britain as well as for France.

Baldwin, who said that he thought the instructions given to Chamberlain on 4 March too rigid, nonetheless felt unable to authorise any change without Cabinet approval. He thought that he could not call another Cabinet for two or three days, but Crowe considered this delay too long. He therefore asked whether Baldwin could authorise Chamberlain to tell Herriot that he personally was impressed with the idea of separate pacts and would commend it to the Cabinet. Baldwin said that he would think this over; but later in the afternoon he summoned Crowe to an informal meeting of ministers at the House of Commons. Those present, besides Baldwin, were Churchill, Birkenhead, Hoare, Worthington-Evans, Bridgeman, Amery, Salisbury, and Cecil.[1]

Crowe's account of the meeting was written next day. He told Chamberlain that, invited by Baldwin to explain the situation, he had said that the immediate question on which Chamberlain asked for guidance was whether Herriot should be threatened with British withdrawal from the Rhineland. But it was clear to him that the issue was much wider and graver, and he hoped that ministers would review the whole problem again. There followed an hour and a half's discussion, which Crowe described as 'vague and inconclusive'. Churchill developed his theory that there was no need to do anything, that France would become increasingly amenable, and there was no danger of a breach. Amery said that it was impossible to do anything because the Dominions would never agree. He admitted that he had agreed to the Cabinet resolution on 4 March but he had not really meant it and must now withdraw his consent. Birkenhead said that he remained opposed to a pact of any kind and denied that the Cabinet had ever agreed to one. He agreed that everyone knew that Britain and the Empire would

1 Crowe to Chamberlain, 11 Mar. 1925, C 3569/459/18, FO 371/10728; Crowe to Chamberlain, 12 Mar., Chamberlain Papers, AC 52/240.

not allow France and Belgium to be invaded, but held that it was impossible to say so formally. Salisbury and Hoare said that the most they supported was a unilateral declaration by Britain. Only Cecil expressed himself in favour of a genuine pact, including Germany, and said that he had no doubt that the Empire was ready to fight not only for the Channel ports but for the French eastern frontier. Birkenhead wound up by saying that there was no difficulty in replying to Chamberlain's request for guidance. All that need be said was that ministers entirely approved his statement to Herriot. The result was eminently satisfactory. 'It had been made quite clear to France that the British Government desired no pact, they would in no case commit themselves to anything, either as towards France alone, or to any number of powers, including Germany. All that was intended was that if France would come to some agreement with Germany, under which pledges were given against aggression, then, in the event of aggression nevertheless taking place, Great Britain might possibly consider the question whether they [*sic*] would give an undertaking to take part in any consultation as to what might be done'. All the other ministers except Cecil agreed.[1] Baldwin had as yet said nothing.

Crowe was appalled. He felt that Chamberlain was being let down, and even suspected Birkenhead and Churchill of undermining his position deliberately. When at last Baldwin allowed him to speak he therefore, as he wrote, expressed himself strongly. He contested formally in the name of the Foreign Office the view that there was no danger of a breach with France. But what was much more immediately serious, if the Cabinet's decision was that now stated by Birkenhead and apparently endorsed by the others, Chamberlain's statement to Herriot had been not clear but seriously misleading and laid the Government open to a charge of bad faith. For Chamberlain had clearly conveyed to Herriot that although the British Government could not enter into a pact with France and Belgium alone, they would endeavour to get the

1 Crowe did not report any contribution to the discussion by Worthington-Evans or Bridgeman. Considering that the former, in particular, had been in favour of a pact with France, this is rather surprising: perhaps they could not stand up to the heavyweights of the Cabinet on their own. Bridgeman recorded in his political diary his regret at his colleagues' decision, but in terms that perhaps reflect the confusion of the meeting. Stephen Roskill, *Naval Policy between the Wars,* Vol. I, *The Period of Anglo-American Antagonism* (London, 1968), hereafter cited as *Naval Policy,* 437, summarises and quotes Bridgeman's note as follows: 'to his great regret the Cabinet decided "to continue the policy of refusing any pact with France to join her against a unilateral attack, unless a quadrilateral arrangement could also be made to include Germany". He was entirely in favour of including Germany, but could not understand why Britain should "refuse what we shall be bound to concede if Germany attacked France" - namely "to assist France in order to keep open the Channel ports".' Roskill's account in *Hankey,* Vol. II, 394-7, is also not very clear.

country and the Dominions to approve entry into a pact of which Germany formed part.

At this point Baldwin asked Crowe to leave the ministers to continue their discussion alone, and when Crowe wrote to Chamberlain next day he did not know the outcome. He hoped that perhaps Baldwin had supported Chamberlain after he had left.[1] Baldwin wrote briefly to Chamberlain on 12 March, saying that the meeting felt he had represented the Cabinet's decision firmly and clearly to Herriot, and expressing his own appreciation and sympathy. The question of Cologne would have to be considered very carefully, and it was impossible to say more now on the pact question.[2] However in view of Crowe's report Chamberlain was not satisfied with this letter. He had now made at Geneva the statement approved by the Cabinet, rejecting the Protocol but holding out the prospect of special arrangements to meet special cases;[3] and he telegraphed home that he would resign if the Cabinet went back on their decision and destroyed the whole effect of the conversations he had had since leaving London.[4]

Later, when the trouble was over, Chamberlain thought that Crowe might have misunderstood the ministers on 11 March.[5] But Crowe had long years of experience in recording conversations; his account was highly circumstantial; and the opinions that he reported were exactly in line with those that the ministers in question had earlier expressed in the Committee of Imperial Defence. It is unfortunate that apart from Bridgeman's note Crowe's is apparently the only record of the meeting, but there is no reason to doubt its accuracy. It seems more likely that those ministers who did not want any British commitment had not changed their minds and took the opportunity of an informal meeting to say so. Crowe may indeed have contributed to this result by inviting them to re-examine the whole problem.[6] How far ministers

1 Crowe to Chamberlain, 12 Mar. 1925, Chamberlain Papers, AC 52/240.

2 Baldwin to Chamberlain, 12 Mar. 1925, AC 52/80.

3 Cmd 2368 of 1925. W.N. Medlicott, *British Policy since Versailles,* 2nd edn (London, 1968), 59, is mistaken in saying that it was this statement that was too much for some members of the Cabinet. Chamberlain had also spoken to Briand and Hymans, and had authorised Herriot to inform the Allied ambassadors in Paris of the nature of his communication; and Crowe had done the same in London: Chamberlain to Crowe, 8 Mar. 1925, C 3327/459/18, FO 371/10728; Chamberlain to Crowe, 9 Mar., W 2096/9/98, FO 371/11065; Crowe to Chamberlain, 11 Mar.; Chamberlain to Crowe, 12 Mar., C 3569, 3726/459/18, FO 371/10728; *DDB,* Vol. II, Nos. 34-6.

4 Chamberlain to Crowe, 14 Mar. 1925, Chamberlain Papers, AC 52/241, printed in Petrie, *Life and Letters,* Vol. II, 264.

5 Chamberlain to Mrs Chamberlain, 25 Mar. 1925, AC 6/1/608.

6 Cecil wrote to Baldwin supporting entry into a pact, but also criticising the

really meant to repudiate the decision of 4 March is an open question. At least when Crowe, after receiving Chamberlain's telegram, took it to Baldwin at Chequers, he was somewhat reassured. Baldwin said that there was no question of Chamberlain not having his full confidence, and that what individuals had said at the informal meeting did not in any sense constitute a Cabinet decision. But there were different views on the form of an eventual pact including Germany, and that was why he had warned Chamberlain not to say more about it. When he returned the Cabinet would discuss Britain's contribution again, and Baldwin by no means despaired of bringing Birkenhead, Churchill and Amery round. He assented to Crowe's statement that a promise to consult in case of aggression would not constitute a pact and would not satisfy France.[1]

How Baldwin brought the objectors round is not known. It has been suggested that this was a question in which he was personally interested, and that he could not afford to lose Chamberlain from his Cabinet; or that Crowe convinced them with his parting shot at the meeting.[2] However it was done, Chamberlain had what he described as 'quite a satisfactory talk' with Baldwin when he returned on 17 March, and obtained a promise of support.[3] On 20 March the Cabinet, after another full discussion, congratulated Chamberlain on his handling of the situation.[4]

Thus the German proposals, launched in difficult circumstances and in a manner that did little to ensure a favourable reception, turned out to be fruitful. If their fate is compared with that of the earlier proposals, equally designed to ward off a danger to Germany from the west, the reason for the difference is seen to lie partly in the nature of the proposals but largely in circumstances in France and Britain.

Foreign Office approach: Cecil to Baldwin, 12 Mar. 1925, Cecil Papers, BL Add. MS 51080; Baldwin Papers, F.2 (Vol. 115).

1 Crowe to Baldwin, 14 Mar. 1925, Baldwin Papers, F.2 (Vol. 115); Crowe to Chamberlain, 15 Mar., Chamberlain Papers, AC 52/244.

2 Sybil Eyre Crowe, 'Sir Eyre Crowe and the Locarno Pact', *English Historical Review* 77 (1972), 49-74. This was Crowe's last important act. He soon afterwards went on sick leave and died on 28 April. Sir William Tyrrell succeeded him as Permanent Under-Secretary of State.

3 Chamberlain to Mrs Chamberlain, 19 Mar. 1925, Chamberlain Papers, AC 6/1/605.

4 C 17(25), CAB 23/49: the discussion was not recorded. In his speech in the House of Commons on 24 March, the lines of which were approved by the Cabinet, Chamberlain still did not say that Britain would take part in a pact arising out of the German proposals; but Baldwin, winding up the debate, stated that while it was too soon to say what form such a pact would take or which countries would be included, Britain would be a contracting party: *HC Deb.*, 5th ser., Vol. 182, cols. 307-22, 402-8.

The Cuno offer was ill conceived and badly presented; but it is hard to suppose that any other last-minute security offer could have prevented the occupation of the Ruhr. The attempts in September 1923 and February 1924 to secure concessions in the Ruhr by approaching first Poincaré and then MacDonald were also fruitless, because Poincaré was not interested and MacDonald was both determined to deal with reparations first and opposed to partial security arrangements. The proposals of 1925, certainly better conceived, hardly better presented at first, but then pursued with far greater skill and determination by Stresemann, ultimately achieved their aim because the French Governments concerned were more receptive and because the British Government were at last disposed to do something about western European security and unable to agree on any other plan. That they did eventually agree on this one must be attributed to Chamberlain's refusal to take no for an answer.

4

THE NEGOTIATION OF THE WESTERN SECURITY PACT 1925

The western security pact and its wider ramifications took several months to negotiate. The process can be divided into four stages: from March to the middle of May, preliminary exploration of the ground; from May to the middle of June, Anglo-French negotiations about the form of the pact; from June to the end of August, exchange of views with the German Government; and from September to October detailed negotiations leading to the conference at Locarno.

Preliminary discussions, March - May 1925

When Chamberlain called in Paris on 16 March on his way home from Geneva he found that Herriot had accepted the British refusal to sign a separate Anglo-French or Anglo-Franco-Belgian treaty and was prepared to examine the German proposal seriously. But he had some questions to ask, such as whether Germany would join the League, whether she meant a pact to modify the occupation of the Rhineland, whether Austria's position could somehow be confirmed, and whether Germany would renounce the use of force in the east as well as in the west.[1]

At first the French and the British tried to elucidate the German position by oral enquiry. That the results were not altogether clear was due partly to the fact that D'Abernon was inclined to put glosses on what the Germans said, and partly to the complexity of the German position on some vital matters, including Poland. From the German point of view the eastern frontier had nothing to do with the problems in the west which had prompted the pact offer. Indeed in Stresemann's long-term policy an understanding with France was a means to the end of Germany's restoration and treaty revision.[2] But since he was aware that in French eyes security in the west and in the east were connected, the offer of arbitration treaties with all her neighbours was made to show that Germany did not intend to use security in the west to fall upon Poland. The Germans were not prepared to guarantee the Polish frontier in any way, and regarded a formal declaration that they did not wish to alter it by force as an indirect guarantee. On the other hand they did not intend to raise the question of frontier revision in

1 Records of conversation, 16 Mar. 1925, C 3921/459/18, FO 371/10729; MAE, Grande Bretagne, Vol. 74; Q d'O to Fleuriau, 16 Mar., MAE, ibid.; Herriot, *Jadis,* Vol. II, 187-9.

2 Cf. Michael-Olaf Maxelon, *Stresemann und Frankreich* (Düsseldorf, 1972).

the near future: they did not regard it as ripe for a satisfactory solution and they knew that raising it now would wreck the western negotiations.[1]

The nuances of this position were perhaps not easy to convey. The Poles automatically regarded the security offer to France as a device to enable Germany to attack them, and an arbitration treaty as a trap by means of which the frontier grievance could be raised in a new way. The efforts of Herriot and Chamberlain to reassure the Polish Foreign Minister, Skrzynski, were not very successful.[2] The press calmed down, but the Poles remained deeply distrustful. D'Abernon too appears to have thought that the Germans would raise the frontier question, and started talking about possible compensation for Poland.[3] On the other hand he seems to have believed, until the second week of March, that the German Government were ready to give a formal undertaking not to attempt to alter the eastern frontier by force.[4]

Chamberlain, as has been noted, shared this misconception, and understanding was not advanced by the incident arising out of his speech in the House of Commons on 24 March. After outlining the German proposals Chamberlain said: 'If I understand them rightly, they amount to this: that Germany is prepared to guarantee voluntarily what hitherto she has accepted under the compulsion of the treaty, that is, the *status quo* in the West; that she is prepared to eliminate, not merely from the West but from the East, war as an engine by which any alteration in the Treaty position is to be obtained. Thus not only in the West but in the East, she is prepared absolutely to abandon any recourse to war for the purpose of changing the treaty boundaries of Europe, though she may be unwilling, or unable, to make the same renunciation of the hopes and aspirations that some day, by friendly arrangement or mutual agreement, a modification may be introduced into the East, as she is prepared to make in regard to any modification

1 Hoesch to AA, 7 Mar. 1925; AA to Hoesch, 10 Mar.; memorandum by Schubert, 10 Mar.; Schubert to Dufour, 23 Mar., 4509/E125173-74, E125495-96, E125752-53, E125706-12.

2 Chamberlain to Crowe, 14 Mar. 1925, C 3753/459/18, FO 371/10728; note by Herriot, 18 Mar., MAE, Grande Bretagne, Vol. 74; Hoesch to AA, 6 Mar., 4509/E125194-96; memorandum by Dirksen, 7 Mar., 4509/E125180-81; Rauscher to AA, 27 Mar., K170/K025663-68; Wandycz, *France and her Eastern Allies,* 332-4.

3 Memoranda by Schubert, 10 Feb. and 21 Mar. 1925, 4509/E125048-54, E125740-44; D'Abernon to FO, 14 Feb.; D'Abernon to Chamberlain, 20 Mar., C 2390, 4491/459/18, FO 371/10727, 10729; D'Abernon, *Ambassador of Peace,* Vol. III, 153.

4 D'Abernon to FO, 1 and 12 Mar. 1925, C 3009, 3655/459/18, FO 371/10727, 10728; memoranda by Luther and Schubert, 10, 11 and 12 Mar., 4509/E125484-87, E125472-83, E125459, E125431-39.

in the West'. Sthamer, who with other foreign representatives was listening to the debate, urgently asked to see Chamberlain and told him that the reference to the eastern frontier was not wholly accurate. He did not clearly explain why, but Chamberlain understood him to mean that the German Government did not renounce all possibility of resort to force. Chamberlain said that if this were so the bottom fell out of the whole scheme and he must go back and tell the House. Sthamer protested that the German proposal was not changed, and Chamberlain said no more; but he telegraphed to D'Abernon that the point was a test of German good faith and must be cleared up at once.[1]

The Germans feared that Chamberlain was trying to commit them to some additional obligation such as a non-aggression pact with Poland, but D'Abernon maintained that only a reply to the British Government was needed. After much discussion he obtained a statement that the German Government 'renounce any idea of bringing about by warlike means an alteration to the present German-Polish frontier', and that there was no reason for the British Government to alter their views as expressed by Chamberlain and Baldwin.[2] The incident was then closed. Chamberlain attributed it to a misunderstanding on Sthamer's part: he did not think he would ever be able to negotiate through the ambassador, whom he suspected of not being kept fully informed by Berlin and of not reporting accurately. It is clear from the German records that Sthamer did on the whole report accurately, but he did not always succeed in conveying points clearly to the British. On this occasion he was trying to point out that the German arbitration treaties which Schubert had suggested as models, did not exclude the use of force in all cases of dispute since the awards of the conciliation bodies were not binding: he succeeded only in being blamed for Chamberlain's own confusion.[3]

On the other hand the Germans had some ground for thinking that Britain would not be averse to peaceful change of the Polish frontier. There was a body of opinion in Britain which, not without assistance

1 *HC Deb.*, 5th ser., Vol. 182, cols. 317-18; FO to D'Abernon, 25 Mar. 1925, C 4302/459/18, FO 371/10729; Sthamer to AA, 25 Mar., 4509/E125616-18.

2 Memoranda by Schubert and Stresemann, 26, 27, 28 Mar. 1925, 4509/E125596-98, E125592-95, E125590-91, E125589, E125583-86, E125580-81, E125567-71, E125563-66, E125560-62. In the final German text the verb 'zurückwiesen' was used for 'renounce', rather than the stronger 'verzichten'.

3 Chamberlain to D'Abernon, 26 Mar. 1925; D'Abernon to FO, 28 Mar., C 4491, 4419/459/18. FO 371/10729; D'Abernon to Chamberlain 29 Mar. Chamberlain Papers, AC 52/263, D'Abernon Papers, BL Add. MS 48928; Sthamer to AA, 25 Mar.; AA to Sthamer, 26 Mar., 30 Mar.; Schubert to Dufour, 30 Mar., 4509/E125616-18, E125619, E125519-25, E125514-18; Dufour to Schubert, 31 Mar., 4567/E166085-99; Sthamer to AA, 1 Apr., 4509/E125848-49.

from German propaganda, had come to the conclusion that the treaty settlement was unjust. Discussion of the pact proposals aroused one of the periodical bursts of criticism of the Versailles provisions, notably a denunciation by Lloyd George in the Commons debate of 24 March.[1] The critics were represented in the Foreign Office: Nicolson's description of the Polish Corridor and Upper Silesia as 'dangerous injustices' has been quoted; and an echo of this reached Berlin when Sthamer reported that Chamberlain had informed the Cabinet in a memorandum that the settlement as regards the Corridor and Upper Silesia could not last.[2] Chamberlain himself in fact gave no encouragement to such an idea. He certainly exhorted the Polish Government to try to conciliate Germany;[3] but he also told Sthamer that he would not encourage Germany to seek a change and it would be folly for her to join the League only to invoke Article 19 of the Covenant.[4] In the middle of June Chamberlain sent to D'Abernon and Max Muller, the British Minister in Warsaw, a considered statement of his position to guide their conversations. The solution reached at the peace conference, he wrote, was at least ethnographically correct and represented the most satisfactory of the courses open at the time. Two other solutions had recently been suggested: that Poland should give up the Corridor and receive Memel in exchange for Danzig; and that East Prussia should be neutralised. Neither seemed practicable. The first was ruled out by the international status of Memel and the Polish-Lithuanian quarrel, even if the advantage of removing a cause of constant friction might seem to outweigh the disadvantage of handing back a large number of Poles to German rule. The second assumed that neutralisation would reduce East Prussian resentment at being cut off from the rest of Germany, but there was no evidence that this was so. There was a danger, Chamberlain went on, of assuming that a frontier change was inevitable and that therefore Britain ought to promote it. But it was too soon to say that change was inevitable, and until it was proved to be so as little as possible should be done. Changes would create new problems as well as solving old ones, and the idea that the British

1 *HC Deb.*, 5th ser., Vol. 182, cols. 328-38.

2 No such memorandum exists. Nicolson's description, in his memorandum of 23 January (see p. 77) was not repeated in the shortened version circulated to the Cabinet by Chamberlain on 19 February, the version which leaked to the press. Sthamer's report is accepted as accurate by J. Korbel, *Poland between East and West* (Princeton, 1963), 167-8, and is repeated from Korbel by a more recent writer who could have checked the Cabinet papers: A. Polonsky, *Politics in Independent Poland* (Oxford, 1972), 137.

3 For example FO to Max Muller, 31 Mar. 1925, N 1843/43/55, FO 371/10997, and 19 May, C 6850/459/18, FO 371/10731.

4 FO to D'Abernon, 15 May 1925, C 6652/459/18, FO 371/10731; Sthamer to AA, 15 May, 4509/E126279-83.

Government favoured change would increase insecurity. The object should be to diminish the existing difficulties: 'If the Germans are wise they will let the question sleep for a generation. If the Poles are wise they will make it possible for them to do so'.[1]

The position of Czechoslovakia was less delicate since there was no major cause of dispute with Germany. Beneš told Herriot and Chamberlain that he was quite willing to discuss treaties of arbitration. As in earlier years he regarded secure peace in the west as the best assurance of peace throughout Europe, although he would have liked a treaty of guarantee in the east as well. He was anxious that existing treaties should not be weakened and that the position of Austria in particular should be safeguarded; and he said that Germany should join the League. To the Germans Beneš said that he was willing to start talks on an arbitration treaty.[2] He also made an attempt to improve relations with Poland, visiting Warsaw at the end of April to sign a trade treaty. The Germans were worried by reports that he had made an agreement about joint resistance to frontier revision;[3] but the *rapprochement* did not go far, and later in the summer Beneš was at pains to mark the difference between his country's position and that of Poland.

On the occupation of the Rhineland D'Abernon received another assurance that the German Government would not demand modification of the treaty.[4] As for entry into the League, Schubert had already given D'Abernon papers on Article 16 and the supervision of German disarmament.[5] The Secretary-General of the League, Drummond, visiting Berlin at the beginning of March, got the impression that the Germans were raising new conditions for entry; but D'Abernon considered that if their fear of isolation could be overcome their attitude on Article 16 might change.[6] D'Abernon hoped for a quick

1 FO to D'Abernon and Max Muller, 16 Jun. 1925, C 8063/459/18, FO 371/10733.

2 Chamberlain to Crowe, 12 Mar. 1925, C 3726/459/18, FO 371/10728; Beneš to Chamberlain, 16 Mar., C 3878/459/18, FO 371/10729; note of conversation, and memorandum by Beneš, 16 Mar., MAE, Grande Bretagne, Vol. 74; Herriot, *Jadis,* Vol. II, 189-90; Hoffman (Bern) to AA., 13 Mar., 3147/D654811-12; Koch (Prague) to AA., 24 Mar., 4509/E125675-76. For Beneš's position see also F. Gregory Campbell, *Confrontation in Central Europe* (Chicago, 1975), 143-8.

3 Memorandum by Schubert, 11 May 1925; AA to Sthamer, 11 May; AA to Koch and Rauscher, 13 May, 4509/E126187-92; E126195-97, E126215-24.

4 D'Abernon to FO, 12 Mar. 1925, C 3664/459/18, FO 371/10728.

5 Memoranda by Schubert, 19 and 24 Feb. 1925; Schubert to D'Abernon, 25 Feb., 4509/E124954-59, E124903-09, E124913-22, E124883-89; AA to Sthamer, 25 Feb., 3123/D642371-78; D'Abernon to FO, 27 Feb., C 3053/109/18, FO 371/10717.

6 Memoranda by Schubert, 11 Mar. 1925, 4584/E178270-74; Drummond to

decision on German entry during the March Council meeting, and suggested that the Roman Law maxim 'Ultra posse nemo obligatur' should meet the case on Article 16. But the Germans were in no hurry and laid equal emphasis on the supervision of disarmament.[1] On 14 March the League Council replied to the German Government's letter of the previous December, saying that Germany could expect a seat on the Council and a voice in deciding the application of the Covenant, but could not refuse to take part in economic measures recommended. The matter was then dropped for the time being, the Germans noting to themselves that the evacuation of the Cologne zone and the question of supervision must be settled in Germany's favour before anything more was done, and assurance found that there would not be a breach with the Soviet Union.[2]

No more than that of the Polish frontier did the Germans intend to raise the question of Austria, but it caused recurrent confusion. As over Poland, the French feared that a settlement in the west would leave Germany free to pursue other ambitions. The question was also of obvious interest to the Italians as well as to the Czechs. So far the Italian attitude to a western pact was reserved: they would have disliked an Anglo-Franco-Belgian treaty but were waiting to see what would emerge from the German proposals.[3] At the end of March the French Government informed Rome that their reply to the Germans would not mention other frontiers, and Chamberlain told the Italian Ambassador that he did not think it desirable to raise the Austrian question.[4] But in Berlin D'Abernon seems to have been enquiring about Austria, and both to have got the impression that Italy was not interested and to have given the impression that Britain would not oppose an Anschluss.[5] No sooner was this cleared up (so far as it ever was: Mussolini continued to regard D'Abernon with suspicion) than the Italian Ambassador in Berlin interpreted some remarks by Stresemann about the strength of popular feeling and the impossibility of delaying a solution to mean that the Germans intended to raise the

D'Abernon, 5 Mar.; D'Abernon to Drummond, 8 Mar., Cecil Papers, BL Add. MS 51110.

1 Memorandum by Stresemann, 9 Mar. 1925, 3123/D642576-78; memorandum by Luther, 10 Mar.; memoranda by Schubert, 9, 10 and 12 Mar., 4509/E125484-87, E125143-47, E125472-83, E125431-39.

2 Memorandum by Schubert, 21 Mar. 1925, 4509/E125745-46.

3 Graham to FO, 12 Mar. 1925, C 3624/459/18, FO 371/10728; *DDI*, Vol. III, Nos. 743, 761, 767, 781.

4 Op. cit. Nos. 777, 778, 786; FO to Graham, 1 Apr. 1925, C 4638/459/18, FO 371/10730.

5 *DDI*, Vol. III, Nos. 772, 780, 783; memoranda by Schubert, 2 Apr. 1925; AA to Neurath, 5 Apr., 4509/E125854-56, E125860-61, E125891-93.

question at once. There was uproar in Rome, not much soothed by Stresemann's rapid denial that they had any such intention.[1] The Secretary-General of the Italian Ministry of Foreign Affairs, Contarini, told Graham that the Germans seemed to think that no one would object to an Anschluss, and that Bosdari reported that D'Abernon was not unfavourable and reflected the British Government's view. Some Foreign Office officials shared the sentiment attributed to D'Abernon, but Chamberlain noted: 'I am definitely opposed to Anschluss and shall say so anywhere and every time that the subject is raised. . . Our only chance of peace is to let everyone know that we are opposed to any revision of the treaty settlement - for a generation'; and the Italians, and D'Abernon, were told of his view.[2]

Thereafter, although the French more than once offered to discuss an agreement guaranteeing the Brenner frontier or providing for opposition to an Anschluss, Mussolini resumed a waiting attitude. Presumably he, and Contarini despite differences between them, thought that a pact without German participation would tie Italy too much to France and strengthen French influence in central Europe; it might also mean supporting the *status quo* in other parts of the region and abandoning patronage of revisionism.[3]

The French observations and questions to the German Government in reply to the security proposal were not formulated before Herriot's ministry fell on 10 April, to be succeeded by a government led by Painlevé and with Briand as Minister for Foreign Affairs. When three weeks later still nothing had happened Chamberlain began to show anxiety about French intentions.[4] The Germans had been expressing dissatisfaction for longer: the delay was causing Stresemann trouble with other members of the Government and with the political parties; and the disarmament question seemed likely to come up again

1 *DDI,* Vol. III, No. 846; Vol. IV, No. 13; memorandum by Stresemann, 8 May 1925, 4509/E126171-73; Neurath to AA, 14 May; AA to Neurath, 15 May, 3086/D614036-37, D614038-39.

2 Graham to FO, 15 May 1925; FO to D'Abernon, 2 Jun., C 6680/249/3, FO 371/10660; FO to Graham, 23 Jun., C 8475/459/18, FO 371/10734; *DDI,* Vol. IV, Nos, 26, 28, 29; Margerie to Q d'O, 29 May; Fleuriau to Q d'O, 4 Jun., MAE, Autriche, Vol. 75.

3 See Giampiero Carrocci, *La Politica estera dell'Italia fascista 1925-1928* (Bari, 1969), 42-7; Besnard to Q d'O, 20 Jun. and 2 Jul. 1925; Q d'O to Besnard, 2 Jul.; Besnard to Q d'O, 10 and 14 Jul.; Q d'O to Besnard, 14 and 16 Jul.; Besnard to Q d'O, 23 Jul.; memorandum, 24 Sep., MAE, Grande Bretagne, Vols. 78-80, 83.

4 FO to Crewe, 5 May 1925, C 5969/459/18, FO 371/10731; Chamberlain to Crewe, 12 May; Crewe to Chamberlain, 13 May, Chamberlain Papers, AC 52/211, 212, Crewe Papers, C/8.

in awkward juxtaposition. On 16 March Sthamer told Crowe that if the security proposal looked like succeeding he thought the evacuation of Cologne would take second place; but three days later, on instructions from Berlin, he reversed the order and told Chamberlain that unless satisfaction were obtained on disarmament and evacuation, public opinion might force the German Government to withdraw the security offer.[1] The Allied Military Committee at Versailles did not report on the Control Commission's report until the middle of April; and the British and French Governments did not agree about the procedure to be followed with the Germans until the beginning of May.[2] The Germans had been thinking of sending a note demanding information, and continued to complain of the delay; but Schubert at least was aware that if a disarmament note arrived before the reply on security, public discussion on the former would make the latter question more difficult.[3]

Anglo-French discussion of the reply to the German proposals, May - June 1925

The French Government finally sent their draft reply to the German security proposals to London on 13 May. It stated that before detailed negotiations could begin, clarification and agreement on certain points were needed, and put forward the French view of the bases for negotiation. These were a pact of territorial guarantee between the powers interested in the Rhine (including Belgium); arbitration treaties between Germany and each of these powers, guaranteed by them all; similar arbitration treaties between Germany and her other neighbours who were signatories of the Treaty of Versailles, guaranteed in the same way; German entry into the League of Nations; preservation of all the Allies' rights under the Treaty of Versailles and of their freedom to fulfil their obligations under the Covenant.[4] The intention behind some of the points was not entirely clear to the British, and some raised difficulties for them. From discussion over the next week it emerged that Chamberlain and Briand agreed that German entry into the League was an essential condition for the conclusion of a pact but

1 Sthamer to AA, 16 Mar. 1925; AA to Sthamer, 18 Mar.; Sthamer to AA, 19 Mar., 4509/E125325-26, E125322-23, E125767-69; FO to D'Abernon, 19 Mar., C 4008/459/18, FO 371/10729.

2 FO to Crewe, 17 Apr. and 5 May 1925, C 4764, 5855/21/18, FO 371/10709.

3 AA to Sthamer, 13 Apr. 1925; memorandum by Schubert, 1 May; Sthamer to AA, 1 May; AA to Hoesch, 4 May, 4509/E125955-63, E125115-18, E126119-24, E126138-40.

4 Crewe to FO, 13 May 1925, C 6493/459/18, FO 371/10731; Q d'O to Fleuriau, 13 May, MAE, Grande Bretagne, Vol. 75; Cmd 2435 of 1925.

not a precondition for negotiation; but they differed on the arbitration treaties and the guarantees. Chamberlain doubted whether Britain could sign an arbitration treaty, and was concerned to distinguish between the guarantees for those in the west (which Britain was prepared to undertake) and those in the east (which she was not). Briand saw a distinction between a territorial guarantee and a guarantee of an arbitration treaty. The first necessarily involved resort to force in defence of the territory guaranteed: the second implied the use of means appropriate to the nature of the violation. If, for example, Germany violated the arbitration treaty with Poland Britain need not be involved farther than was appropriate or than she was committed by membership of the League; but France must not be deemed to violate the Rhine pact if she were called upon to help Poland. Briand confirmed that he used 'arbitration' in the most general sense and did not exclude conciliation by the League of Nations, but the peaceful solution must be binding.[1]

The British views, approved by a Cabinet committee representing a fair cross-section of ministerial opinion, were sent to Paris on 28 May. The basic principle was that any new British obligation 'shall be specific and limited to the maintenance of the existing territorial arrangements on the western frontier of Germany. His Majesty's Government are not prepared to assume fresh obligations elsewhere in addition to those already devolving upon them as signatories of the Covenant of the League of Nations and of the Peace Treaties. At the same time, it may be well to repeat that, in seeking means to strengthen the position in the west, His Majesty's Government do not themselves question, or give any encouragement to others to question, the other provisions of the treaties which form the basis of the existing public law of Europe'. The French draft did not accurately convey the extent and character of the obligations that the British Government were ready to assume, and it had therefore been amended. The new draft envisaged a pact of territorial guarantee relating to the western frontier of Germany; arbitration treaties between France and Germany and Belgium and Germany, guaranteed by each of them and by Britain; arbitration treaties between Germany and her other neighbours who were signatories of the Treaty of Versailles but without guarantees; and, like the French, German

1 FO to Crewe, 14 May 1925; French memorandum, 18 May; memorandum to Fleuriau, 19 May; memorandum from Fleuriau, 22 May, C 6558, 6708, 7063/459/18, FO 371/10731, 10732; MAE, Grande Bretagne, Vols. 75-6; Cmd 2435 of 1925.

entry into the League and preservation of all the Allies' rights and obligations.[1]

Although they accepted the British refusal to undertake new obligations beyond the western frontier of Germany and welcomed an informal explanation that the British considered the Covenant entitled France to go to the help of Poland or Czechoslovakia if either were attacked by Germany, the French thought it necessary to state clearly that France must retain freedom to do so. They therefore produced a new draft which included the idea of guarantees for the eastern arbitration treaties by any signatory of the Rhine pact who wished to give one, and said that action on such a guarantee would not be a breach of the Franco-German arbitration treaty.[2] After considering the French amendments Chamberlain told Baldwin that he thought they could all be accepted apart from one about the rights and obligations attaching to membership of the League. He wished to retain the British version, which was wider and would apply to Germany's rights once she joined the League. Baldwin agreed that Chamberlain might so inform Briand at Geneva, where both were going for the June Council meeting.[3]

At Geneva Chamberlain and Briand rapidly reached agreement, Chamberlain's one condition being accepted.[4] The speed of their agreement caused surprise and speculation in the press, which had been pessimistic about the Anglo-French correspondence and therefore assumed that one or other had sacrificed something important. A Havas agency message caused alarm in Berlin and trouble in Rome because it implied that a virtual Anglo-Franco-Belgian alliance had been decided. Mussolini and the Italian press only calmed down on being assured that the message was inaccurate and the British and French Governments would be very glad if Italy joined a Rhine pact.[5] The Germans remained uncertain despite reassurances about the

1 FO to Crewe, 28 May 1925, C 7174, 7265/459/18, FO 371/10732; Crewe to Briand, 28 May, MAE, Grande Bretagne, Vol. 76; Cmd 2435 of 1925. The Belgian and Italian Governments were also informed.

2 Briand to Fleuriau, 4 Jun. 1925, MAE, Grande Bretagne, Vol. 76; FO to Crewe, 5 Jun., C 7565, 7577/459/18, FO 371/10732; Cmd 2435 of 1925. The point about the Covenant was discussed between the Quai d'Orsay and the Foreign Office; C 7296, 7512/459/18, FO 371/10732; minute by Laroche, MAE, Grande Bretagne, Vol. 76.

3 Minutes on C 7806/459/18, FO 371/10733.

4 Chamberlain to Briand, 8 Jun. 1925, C 7743/459/18, FO 371/10732; MAE, Grande Bretagne, Vol. 76; Chamberlain to Tyrrell, 8 Jun.; Crewe to FO, 11 Jun., C 7862, 7884/459/18, FO 371/10733.

5 D'Abernon to FO, 9 Jun. 1925. Grahame to FO, 9 Jun.; FO to D'Abernon,

prospects for the negotiations. At the beginning of June Schubert believed that the central problem of the Anglo-French discussions was the relation between a Rhine pact and France's obligations to Poland and Czechoslovakia.[1] Agreement between Chamberlain and Briand that France might guarantee the eastern arbitration treaties did not, of course, solve the problem for the Germans. Nor had they made progress with the Soviet Government about Germany's entry into the League. In conversation with D'Abernon Stresemann suggested that the western powers would have to compensate Germany for worsened relations with the Soviet Union by extra concessions such as return of Eupen and Malmédy, evacuation of the whole Rhineland, or a colonial mandate.[2] However the Allied note on disarmament, which arrived at this moment, was received calmly despite the evident possibility of friction between the army and the Auswärtiges Amt on the subject.[3]

Correspondence with Germany and drafting the pact, June - August 1925

The French Government's reply on a security pact, in the terms agreed with the British, was delivered in Berlin on 16 June.[4] The Germans now had to decide whether to pursue negotiations on this basis. The Government were divided and for a time Luther's support of Stresemann was in doubt.[5] Even after the Cabinet approved Stresemann's policy the arguments continued and the tone of the press was unfavourable. When towards the end of June D'Abernon returned to Berlin from leave Chamberlain told him to use all his influence to prevent the Germans from destroying their own work, and despite doubts as to the usefulness of talking to a 'feather bed' Sthamer was exhorted to urge his Government to send a speedy and

9 Jun.; Graham to FO, 10 Jun.; Chamberlain to Graham, 11 Jun.; Chamberlain to Tyrrell, 12 Jun.; Graham to FO, 13 Jun., C 7752, 7754, 7785, 7848, 7849, 7957, 8052, 8199/459/18, FO 371/10733, 10734; *DDI,* Vol. IV, Nos. 21, 23, 24, 27, 29, 32.

1 Sthamer to AA, 26 and 28 May 1925; AA to Hoesch, 2 Jun.; Hoesch to AA, 4 Jun., 4509/E126407, E126437, E126478-84, E126507-10.

2 Memorandum by Stresemann, 10 Jun. 1925, 3123/D643483-85, extract in *Vermächtnis,* Vol.II, 101-3; D'Abernon, *Ambassador of Peace,* Vol.II, 167-70.

3 See Salewski, *Entwaffnung und Militärkontrolle,* 305-7.

4 MAE, Grande Bretagne, Vol.77; C 7884/459/18, FO 371/10733; Cmd 2435 of 1925; *Locarno-Konferenz,* No.14.

5 See Henry A. Turner, *Stresemann and the Politics of the Weimar Republic* (Princeton, 1963), 204-7; Max von Stockhausen, *Sechs Jahre Reichskanzlei* (Bonn, 1954), 165-7; Hans Meier-Welcker, *Seeckt* (Frankfurt, 1967), 470-7.

uncontentious reply.[1] After talking to Stresemann and Schubert D'Abernon sent pessimistic reports: he believed that Stresemann was still wholeheartedly behind the negotiations but the opposition, fanned by the Russians, was unexpectedly strong.[2] Chamberlain replied that these reports, contrasting with D'Abernon's earlier optimism, made him wonder whether he was 'being used as a dupe in a negotiation in which the German proposals were only put forward to divide the Allies or get a better price from Russia. . . If Germany refuses or delays acceptance the opportunity may pass for ever and the blame will be hers'.[3]

The points that caused the greatest objections in Germany were the insistence on German entry into the League, the proposed guarantee of the eastern arbitration treaties, the unlimited nature of all the arbitration treaties, and the retention of the Allies' rights under existing treaties. Some of the objections reflected fears of what might theoretically happen if legal loopholes were left, but some expressed important political considerations. Thus the objection to unlimited arbitration, which Schubert said 'presented a problem of extraordinary difficulty', was worded as a technical one about the unsuitability of arbitral tribunals for dealing with non-juridical disputes. In fact the French were thinking of arbitration in the broad sense including conciliation procedures, whilst the Germans disliked the idea of submitting disputes that might involve vital interests to outside decision, and wished to avoid formally renouncing the use of force against Poland. The objection to a guarantee of the eastern arbitration treaties was worded as a fear that it would allow France to act against Germany without waiting for a League decision in the event of trouble caused by the German minority in Poland; but it was really due to repugnance at acknowledging any French title to a voice in German-Polish relations.[4]

D'Abernon pooh-poohed Schubert's assertion that the Germans were threatened with another dictated treaty, and hoped that when

1 Chamberlain to D'Abernon, 26 Jun. 1925, Chamberlain Papers, AC 52/280; Addison to Lampson, 26 Jun.; FO to D'Abernon, 30 Jun., C 8804, 8805/459/18, FO 371/10735.

2 D'Abernon to FO, 28 and 29 Jun. 1925, C 8699, 8770/459/18, FO 371/10735; memorandum by Schubert, 27 Jun., 4509/E126878-87; memorandum by Stresemann, 28 Jun., 3123/D643748-54.

3 FO to D'Abernon, 30 Jun. 1925, C 8770/459/18, FO 371/10735.

4 D'Abernon to FO, 1 Jul. 1925, C 9066/459/18, FO 371/10735; memoranda by Schubert and correspondence with D'Abernon, 30 Jun. and 1 Jul., 4509/E126932-33, E126988-91, E126992-127006, E126592-99. Internal German correspondence about arbitration treaties in 4509/E127720-45, E127880-88; 4562/E155860-67.

the drafting stage was reached it would not be difficult to meet most of their objections. But he admitted that Schubert and Gaus said that the pact as proposed would put Germany in a worse position than if she simply joined the League, and that the French had twisted the offer of a short and simple agreement out of all recognition. Chamberlain was sufficiently worried by the German attitude to set out his impressions in a despatch which could be published if the negotiations failed. He agreed that most of the objections were theoretical rather than practical, and should not in themselves cause great difficulty. He would not give further explanations now, lest there be further delay and the correspondence be prolonged. But two points must be made. First, the statement that the proposal of unlimited arbitration treaties presented a problem of extraordinary difficulty was itself extraordinary, since it was the Germans who had first suggested comprehensive arbitration treaties providing for the peaceful settlement of all disputes.[1] Secondly the Germans were creating difficulties in the language of the French note. They might have contemplated a short and simple agreement, but their proposals were comprehensive and elastic and the French note was an attempt to carry further tentative suggestions which had been taken as aimed at 'the preservation of peace, the removal of the prevailing sense of insecurity and the cultivation of more friendly relations between the nations recently at war. . . If, at this stage, the German Government draw back, the world will quickly revise its estimate of the nature and purpose of their original proposals. . . I cannot suppose that any responsible statesman, realising what this would mean, will enter upon so disastrous a course'.[2]

The original objects of the German proposals were in fact a good deal narrower than the preservation of peace and the cultivation of more friendly relations; but these more limited aims had in large measure been achieved by the summer, as Hoesch pointed out in a despatch urging the continuation of negotiations. The pact proposals, he maintained, had had a significant effect on the disarmament note, it had separated the question of the evacuation of the Cologne zone from that of future supervision under Article 213, and had killed the idea of an Anglo-Franco-Belgian alliance. Hoesch thought that unlimited arbitration treaties in the west would be advantageous to

1 Article 1 of the German-Swiss arbitration treaty was quoted in support of this argument, which suggests that the British were still ignoring the fact that under this treaty the awards of the counciliation body were not binding.

2 FO to D'Abernon, 17 Jul. 1925, C 9066/459/18, FO 371/10735. The warning in the last sentence was meant to be conveyed to the German Government.

Germany, and since it would obviously be difficult to find convincing reasons for concluding a different kind of treaty in the east the point might have to be conceded. But even though a French guarantee of the eastern treaties would probably give France no greater right to intervene in a German-Polish conflict than she possessed under the Covenant, Hoesch thought that it should be resisted on principle.[1]

Since the German objection to a French guarantee of the eastern arbitration treaties was one of principle, it was difficult to reassure them about it, and D'Abernon's attempts to do so were both indiscreet and unsuccessful.[2] The German note delivered in Paris on 20 July rejected such a guarantee. It described the statement that the peace treaties would not be modified by the pact as unnecessary and undesirable: the German Government believed that a pact would have an effect on the occupation of the Rhineland. Further, they objected to unlimited arbitration treaties coupled with the right to take action in case of breaches of existing treaties, to the possibility that a guarantor of a western arbitration treaty could decide who had been the guilty party, and to the demand for German entry into the League of Nations. The last letter from the Council, the note said, did not meet the difficulty over Article 16: Germany was disarmed and exposed and could not be regarded as enjoying equal rights until her disarmament was followed by general disarmament.[3]

Although the note ended with an expression of hope that further discussion would lead to a positive result, its tone was more suited to pleasing right-wing opinion in Germany than to encouraging the western governments. Chamberlain and Briand made the best of it to each other, but both were concerned at the continued German objection to joining the League, and Chamberlain commented that the German Government appeared no longer 'in the role of a far-seeing contributor to the general cause of peace, but rather in that of a somewhat unwilling participant, who acquiesces in a scheme, not because of its intrinsic merits, but merely in the hope that consent will

1 Hoesch to AA, 30 Jun. 1925, 3123/D643769-81.

2 D'Abernon to Lampson, 3 Jul. 1925; Lampson to D'Abernon, 5 Jul., C 8939/459/18, FO 371/10735; memorandum by Schubert, 8 Jul., 4509/E127066-70.

3 Note from the German Government, 20 Jul. 1925, 3123/D643918-33; C 9581/459/18, FO 371/10736; MAE, Grande Bretagne, Vol. 79; *Locarno-Konferenz,* No. 16; Cmd 2468 of 1925, *Reply of the German Government to the note handed to Herr Stresemann by the French Ambassador at Berlin on June 16, 1925, respecting the proposals for a pact of security.*

enable him to drive a bargain in other directions'.[1] When D'Abernon reported Schubert's hope that there would not be another French note Chamberlain retorted that the Germans should have thought of that before publishing 'an election manifesto'. They were now asking the Allied Governments to show 'a patience, forbearance and statesmanship, not to say a courage, in face of public opinion, of which in effect they avow themselves incapable'.[2]

In the mean time the British and French Governments had begun to discuss drafts of a treaty. The initiative was taken by the Foreign Office, with the dual purpose of producing a basis for discussion and of forestalling any French attempt to reintroduce points that had been rejected in May. One point which the British had to decide was whether the obligations of the pact should apply to the Dominions unless they contracted out, or whether, as in the proposed Anglo-French pact of 1922, the obligations should be inapplicable unless the Dominions chose to accept them. During the discussion of this problem, in which the chief concern was to preserve the outward unity of the Empire, the Australian Prime Minister, Bruce, questioned whether security was anything but a continental question which could be better solved by Germany joining the League. Chamberlain replied that he was sure a Franco-German agreement was impossible without British participation and Germany would only join the League if her entry were insisted on as a condition of the pact. Moreover security was not a purely continental question: Britain had a vital interest in the Channel coast and could not remain unaffected by any major European conflict. If Britain withdrew from Europe there would be no chance of permanent peace; and 'I at any rate would not be responsible for attempting to conduct the foreign policy of this country in conditions which to my mind make war inevitable'.[3]

Bruce was, as Amery said, likely to back British policy more strongly than any other Australian Prime Minister and certainly more strongly than any Canadian or South African Prime Minister. It was presumably with his views in mind that Chamberlain decided that the obligations of the proposed treaty should not apply to the

1 FO to D'Abernon, 28 Jul. 1925, C 10034/459/18, FO 371/10737. Chamberlain also regarded the reference to the occupation as both foolish and near to a breach of Stresemann's promise that the question would not be raised as a condition of the pact: Chamberlain to D'Abernon, 29 Jul., Chamberlain Papers, AC 52/289, D'Abernon Papers, BL Add. MS 48929.

2 D'Abernon to FO, 28 Jul. 1925; FO to D'Abernon, 30 Jul., C 9992/459/18, FO 371/10737.

3 Bruce to Amery, 6 May 1925; Amery to Chamberlain, 15 Jun.; Amery to Baldwin, 15 Jun., Baldwin Papers, F.2 (Vol. 115); Chamberlain Papers, AC 52/32, 37; Chamberlain to Amery, 19 Jun., AC 52/38.

Dominions or India unless they contracted in.[1] Except for the New Zealand Government, who said that they would follow Britain, none of the Dominion Governments expressed an official opinion on the information sent to them about the pact before the debate on it in the House of Commons on 24 June. One of the strongest pleas in Chamberlain's speech was that isolation was impossible for Britain, who was a member of the League, had rights and duties under the Treaty of Versailles, and was geographically closely linked to Europe. Most speakers on both sides of the House agreed; and although MacDonald still hankered after some general instrument, the policy set out in the now published correspondence with the French Government was approved. Anxiety was, however, expressed about the relationship between the guarantee and the machinery of the League.[2] After the debate Chamberlain wrote to Crewe that he was well satisfied and believed that so far as British opinion was concerned 'we really have the pact in our pocket' - provided that the principle was maintained that except to repel invasion no party should resort to war until the methods of settlement by the League had been exhausted.[3]

The first British draft of the mutual security pact therefore provided that alleged breaches of the undertaking by France and Belgium and Germany not to go to war except in resistance to attack or when authorised by the League, would be submitted to the Council of the League, as would alleged violations of the demilitarisation of the Rhineland and breaches of the western arbitration treaties. If the Council established the existence of a breach it would inform the guarantors, who would then come to the help of the injured party; but if the country breaking the arbitration treaty resorted to war, the guarantors would act immediately.[4] After approval by the Committee of Imperial Defence and the Cabinet, the draft was sent to the French Government.[5]

They however, and the Belgian Government, objected to subordinating the operation of the guarantee to decision by the Council, especially in case of a sudden attack; and the French feared that the draft weakened the provisions of the Treaty of Versailles relating to the Rhineland.

1 Harding (Colonial Office) to Lampson, 24 Jun. 1925; Lampson to Harding, 30 Jun., C 8530/459/18, FO 371/10734.

2 *HC Deb.*, 5th ser., Vol 185, cols. 1555-1671.

3 Chamberlain to Crewe, 27 Jun. 1925, Chamberlain Papers, AC 52/221, Crewe Papers, C/8.

4 CP 311(25), 312(25), 27 Jun. 1925, CAB 24/174.

5 CID 201st meeting, CAB 2/4; CP 318(25), CAB 24/174; C 33(25), CAB 23/50; FO to Crewe, 4 Jul. 1925; Chamberlain to Fleuriau, 4 Jul., C 8861/459/18, FO 371/10735.

Chamberlain maintained that there must be machinery to decide whether the *casus foederis* had arisen, and that the guarantors were free to act if Germany violated the frontier before the League could reach a decision;[1] but in order to sort out the problem the legal adviser to the Quai d'Orsay came to London. Fromageot arrived almost simultaneously with the German note of 20 July, with its objection to the possibility of action by any of the parties without a carefully regulated procedure. It emerged from the discussion with him that the French were anxious about the risk both of delay in getting a Council decision and of failure to reach a decision (since unanamity would be required and some of the smaller powers might not dare to pronounce Germany the aggressor) preventing the guarantee coming into play. Fromageot wanted some provision that would allow Britain to go to the help of France at her own discretion and subject only to subsequent endorsement by the League, and he refused to accept a distinction between an attack on French territory and infringement of the demilitarised zone.

Some members of the Central Department thought that the French request should be rejected; but Chamberlain held that a provision of this kind was desirable and could be justified to Parliament as preserving Britain's freedom of action. It was agreed that Hurst should try to get Fromageot's consent to an article so worded as to make it clear that the guarantor would only act in advance of a Council decision in cases where hostilities had actually broken out or when the armed forces of either side had indubitably entered the demilitarised zone. If Fromageot accepted he was still to be warned that the Cabinet might well not agree.[2]

This was the inception of the idea of a flagrant violation of the demilitarised territory. Chamberlain told Fleuriau and Fromageot that he thought it was in the Government's power to give with general national approval a guarantee that would operate effectively in case of a serious threat from Germany; but he warned them against two dangers. The first was that popular British acceptance of the obligation depended on the guarantee being clearly limited to the case against which it was meant to provide. Chamberlain was worried lest attempts to fill every gap might so confuse and alarm public opinion that the real guarantee might slip through France's grasp. The second danger lay

1 Minute by Chamberlain, 6 Jul. 1925, C 9186/459/18, FO 371/10736; Q d'O to Fleuriau, 9 Jul., MAE, Grande Bretagne, Vol. 79; Chamberlain to Fleuriau, 11 Jul.; FO to Grahame. 14 Jul.; Grahame to FO, 17 Jul., C 9216, 9411, 9539/459/18, FO 371/10736; *DDB*, Vol. II, Nos. 76, 78, 79.

2 Minutes, 21 Jul. 1925; record of meeting, 22 Jul., C 9581, 9693, 9784/459/18, FO 371/10736; note by Fromageot, 23 Jul., MAE, Grande Bretagne, Vol. 80.

in the eastern arrangements. It was on them that it was likely to be most difficult to reach agreement with Germany; but he trusted that the western pact would not be allowed to founder on them, for if it did there would be no British guarantee at all.[1]

Although the German note required a written reply, it was likely that discussion with the Germans could begin soon afterwards. The British idea was to put forward the draft treaty as a British text which committed no one, and to invite the German legal adviser Gaus to meet Hurst and Fromageot to see how far they could agree, leaving the ministers to come in and take the final decisions. There were obvious objections to a ministerial meeting before success was reasonably assured, and the French dislike of conferences had to be borne in mind. But the Germans wanted the ministers to meet and agree on principles before the drafting was done. They evidently feared that Gaus might be led into making political decisions, and said that he would be at a disadvantage in discussing a text which he supposedly would not have seen in advance.[2] Despite encouragement from Paris and London, and the completion of the evacuation of the Ruhr and the 'sanctions towns' originally occupied in 1921, Schubert's attitude remained stiff. D'Abernon thought, wrongly, that the German objections to joining the League were receding; but he reported continued insistence on a procedure for impartial decision before any forcible intervention could take place under the treaty, and continued rejection of a French guarantee for the eastern arbitration treaties.[3]

Briand was prepared to consider a meeting with Stresemann, but only after he had reached full agreement with the British; and for this purpose he suggested visiting London. He told Phipps, the British Chargé d'Affaires in Paris, that he would accept any provision that would save justified measures against German aggression from being prevented

1 FO to Phipps, 23 Jul. 1925; C 9802/459/18, FO 371/10736; Fleuriau to Laroche; note by Fleuriau, MAE, Grande Bretagne, Vol. 80.

2 D'Abernon to Chamberlain, 25 Jul. 1925; Chamberlain to D'Abernon, 29 Jul.; D'Abernon to Chamberlain, 7 Aug., Chamberlain Papers, AC 52/288, 289, 290, D'Abernon Papers, BL Add. MS 48929; FO to D'Abernon, 31 Jul., 6 Aug., C 10255, 10531/459/18, FO 371/10737, 10738; memoranda by Schubert, 24 and 31 Jul., 4509/E127412-14, E127458-62; Sthamer to AA, 28 Jul., 1 Aug., 4509/E127488, E127479-80; memorandum by Stresemann, 3 Aug., 3123/D644145-48, *Vermächtnis,* Vol. II, 163-6; AA to Sthamer and Hoesch, 4 Aug., 3123/D644155-56, D644149-50; Dufour to AA, 6 Aug., 4509/E127525-27. Gaus had in fact seen the British draft by 5 August: a copy of it, as approved by the Cabinet and sent to the Dominions, was given to the German Consulate-General in Dublin by an Irish informant: 4509/E127388-90, E128723-26.

3 Hoesch to AA, 6 Aug. 1925; Dufour to AA, 7 Aug.; memoranda by Schubert, 8, 9, 10 Aug., 4509/E127540-44, E127551-55, E127563-71, E127574-76. E127588-91; D'Abernon to FO, 10 Aug., C 10554/459/18, FO 371/10738.

by one dissentient vote on the Council.[1] A new French text allowed for resort to war in resistance to 'hostile acts' as well as to invasion or attack, and provided for action in case of 'manifest violation' of the demilitarisation of the Rhineland.[2] At their first meeting on 11 August Chamberlain and Briand agreed on a reply to the German note, including an invitation to verbal negotiations. Chamberlain put forward the idea of inviting Gaus to meet Hurst and Fromageot, and perhaps the Belgian legal adviser Rolin Jaecquemins, to exchange ideas and information. Briand, who said that he did not want to give the impression that the French and British had arranged everything before the curtain rose, but was also averse to a formal conference, agreed that this was the best solution.[3]

The discussion of the French redraft of the treaty was less simple. The chief problem was 'hostile acts'. Chamberlain asked that the expression be omitted, since he wished to avoid the reproach that he was promising armed assistance to France and Belgium in cases where it was not called for. Fromageot explained that the expression was that of the Treaty of Versailles and really covered two categories of act. Minor breaches of demilitarisation such as the discovery of a railway siding overlooked by the Control Commission clearly could not be regarded as hostile acts, but positive actions such as the assembly of armed nationalist associations could, and France would be allowed to act without waiting for the League. Chamberlain said that in the British view, although the Treaty of Versailles gave the Allies the right to respond to a violation of the demilitarised zone by hostilities, they were bound by the Covenant not to resort to hostilities in any case until the procedure for peaceful settlement had been exhausted. Just because the term 'hostile acts' might cover minor cases, it ought not to be used. As a general rule the Council ought to be called on to decide whether the alleged violation was important, and Chamberlain wished to reserve the immediate operation of the guarantee for cases where urgent action was clearly necessary. If they tried to reserve rights which were not going to be exercised in practice, something vital might be lost. Briand said that he for one would not dream of losing the substance for the shadow: no one could possibly hesitate if the choice lay between a defensive war against Germany with Great Britain acting on the side of France, and an independent war by France, unsupported by Great Britain, for reasons of minor importance. Chamberlain said

1 Phipps to FO, 27 and 28 Jul. 1925, C 9984, 9994/459/18, FO 371/10737.

2 Q d'O to Fleuriau, 29 Jul. 1925, MAE, Grande Bretagne, Vol. 80; Fleuriau to Chamberlain, 31 Jul., C 10146/459/18, FO 371/10737.

3 Notes of conversation, 11 Aug. 1925, C 10609/459/18, FO 371/10738.

that when there was time every method of conciliation must be exhausted before action was taken, but they must provide for immediate action when there was not time for the conciliation machinery to operate without prejudicing the position of the injured country. The French agreed that it should be possible to find a suitable wording.

A second problem was the possible termination of the treaty. The British draft, in order to avoid specifying a time limit, had provided that the treaty should remain in force until the Council of the League decided, on the application of one of the parties, that the League itself afforded sufficient protection. The French had deleted the passage because, they said, under it a majority of the Council could bring to an end not only the guarantee but also the undertaking not to go to war and the arbitration treaties.[1]

Next day various amendments worked out overnight were approved. The undertaking not to resort to war was now not to apply (in addition to the case of resistance to invasion or attack) to a case of 'a flagrant violation of Articles 42, 43 or 180 of the Treaty of Versailles, if such violation constitutes an unprovoked act of aggression and by reason of the assembly of armed forces in the demilitarised zone, immediate action is necessary'; and in this case too the guarantors would act immediately. For the treaty to be terminated at least two of the parties would have to ask the Council to decide that the League afforded sufficient protection.[2]

The Cabinet approved the new text, and the reply to the German note, on 13 August. In the discussion it was emphasised that the guarantee would not operate automatically if Germany attacked Poland, France in consequence attacked Germany, her troops were driven back, and then Germany invaded France.[3] At the end of the first meeting with Briand Chamberlain had written off to tell D'Abernon how well things were going, how admirable was the attitude of the French, and how it was Briand who insisted that they must prepare for a real discussion with the Germans. The object of inviting Gaus was to give him a copy of the form into which the British and French had put their ideas, and all necessary explanations of their intentions. Gaus would not be asked to commit himself to anything: he would go home and discuss the plan and after that Stresemann and any other German representative could meet Chamber-

1 Notes of conversation, 11 Aug. 1925, C 10610/459/18, FO 371/10738.
2 Notes of conversation, 12 Aug. 1925, C 10611/459/18, FO 371/10738.
3 C 45 (25), CAB 23/50.

lain, Briand and the Belgian Foreign Minister Vandervelde for conversations. After the second meeting with Briand Chamberlain added to his letter an outline of the treaty, stressing that it was Britain who would have to be satisfied that a flagrant act had taken place and there was immediate danger. Germany ought not to find anything to object to in such a treaty. As for the eastern guarantee, 'Don't the Germans see that this is the way and the only way of rewriting the Franco-Polish Alliance? It is all in the German interest, and ours'.[1]

But although D'Abernon quoted this letter to Schubert, and expressed a hope that the ministers could meet in time for Germany's entry into the League to be fixed at the Assembly in September, Schubert was still in no hurry to send Gaus to London.[2] The Germans had not yet made up their minds about a number of fundamental problems, of which the obligations of Article 16 of the Covenant was one. Entry into the League was now accepted as inevitable; but as Gaus wrote, the practical problem was to enable Germany to keep out of conflicts involving her neighbours. A formal amendment to Article 16 was neither possible nor desirable, but Germany's right to decide whether to participate in joint League action without incurring charges of disloyalty must be secured. The provision of the Geneva Protocol referring to a country's geographical position and military situation might serve as a starting point, but it did not go far enough to allow Germany to refuse to take part in economic measures or allow passage of troops. Another problem was the operation of the guarantee in the west. It was a nice question, Gaus thought, whether Germany had a greater interest in a promise of immediate British assistance against France, or in protection against a French assertion that peace was endangered by a German violation of the demilitarised zone. The best solution would be that the guarantee should only operate automatically in the event of French forces crossing the frontier or German forces entering the demilitarised zone: in all other cases there should be a prior decision by the Council. On the arbitration treaties Gaus suggested that the final decision should depend on whether the advantage of having unlimited treaties with France and Belgium were held to outweigh that of retaining some freedom in the east. As for the French guarantee of the eastern arbitration treaties, Gaus thought that provided the right of unilateral action by the guarantor was removed

1 Chamberlain to D'Abernon, 11 Aug. 1925, FO 800/258, D'Abernon Papers, BL Add. MS 48929, Petrie, *Life and Letters,* Vol. II, 281-3.

2 Memoranda by Schubert, 14 and 24 Aug. 1925, 4509/E127648-53, E127772-74.

a guarantee would make little practical difference: it was, however, politically undesirable. [1]

Hoesch's comments on an earlier version of this paper were naturally more political than juridical. He agreed that the French claim to guarantee the eastern arbitration treaties was unjustified, and suggested that it would have to be decided whether in the last resort it was worth wrecking the whole pact on this point. He repeated his earlier view that unlimited arbitration treaties would have to be accepted, and thought that a formal release from Article 16 was impossible. The whole point for the western countries was to remove not only the possibility of joint German-Russian military action against Poland but also the possibility of Germany acting as a bulwark for Russia against the League and ensuring by benevolent neutrality a Russian destruction of Poland. Hoesch thought that some of Gaus's fears were unfounded, since Russia was unlikely simply to attack one of her neighbours; but his discussion of a Hungarian-Czechoslovak conflict raised in Hoesch's mind the question of Germany's whole attitude to the League. If she joined, she would have to accept its basic purpose and give up ideas of promoting or helping Hungarian aggression. [2]

The jurists' meeting and the approach to Locarno, August - October 1925

The French reply to the German note of 20 July was delivered in Berlin on 24 August. It ended with an invitation to negotiations, and the German reply of 27 August was a brief acceptance of the invitation to a meeting of legal experts.[3] This meeting, to which Mussolini decided to send a representative, was held in London from 1 to 4 September. The jurists agreed to a number of amendments to the Anglo-French draft treaty, being clear, however, that these were not binding on their governments.

On the form of the western arbitration treaties Gaus secured what he regarded as a return to the German system, since the agreed new version provided for judicial arbitration for questions with regard to which the parties were in conflict as to their respective rights, with binding awards; a conciliation commission for other disputes; and, if its recommendations were not accepted by both parties, submission of the dispute to the League of Nations. As for the guarantee, Gaus asserted that the provision for action in advance of a Council decision

1 Memorandum by Gaus, final version, 21 Aug. 1925, 4509/E127720-45; an earlier version, 6698/H108347-74.

2 Hoesch to Schubert, 8 Aug. 1925, 4509/E127579-87.

3 *Locarno-Konferenz*, Nos. 17-18.

would operate one-sidedly, since it required all the parties other than the attacker and the victim to agree and Belgium was unlikely ever to pronounce against France. The other jurists at first described this objection as unjustified but later, to Gaus's surprise, accepted that each guarantor should act alone if it agreed that a flagrant violation had taken place. The probable reason for this change was the new prospect that Italy would join the pact, which made it desirable that Britain should be able to act without needing Italian agreement. Gaus now regarded placing the responsibility on the individual guarantor as preferable to a search for an objective test of the conditions for the operation of the guarantee.

No agreement was reached about the guarantee for the eastern arbitration treaties. Gaus set out the German objections and said that he did not think any German Government could sign an agreement which recognised such a guarantee. Fromageot replied that arbitration treaties with the eastern neighbours were part of the original German proposals, and he did not think that Poland would sign one unless it was guaranteed by France. Hurst explained that although Britain was not prepared to guarantee the eastern treaties Chamberlain had accepted the idea of a French guarantee because the Franco-Polish alliance existed and France was bound by it. If Poland, relying on French support, acted so unwisely as to precipitate a conflict with Germany France would be in a difficult position with a possible conflict of obligations under the Covenant and the alliance. The proposed guarantee would not only reduce the risk of armed conflict but would bring the existing alliance more into harmony with the League and would enable France to exercise a moderating influence on Poland. Gaus, however, continued to maintain that either the guarantee added nothing to the Covenant, in which case it was superfluous, or it gave France a special right in regard to Germany, in which case it was impossible. When Hurst asked whether Germany might prefer to sign a renunciation of warlike measures in respect of Poland as well as of France and Belgium, Gaus replied that Germany saw no reason to go beyond the arbitration treaty and the Covenant.[1]

In the face of this clear German refusal some other way of protecting the eastern arbitration treaties had to be sought. Hurst thought that France might give a unilateral guarantee of the arbitration treaty, which would be communicated to the League and would enable her

1 Report by Hurst, 4 Sep. 1925; note by Hurst, 5 Sep., C 11425, 11455/459/18, FO 371/10739; report by Gaus, 4509/E128045-67, *Locarno-Konferenz*, No. 20; report by Rolin, *DDB*, Vol. II. No. 104.

to take action, under Article 16, if Germany attacked Poland in breach of the arbitration treaty. Briand suggested that the arbitration treaties might somehow be guaranteed by the League, with France to act as its agent.[1] Skrzynski had been suggesting a Franco-German-Polish treaty of mutual guarantee identical with the western pact; but although he was optimistic that Germany would agree if pressed by Britain, the French were more realistic and did not raise the suggestion.[2]

Another problem was how the eastern treaties were to be negotiated. At Geneva on 9 September Chamberlain, Briand, Vandervelde, and the Italian delegate Scialoja agreed to ask Mussolini where in Switzerland he would go, and then to invite the Germans to a meeting. Chamberlain suggested that it should start with discussion of the western pact and then Polish and Czechoslovak representatives should be invited to join in. Skrzynski and Beneš were anxious that the negotiations should take place, and all the treaties be signed, simultaneously. The Quai d'Orsay were anxious about the effect on the western pact if the German-Polish negotiations failed.[3] They were preparing a draft treaty when on 18 September Stresemann said at a press conference that neither Poland nor Czechoslovakia had approached Germany about one. So far as Czechoslovakia was concerned this was only half true: Beneš had not hitherto formally proposed negotiations, but he had told the German Minister in Prague as early as March that he was willing to conclude an arbitration treaty, and had referred to possible terms on more than one subsequent occasion.[4] He now informed the German Government that his Government were ready to open negotiations. Since it was a weekend the Poles did not receive advance warning: Skrzynski was upset, and was further taken aback when told that the French and British Governments did not wish to deter him from taking similar action.[5] The Germans

1 Note by Hurst, 5 Sep. 1925; memorandum by Chamberlain, 9 Sep., C 11455, 11670/459/18, FO 371/10739.

2 Memorandum by Laroche, 13 Aug. 1925; Panafieu (Warsaw) to Berthelot, 21 Aug.; memorandum by Laroche, 4 Sep.; *aide-mémoire* from Skrzynski, 6 Sep., MAE, Grande Bretagne, Vols. 81-2.

3 Memoranda by Chamberlain, 9, 11 and 12 Sep. 1925, C 11670, 11813, 11814/459/18, FO 371/10739, 10740; *aide-mémoire* from Skrzynski, 6 Sep.; Massigli to Laroche, 8 Sep.; Beneš to Berthelot, 20 Sep., MAE, Grande Bretagne, Vols. 82-3.

4 Koch to AA, 24 Mar., 3 Apr., 25 Jul. 1925, 3123/D642837-38, D643012-14, D644114-17.

5 Memorandum by Schubert, 20 Sep. 1925, 4509/E128090-94; Max Muller to FO, 23 Sep.; FO to Max Muller, 25 Sep.; Max Muller to FO, 28 Sep., C 12148, 12339/459/18, FO 371/10740; Q d'O to Panafieu, 24 Sep., MAE, Grande Bretagne, Vol. 83.

were prepared to take up Beneš's approach in the hope of preventing Polish and Czechoslovak participation in the conference; but this was not Beneš's intention, and the interval before the conference was now too short for any German action to be developed.[1]

The western invitations to a meeting of ministers were delivered in Berlin on 15 September. The German Government's decision to accompany their acceptance with a repudiation of war guilt and an insistence on the evacuation of the Cologne zone before the pact was concluded, greatly annoyed Chamberlain. He wrote angrily to D'Abernon: 'Your Germans - I use the possessive pronoun as one says to one's wife: *Your* housemaid - are very nearly intolerable. From first to last very nearly every obstacle to the Pact negotiations has come from them. Briand has almost taken my breath away by his liberality, his conciliatoriness, his strong and manifest desire to promote peace. The German attitude has been just the contrary - niggling, provocative, crooked. . . I have chosen my path within the limits set to me by forces beyond my control. God forgive me if I allowed myself to be duped by the Germans, but either Stresemann is crooked and a coward, or the value of any Pact which may be made is *for the present* singularly discounted by the opposition which he meets'.[2]

The repudiation of war guilt might be represented as a sop to nationalist opinion without much external significance; but the evacuation of the Cologne zone was a point on which the German delegates were instructed by the Government to insist. Other points laid down were that before the pact was concluded the question of German disarmament must be cleared up and the occupation régime in the Rhineland revised; efforts must be made to secure a shortening of the occupation of the second and third zones; before Germany joined the League the problem of general disarmament must be tackled seriously; and, on the pact itself, the renunciation of war in the west must not

1 Memorandum by Schubert, 21 Sep. 1925; memorandum by Stresemann, 25 Sep.; memorandum by Schubert, 30 Sep.; Koch to AA, 2 Oct., 4509/E128100-07, E128201-04, E128413-15, E128443-45; instructions to Koch, 1 Oct., K1885/K478840-42. During the summer there had been some talk of a meeting between Beneš and Stresemann, but it did not take place. According to the German archives the initiative came from Beneš, but the French Embassy in Berlin believed that it came from Stresemann: L417/L120587-89, L120610; 3086/D617797-801, D617810-11, D617813-15; 4509/E127107-08; Margerie to Q d'O, 15 and 22 May, MAE, Tchécoslovaquie, Vol. 69.

2 Chamberlain to D'Abernon, 30 Sep. 1925, Chamberlain Papers, AC 52/297, D'Abernon Papers, BL Add. MS 48929: words italicised underlined in original. German note and declaration, *Locarno-Konferenz,* Nos. 21-2. German correspondence, 3123/D644614-644744, *passim* and 4509/E128193-128383, *passim;* British correspondence, FO 371/10740; French correspondence, MAE, Grande Bretagne, Vol. 83; *DDB*, Vol. II, Nos. 107-8.

imply any renunciation of German territory, a French guarantee of the eastern arbitration treaties must be refused, and the German objections to Article 16 must be met.[1] In accordance with this policy Luther, who with Stresemann was going to Locarno, held forth to D'Abernon about Germany's grievances and his doubts whether the pact would satisfy the Reichstag.[2] Chamberlain, however, set off for the conference in a spirit of 'sober hopefulness'. He told his colleagues that completing the western pact was not likely to be difficult, but the eastern problems would be much harder to solve. Since full European security could not be attained without an arrangement in the east he must take an interest in these negotiations, and would not conclude the western negotiations until the eastern situation had developed.[3]

The Russian factor, December 1924 - October 1925

Throughout the negotiations for the western security pact the question of relations with the Soviet Union was of the first importance for the German Government; but it was not of prime significance for the French or the British. The latter in particular, although aware of the problem for Germany, regarded it as possible to deal with western European security without reference to the Soviet Union and to keep Anglo-Soviet relations in a separate compartment.

The question was important for Germany owing to her geographical position and the political and economic relationship built up since 1921 and symbolised by the Treaty of Rapallo. Any substantial alteration of Germany's relations with the western powers would inevitably have repercussions on those with the Soviet Union.[4] In the summer and autumn of 1924, with agreement on reparations achieved and Germany's entry into the League being canvassed, such a substantial alteration seemed to be in view. It appears to have been anxiety on this score, and the failure to achieve an Anglo-Soviet agreement, that prompted the Soviet Government to propose to the German Embassy in Moscow in December an understanding on Poland and an agreement that the two countries would concert their action on joining the League and would not enter any combination

1 *Locarno-Konferenz,* No. 24; 3123/D645128-29.

2 D.Abernon to FO, 2 Oct. 1925, C 12490/459/18, FO 371/10741.

3 Memorandum by Chamberlain, 2 Oct. 1925, C 12491/459/18, FO 371/10741.

4 The literature on German-Soviet relations in the 1920s is large: one of the fullest accounts of the period under consideration here is Kurt Rosenbaum, *Community of Fate.* The interaction between German eastern and western policy is discussed by Eleonore Breuning, 'Germany's Policy between East and West', Oxford D. Phil. thesis, 1965; Martin Walsdorff, *Westorientierung und Ostpolitik. Stresemanns Russlandpolitik in der Locarno-Ära* (Bremen, 1971).

directed against the other. The then State Secretary, Maltzan, was ready to discuss an agreement on Poland; but the German attitude to the larger proposal was cautious and no answer had been given by the time that the security proposals were made to the western powers.[1]

The news of these proposals alarmed both the Russians and Brockdorff-Rantzau, the German Ambassador in Moscow, who, although sceptical of the possibility of close collaboration with and opposed to any far-reaching treaty commitment to the Soviet Union, was also violently opposed to any German commitment to the west since he believed that it would subject Germany to western hegemony. Brockdorff-Rantzau was not convinced by Stresemann's argument that the negotiations with the western powers need not affect the development of German-Soviet relations since Germany had no intention of guaranteeing or recognising her frontier with Poland, and entry into the League, if accepted at all, would only take place on conditions that would allow Germany to remain neutral in a conflict between the League and the Soviet Union and would enable her to frustrate League action.[2] Enjoying as he did a position of unusual independence of the Auswärtiges Amt, Brockdorff-Rantzau virtually declined to pursue with the Soviet Government the discussion, which Stresemann wanted, of the effects of German entry into the League; and he returned to Berlin in the middle of April. Here he remained until the end of June, warning against subservience to the west but unable to suggest any alternative policy that would secure Stresemann's aims.[3]

Discussions continued through the Soviet Embassy in Berlin. After another attempt to convince the Russians that the conclusion of a western security pact would not mean a reorientation of German policy, that Germany would not enter the League unconditionally and that the chances of her being compelled to act against the Soviet Union were remote, produced merely a repetition of the Soviet view that Germany would become an instrument of British anti-Soviet policy, the Germans decided at the end of June to offer a preamble to be attached to the trade treaty being negotiated in Moscow.[4]

1 Rosenbaum, *Community of Fate,* 121-8; Walsdorff, *Westorientierung und Ostpolitik,* 59-70.

2 Rosenbaum, *Community of Fate,* 129-36; Walsdorff, *Westorientierung und Ostpolitik,* 70-90; Stresemann to Rantzau, 19 Mar. 1925, *Locarno-Konferenz,* No. 9.

3 Rosenbaum, *Community of Fate,* 138-42; Walsdorff, *Westorientierung und Ostpolitik,* 91-5; Addison to Lampson, 26 Jun. 1925, C 8804/459/18, FO 371/10735.

4 Rosenbaum, *Community of Fate,* 142-5; Walsdorff, *Westorientierung und Ostpolitik,* 95-8, 108-17.

This preamble would pledge the two governments to friendly political and economic collaboration in the spirit of Rapallo, and would be supplemented by a verbal declaration that even if Germany did not secure formal release from the obligations of Article 16 she would maintain her standpoint on it and would conduct herself on those lines as a member of the League. Brockdorff-Rantzau returned to Moscow with the preamble and accompanied by Dirksen of the Eastern Department of the Auswärtiges Amt. Although the Russians did not accept the preamble and virtually repeated their December proposal, the offer seems to have prevented a crisis of confidence. At the end of August it was agreed not to hold up the trade treaty; and Litvinov, the Deputy Commissar for Foreign Affairs, stated that the Soviet Government were willing to continue the political negotiations even if Germany had to join the League.[1]

The British and the French knew that anxiety about relations with the Soviet Union was the main ground for the German objections to joining the League. They were also well aware of the Soviet charge that Britain was trying to build up an anti-Soviet coalition and intended to harness Germany for it. Anglo-Soviet relations certainly deteriorated under the Conservative Government, with the abandonment of the general agreement negotiated by MacDonald and the official acceptance of the Zinoviev letter as genuine. But there is no evidence that the Government ever thought of organising a crusade against the Soviet Union; and although the fear of the Soviet leaders that they would do so seems to have been genuine, at least initially, the evidence they produced for the belief was either thin or spurious.

When Chamberlain visited Paris and Rome at the beginning of December 1924 the Soviet press claimed, apparently on the basis of one French newspaper report, that the purpose of his journey was to start an anti-Soviet campaign. There is no record of Chamberlain mentioning the Soviet Union in Rome. In Paris the main subjects of his conversation with Herriot were the Geneva Protocol and the evacuation of the Cologne zone: the possibility of exchanging information about communist activities was, however, mentioned.[2] On 19 March the Commissar for Foreign Affairs, Chicherin, gave Brockdorff-Rantzau a

1 Rosenbaum, *Community of Fate,* 155-76; Walsdorff, *Westorientierung und Ostpolitik,* 117-23, 127-9.

2 Record of conversation, 5 Dec. 1924, N 9233/44/38, FO 371/10471; minute by Tyrrell, 18 Dec., N 9371/108/38, FO 371/10480; minute by Herriot, 5 Dec., MAE, Grande Bretagne, Vol. 71; minute by Laroche, 13 Dec., Grande Bretagne, Vol. 57. Louis Fischer, *The Soviets in World Affairs* (London, 1930), 578-9, states that Chamberlain offered Herriot an Anglo-Franco-Belgian pact in return for French participation in an anti-Soviet policy: the latest writer to accept this

paper purporting to be a translation of a memorandum addressed by Chamberlain to the French Government on 7 March, advocating political treaties binding a number of states to mutual defence, non-aggression and prevention of revolution, and including Germany to forestall a German-Soviet alliance. This document is an obvious fabrication, and an amateurish one at that. In addition to the inherent improbability that the British Government would have been advocating a large-scale alliance at the moment when they were about to reject the Geneva Protocol, the memorandum does not even mention the Protocol as a genuine document of this date obviously would have done; and some of the terminology (for example 'national chauvinists') would never have been used by British politicians or civil servants. The Auswärtiges Amt regarded the document as spurious on internal evidence alone.[1]

Then, however, came the publication in American newspapers of Nicolson's memorandum with its statement that a security system should be framed in spite of, or even because of the Soviet Union.[2] Members of the British Government, notably Birkenhead and the Home Secretary Joynson-Hicks, were given to making anti-communist speeches; and Chamberlain more than once turned down Soviet suggestions of discussions to explore what agreements could be substituted for the abandoned treaties of 1924.[3] Such actions were enough to keep Soviet uneasiness alive; but Chamberlain had no desire for a breach. Twice in the summer he sought and obtained Cabinet approval for his policy of maintaining relations but ignoring the Russians: his hope was that a demonstration that Europe could do without them would have a salutary effect on Soviet policy.[4] Furthermore, even though he had discussed with Herriot the possible exchange

story without examination is Spenz, *Die diplomatische Vorgeschichte des Beitritts Deutschlands zum Völkerbund*, 52-3; but Spenz's sources for his account of British policy are inadequate.

1 Rantzau to AA, 21 Mar. 1925, 4562/E155106-13. A. Anderle, *Die deutsche Rapallo-Politik* (Berlin, 1962), 118-20, treats the document as genuine. Reports reaching Berlin in May of Anglo-Franco-American discussion of a plan of intervention against the Soviet Union led to enquiries being made of the German Embassies in London, Paris and Washington. All three dismissed the reports as invention: one particularly improbable feature, as Hoesch pointed out, was the suggestion that the United States Government had offered to take over the Russian debt to France and cancel the French debt to the United States: 4562/E155288-89, E155297-98, E155306; 2860/D555211.

2 See pp. 75-6.

3 FO to Hodgson (Moscow), 1 Apr. and 13 Jul. 1925, N 1852, 4021/102/38, FO 371/11015-16.

4 Memorandum by Chamberlain, 10 Jun. 1925, N 3432/102/38, FO 371/11016; Chamberlain to Baldwin, 24 Jul.; note by Chamberlain, 30 Jul., Chamberlain Papers, AC 52/18; C 36(25), C 43(25), CAB 23/50.

of information about communist activities, this form of anti-Soviet collaboration seems to have been avoided in practice. The discussion with the French appears not to have been followed up; and when in the summer the Portuguese Government suggested co-operation in combatting communism the Foreign Office and the Home Office agreed that, while there was no objection to ordinary police collaboration over known criminals, it was particularly desirable at present, in view of the allegation that Britain was engaged in creating an anti-Soviet *bloc,* not to depart from the practice of deprecating arrangements with other governments about communist activities. Again at the end of the year, when a similar enquiry came from the Swiss Government, the Foreign Office replied: 'We are anxious to avoid being involved in anything which could be regarded as a concerted anti-Bolshevik movement or as tending to the organisation of or participation in an anti-Bolshevik bloc'.[1]

Although the Foreign Office rejected a suggestion from R.M. Hodgson, the Chargé d'Affaires in Moscow, that they should issue a formal denial of the story of an anti-Soviet coalition, on the ground that a denial would not convince the Russians and would only lend importance to the story, Max Muller was instructed in August to give a denial to Skrzynski since the Poles appeared to believe the tale. Skrzynski said that he had never believed in the *bloc* story although he thought that the Russians had really done so until recently. But he found it hard to believe that the British Government would not think it in their interest to detach Germany from the Soviet Union.[2]

How large a factor in British policy on the security pact such a desire was, is not easy to determine. The fear of a Russo-German alliance, or of a harsh Allied policy driving Germany into the arms of Russia, was expressed at intervals in Britain from Lloyd George's Fontainebleau memorandum of March 1919 onwards. One consideration, though not the main one, in taking up the policy of mutual security in western Europe was certainly a desire to convince Germany that she had more to gain from friendly relations with the west than from a commitment to the Soviet Union. It is much less certain whether it was thought that Germany would have to choose between east and west, or whether it was expected that she would continue to tread the narrow path between the two. On the one hand one has assurances to the Germans that Britain understood the necessity for Germany to

1 N 3600, 4225, 5536, 6173, 6282, 6930, 7081/29/38, FO 371/11010-11.

2 Hodgson to FO, 7 Aug. 1925; FO to Hodgson, 12 Aug.; Chamberlain to Max Muller, 12 Aug.; Max Muller to Chamberlain, 25 Aug., N 4519, 5059/102/38, FO 371/11016.

have regard to her relations with the Soviet Union and did not wish to promote a breach. On the other hand one has words like those used by Chamberlain to the Polish Minister in London about 'the European Powers on the one hand and the Soviet Government on the other fighting for the soul of the German people'.[1] Perhaps the best answer is that provided Germany was not thrown into the arms of the Soviet Union the question in British eyes did not present itself as one of a hard and fast choice for Germany. It was probably assumed and hoped that better relations with the west and return to the European political community would weaken Germany's political ties with the east. The importance to Germany of her economic ties with the Soviet Union was acknowledged and there was no suggestion that they should be broken; but despite the disappointing experience of Anglo-Soviet trade since 1921 the intimate connexion, in both Soviet and German eyes, between economic and political relations was probably not appreciated in Britain.

In French policy, in addition to the possibility of detaching Germany from the Soviet Union, there was a second element not paralleled on the British side, that of possibly detaching the Soviet Union from Germany and so strengthening stability in eastern Europe. In October 1924 Herriot's Government recognised the Soviet Union and re-established full diplomatic relations for the first time since the revolution; and Herriot told Chamberlain that one of his reasons for doing so was the fear lest left to herself the Soviet Union should combine with Germany.[2] The new French Ambassador, the publicist Jean Herbette, advocated a Franco-Soviet entente for the sake of eastern European security;[3] but although Briand, like Herriot, was willing to contemplate a general agreement with the Soviet Union and in particular to encourage better Soviet-Polish relations,[4] no progress was made before the end of 1925. The conference on outstanding questions (notably Russian debts and claims) which had been intended

1 FO to D'Abernon, 15 May 1925, C 6652/459/18, FO 371/10731; FO to Max Muller, 7 Jul., C 9132/459/18, FO 371/10735. An argument addressed to the Poles on such a subject was, however, always a special one.

2 Record of conversation, 5 Dec. 1924, N 9223/44/38, FO 371/10471.

3 Herbette to Q d'O, 29 Jun. 1925, MAE, Russie, Vol. 332; Herbette to Q d.O, 26 Aug., Grande Bretagne, Vol. 82; Herbette to Herriot, 24 Oct., Herriot, *Jadis*, Vol. II, 290-1.

4 Cf. his remarks reported in Chamberlain to Tyrrell, 4 Oct. 1925, N 5714/710/38, FO 371/11022. In the summer Chicherin dropped hints to Herbette about a mutually guaranteed Polish-Soviet non-aggression pact: Herbette to Q d'O, 26 Aug., MAE, Grande Bretagne, Vol. 82; *Dokumenty Vneshnei Politiki SSSR*, Vol. VIII (Moscow, 1963), n. 128 and No. 272: I am indebted for this reference and that in p. 130, n. 2 to Dr. E.C.M. Breuning.

to start in January, was delayed by technical complications; and the Soviet pressure on Germany against the security pact, and increased anti-French propaganda in the French empire and Morocco raised doubts about the sincerity of Societ desires for better relations.[1]

Chicherin's visits to Warsaw and Berlin on the eve of the Locarno meeting did not alter matters. In Warsaw he talked about the desirability of a Franco-Soviet *rapprochement* and a Polish-Soviet non-aggression pact: Skrzynski replied that he was ready to sign a non-aggression pact with any country at any time but a Polish agreement with the Soviet Union must not endanger or ignore the Baltic States or Rumania. Max Muller, meeting Chicherin at a reception, told him that the story of Britain promoting an anti-Soviet front was pure invention.[2] In Berlin Chicherin did not succeed in deterring or frightening the German Government off the western pact, by allegations that it was Germany who in the previous December had proposed an alliance against Poland, by threatening a Franco-Polish-Soviet *rapprochement,* or by repeating his fears that Germany was becoming a vassal of British policy - the only evidence that he could produce being a report that a British bank (not the Bank of England) had advised a German bank not to give credits to the Soviet Union. Stresemann was not impressed by these threats and warnings, but he repeated his assurance that Germany as a member of the League would so deal with Article 16 that a war against the Soviet Union was excluded; and on 2 October the German Government announced that agreement in principle had been reached on the signature of the German-Soviet trade agreement.[3] Germany was not being detached from the Soviet Union.

1 Q d'O to Herbette, 28 Jun. 1925, MAE, Russie, Vol. 332. For the Franco-Soviet financial negotiations see *Survey of International Affairs, 1924,* 251-6; *1927,* 278-81.

2 Max Muller to FO, 29 Sep. 1925, N 5575/102/38, FO 371/11016; N 5570/1805/55, FO 371/11005; Chamberlain to FO, 9 Oct., C 12818/459/18, FO 371/10742; *Dokumenty Vneshnei Politiki SSSR,* Vol. VIII, No. 323; Korbel, *Poland between East and West,* 162-6.

3 Rosenbaum, *Community of Fate,* 178-84; Walsdorff, *Westorientierung und Ostpolitik,* 132-8. Chicherin's press interviews in Berlin in *Soviet Documents on Foreign Policy,* ed. Jane Degras, Vol. II (London, 1952), 57-9, 60-1. Stresemann's account to Chamberlain of his conversations with Chicherin in Chamberlain to FO, 8 Oct. 1925, FO 840/1/5. The German-Soviet trade agreement was signed on 12 October, during the conference at Locarno.

5

THE CONFERENCE AT LOCARNO AND THE SIGNATURE OF THE TREATIES 1925

Although by the end of the jurists' meeting most of the terms of the mutual security pact had been agreed, some important features were still unsettled. The conference at Locarno of the Foreign Ministers and delegates of Great Britain, France, Germany, Belgium and Italy was therefore one for substantial negotiation. At the end of the conference a protocol, eight treaties or conventions, and one collective note were initialled, and were to be signed in London six weeks later. While there was little doubt that the results would be accepted in the other countries, the outcome in Germany was less certain. During the interval between the conference and the signature, therefore, attention centred mainly on the domestic position of the German Government and the extent to which they could satisfy their critics by the attainment of additional advantages or by interpreting away what they had undertaken.

The conference, October 1925

Between 5 and 16 October there were nine conference meetings, two of them attended by the Polish and Czechoslovak Foreign Ministers, and a number of informal conversations. Even the conference meetings were kept as informal as possible: there was no chairman,[1] and no official record was made.[2] The question of the French guarantee of the eastern arbitration treaties was tackled at once. At the second conference meeting, on 6 October, Stresemann asked for explanations, particularly

1 This had been Chamberlain's idea before he left London. On arriving at Locarno he found that Briand favoured British chairmanship but the Germans, to stress equality, were opposed to any permanent chairmanship. It was therefore agreed to have none: Chamberlain to Tyrrell, 4 Oct. 1925, N 5714/710/38, FO 371/11022; Chamberlain to FO, 5 Oct., C 12661, 12662/459/18, FO 371/10741.

2 The secretary to each delegation, however, compared his notes with those of the other secretaries: all the resulting sets of notes can therefore be regarded as semi-officially agreed. *Lokarnskaya Konferentsiya* (Moscow, 1959) contains a Russian translation of all the secretaries' notes; the German notes are printed in *Locarno-Konferenz;* the French notes are in MAE, Grande Bretagne, Vol. 85; the British notes are in FO 371/10742-44. The following account is based mainly on the British record, which is the fullest, and on British and German accounts of informal conversations. *DDB,* Vol. II, contains some reports from Vandervelde; *DDI,* Vol. IV, contains only a few telegrams from Scialoja. Later accounts by participants include H. Luther, *Politiker ohne Partei* (Stuttgart, 1960), 368-85 and Schmidt, *Statist auf diplomatischer Buhne,* 76-91. Suarez, *Briand,* Vol. VI, 104-32, gives an account of the atmosphere rather than of the proceedings.

on how the treaties were to be concluded and how a state could guarantee a treaty to which an ally was a party. Briand said that the French position had been fully explained. France had treaties with certain countries, by which she was bound. While seeking to secure her own frontiers she could not forget her obligations to others. If the problem was one of form, of finding a different way of doing the same thing, agreement ought to be possible; but if the objection were fundamental and France were asked not to give a guarantee at all, it would be impossible to conclude the western pact. It was a matter not of an old-style alliance directed against another country, but of mutual protection. There were to be arbitration treaties in the west and the east: if they ruled out resort to force in all cases, he could not understand the objection to the obligations being guaranteed. Of course public opinion had to be taken into account, but on both sides. The guarantee was already implied in the Covenant: if the worst happened no one would be surprised if some countries interpreted Article 16 as involving for them the obligation to use armed force. The Germans must consider what a change had taken place in the way of looking at the western guarantee. The 1919 treaties had provided for a guarantee of one side only: now they envisaged a mutual one. It had taken a lot of work to get French opinion to accept the change: similar work should be done on the German side, for there was no reason why the principle should not be applied to the other frontier.

Stresemann replied that German opinion too had moved since the Cuno offer. The necessity of taking into account France's relationship with Poland had been accepted, and this was why the arbitration treaties had been proposed. France had demanded that Germany should guarantee peace in the east and join the League. Despite conflict at home the German Government had agreed to the latter demand and her entry would provide additional guarantees. He would like to be clear on two points: how the French guarantee would operate under the Covenant, and why it was necessary if it did not go beyond the Covenant.

Briand replied that the second question might be asked about the guarantee for the Rhine frontier. As to the first, the terms of Article 16 were not as clear as those of the pact and it did not fully safeguard security. It was natural and logical to give a special guarantee to the arbitration treaties. France had binding agreements with Poland and Czechoslovakia and her own security was involved. Stresemann might say that there was no danger on the eastern frontier, and Briand did not doubt the present German Government's desire for peace. But one day there would be another government, and when public opinion became heated who knew what might happen. It was necessary to take precautions even if the eventuality was never likely to arise. If the difficulty was one of form he was ready to seek the wording that came nearest to the Covenant.

Luther said that what they were discussing seemed to be whether it was a matter of form. The German Government had not discussed a formula: perhaps the French could suggest one. Briand said that they had tried to meet the Germans in drafting the article in question. If the Germans would not accept it they should, he indicated, help to find another solution. They had accepted the necessity of some special provision in the west: so long as the gap remained it was logical to try to fill it.

Chamberlain interposed to explain the British position. It was understood, he said, that the British Government could not undertake any new obligation in the east, but they were not uninterested in the situation there. Britain's greatest interest, like that of all the world, was peace; and no one could say where a war, once started, would end. Moreover Britain was a member of the League and had undertaken all the obligations of the Covenant, including Article 16. These obligations were not clearly defined and might be interpreted differently according to the circumstances of a given case. What Britain might do in, for example, a South American conflict would obviously not be the same as what she would do in a western European one. The British Government were in effect prepared to put all their forces at the disposal of the League for the support of Germany or of France if the other committed the flagrant aggression defined in the pact. This was more definite than Article 16. In the same way it seemed necessary to supplement Article 16 by a special guarantee in the case of Germany's eastern frontier.[1]

After the meeting Chamberlain tried to persuade Luther that a French guarantee of the arbitration treaties would limit France's obligations to Poland and Czechoslovakia, and urged him to discuss the problem with Briand. Luther replied that no German Government could accept the idea of a guarantee.[2] Next day he said the same to Briand, who answered that he would try to find a new proposal but he had already gone a long way and did not know whether more could be done.[3] At the next conference meeting the relevant article of the western pact was referred to the jurists. Hurst suggested that the difficulty might be met by amending the article under which France and Belgium and Germany undertook not to go to war except in resistance

1 Second meeting, 6 Oct. 1925.

2 Chamberlain to FO, 7 Oct. 1925, C 12746/459/18, FO 371/10741.

3 Memorandum by Luther, 7 Oct. 1925, 3123/D645137-38.

to invasion or attack or to flagrant violation of the demilitarised zone or with the authority of the League. Gaus said that the German delegation might accept such an amendment, and it was presumably this that allowed Chamberlain to report home that the jurists were thought to have nearly reached a solution.[1] But next day Gaus again said that no guarantee of the eastern treaties was acceptable, and in addition Hurst found that the Germans wanted provision against individual action by France in a case where, the League having failed to agree, members recovered their freedom of action under Article 15(7) of the Covenant. The Germans professed to fear that in such a case France would falsely accuse Germany of attacking Poland, and they wanted an impartial procedure to identify the aggressor.[2]

This demand was discussed by the principal delegates on the boat trip which they took on Lake Maggiore on 10 October, but without result. Chamberlain and Hurst pointed out to the Germans that they could not both refuse to limit their country's freedom of action by undertaking in no case to go to war with Poland, and demand that France's freedom of action under the Covenant be limited. As a result Gaus agreed to try to get his ministers to drop the demand.[3] He evidently succeeded, for at the conference meeting on 13 October Hurst was able to produce an agreed final version of Article 2 of the western pact, giving France the additional right to act against Germany in pursuance of Article 16 of the Covenant or a decision by the Council or the Assembly, or in pursuance of Article 15(7) provided that Germany had been the first to attack. This, Hurst said, fully safeguarded France's right to help Poland and Czechoslovakia, and a separate reference to a guarantee for the eastern arbitration treaties was no longer needed.[4] The Polish and Czechoslovak representatives consented to this solution: Beneš had suggested something of the kind before the conference met, and Skrzynski's impracticable suggestion of a tripartite guarantee treaty between France and Germany and Poland was not mentioned again.[5] To the extent that a French

1 Third meeting, 7 Oct. 1925; Chamberlain to FO, 8 Oct., C 12780, 12791/459/18, FO 371/10741.

2 Minute by Hurst, 8 Oct. 1925, FO 840/1/6; German delegation to AA, 9 Oct., 4509/E128590-92.

3 Minutes by Hurst, 11 and 12 Oct. 1925, FO 840/1/7; Chamberlain to FO, 12 Oct., C 12899/459/18, FO 371/10742.

4 Seventh meeting, 13 Oct. 1925.

5 Beneš to Berthelot, 20 Sep. 1925, MAE, Grande Bretagne, Vol. 83. Skrzynski mentioned his idea early in the conference to Chamberlain, who advised him to discuss it with Briand: British delegation meeting, 9 Oct., FO 840/1/6. The British delegation discussed further solutions among themselves, but there is nothing to show that they were put to others.

guarantee of the eastern arbitration treaties was not mentioned in the western pact the Germans had won their point. They could not, however, prevent France from concluding the Franco-Polish and Franco-Czechoslovak treaties initialled on the same day as the pact; and since they were referred to in the final protocol of the conference, to that extent the German Government acknowledged their existence.

Two other substantial amendments to the western pact were made at German suggestion. In the first place the Germans wished, in the provision about flagrant violation of the demilitarised zone, to specify 'German, French or Belgian' forces in order to emphasise the mutual character of the guarantee and forestall any British excuse for not helping Germany. The point was partly met by specifying the crossing of the frontier (as well as the outbreak of hostilities or the assembly of armed forces in the demilitarised zone) as a case which might make immediate action necessary. Secondly the Germans proposed that only one of the parties need approach the League for a decision that the treaty had become unnecessary - a return to the original British draft which the French had disliked. Stresemann explained that the present article smacked of inequality, since the Allies were a group in which it would be easy to find a seconder whereas Germany was on her own. His wish was eventually met, but it was provided that a two-thirds majority of the Council would be needed to terminate the treaty.[1]

Another substantial amendment was proposed by Vandervelde. He had at the end of July sent to Briand and Chamberlain comments on the draft treaty which proposed something like a return to the Geneva Protocol, to Briand's annoyance and the Foreign Office's surprise.[2] Now he put forward an amendment to the article of the pact dealing with the western arbitration treaties, the effect of which was to reintroduce unlimited arbitration. Vandervelde explained that he was worried lest a conflict might arise for which no solution could be found. Disputes of a political nature were to be submitted to a conciliation commission and then, if their recommendations were not accepted by the two governments concerned, would go to the Council of the League. But if the Council failed to agree there would be an impasse, and the Belgian Government proposed that in such a situation the dispute should go for final decision to some other form of arbitration. This return to an argument of the summer was no doubt disconcerting to the other delegates; but the Germans kept silent and it was Briand who replied that France and Belgium and Germany were undertaking in no

1 First, Third and Fifth meetings, 5, 7 and 10 Oct. 1925.

2 *DDB*, Vol. II, Nos. 86, 92-3; C 10020, 10406/459/18, FO 371/10737; MAE, Grande Bretagne, Vols. 80-1.

case to attack each other or resort to war, so that there really was no gap. Chamberlain said that if war were excluded and forcible measures put outside the bounds of possibility, a case where a settlement could not be reached would be very improbable. At Briand's suggestion the amendment was postponed until the arbitration treaties were discussed: it could be discussed then if there seemed to be a loophole.[1]

Discussion of the second major obstacle to the western pact, Germany's entry into the League, began in private conversations. Luther told Briand on 7 October that Article 16 was the most serious problem. He explained that it was not simply a matter of military action: economic measures too involved the risk of war, and there were dangers in allowing the transit of other countries' troops.[2] Next morning Stresemann asked Chamberlain for his interpretation of Article 16. Chamberlain said that he supposed that when the Covenant was drafted its authors, expecting the United States to be a founder member of the League and Germany to be admitted shortly, had thought that a unanimous Council decision would carry so much moral force that no country would be likely to defy it, and the economic pressure on a recalcitrant state would be so overwhelming that resistance would be obviously hopeless. It must therefore have seemed most improbable that military measures would ever be needed. But the force of economic sanctions had been greatly weakened by the abstention of the United States from membership of the League, and British Governments had had to think about what would happen if such measures had to be enforced by sea power and conflict arose with the United States. All the same he thought it impossible to define Article 16 more precisely than the Council had done in its letter to the German Government the previous March. As regards military measures the Council would make recommendations but each government would decide whether and how much it could contribute. As regards economic sanctions members had some freedom to decide the extent and even the timing of their co-operation, but could not decide not to co-operate at all. Stresemann asked whether there could be an interpretation applying to the disarmed countries. He suggested, as he did again later in the day, an exchange of letters between the German Government and the League supplemented by a secret exchange between Germany and the principal Allies, in which they would explain that in their opinion the special consideration for Germany, which the public correspondence acknowledged as necessary, would make it unreasonable to expect her

1 Third and Fifth meetings, 7 and 10 Oct. 1925.

2 Memorandum by Luther, 7 Oct. 1925, 3123/D645137-43; Chamberlain to FO, 7 Oct., C 12720/459/18, FO 371/10741.

to participate in any measures taken in the event of aggression by the Soviet Union.[1]

At the conference meeting that afternoon, 8 October, Stresemann began by outlining the history of Germany's attitude to the League and the correspondence with the Council. This had given satisfaction on some points but the question of Article 16 remained open. Not only could Germany not take part in military measures: it was impossible to envisage her taking indirect military action such as allowing the passage of troops, and she could not co-operate in an economic boycott. He would take the example of a war between Poland and Russia - but not because there was any secret agreement between Germany and Russia: there were no agreements other than the Treaty of Rapallo. Without doubt Moscow would answer a German boycott with a declaration of war. In 1920 Germany had only been saved from serious difficulties by the halting of the Russian advance in Poland. If the Russians advanced again Germany was defenceless. She was in a special position and asked not for privileges but for special treatment in a transitional period. If greater progress had been made with general disarmament there would be no difficulty; but so long as some countries were armed and others unarmed, each country must be able to decide whether to participate in action under Article 16. The question of German participation must be deferred until general disarmament was complete. There would have to be further exchanges of notes. If Germany were assured that it was for her alone to decide on the extent of her participation she would be willing to promise to co-operate to the utmost of her power.

Briand replied that this was the central point of the negotiations. The whole pact turned on the League, and if that pivot were broken or put out of joint all their combinations became impossible or inoperative. The League was an association for mutual assurance against war, and was trying to bring in a system based on that equality on which the Germans set so much store. But equality must apply to the unpleasant as well as the pleasant features. Article 16 did not provide enough organised force; security was not yet organised; only when it was could disarmament be contemplated. If countries could refuse their support the better armed were less likely to be able to reduce their forces. Germany was militarily not negligible and economically strong: if she could not give anything even in the economic sphere the League would be positively weakened. If Russia committed aggression the League would be at war with her: to refuse economic help to the League would be equivalent to giving support to the aggressor. But nothing

1 Chamberlain to FO, 8 Oct. 1925, C 12881/459/18, FO 371/10742.

was being aimed against Russia: the agreements were directed against war, and she could join the League. If she had no aggressive intentions there was no problem. If she had aggressive intentions the very danger of which Stresemann spoke should remove Germany's hesitations, for she would be much safer in the League. She would also be in a stronger position to discuss Article 16 on a footing of equality in order to promote general disarmament; but if she started on a footing of wilful inequality her voice would be weakened. In any case these questions were outside the competence of the delegations at Locarno. The great powers could not do what they liked at Geneva and could not bind the League. Briand begged the Germans to think again.

Chamberlain said that the reason why British opinion, which had at first been doubtful, now supported the pact was that it meant that Germany would join the League. He understood the German anxieties, and he supposed that in any case of war the League would have to consider the situation of each country upon which it made demands. But for a country to say that it would join the League and enjoy all the privileges and guarantees of membership and at the same time refuse in advance all help in certain cases, was to take up an impossible position. If the League agreed, all the countries which had disarmed voluntarily, as well as those which had been disarmed, could demand the right to be neutral. Chamberlain confirmed that the permanent members did not control the Council, and he was sure that Scialoja, as a regular representative on the Assembly, would say how jealous it was of the Council. Finally, said Chamberlain, he would state clearly and categorically that it had never entered the British Government's head to make any kind of alliance or *bloc* against the Soviet Union, through the League or through the pact.

Scialoja supported Chamberlain and then Luther took up the debate. He emphasised again that there were no special bonds with the Soviet Union, but Germany could not change her geographical position and her disarmed state made it worse. There was no danger in Article 16 for Britain and France. When Briand and Chamberlain at once contested this statement Luther maintained that Germany was particularly affected and a formula must be found that would give her a feeling of safety.

Briand replied that if war broke out in the east the countries lying between Germany and the war zone would be fighting for her as well as for themselves. Germany would be affected in any event, but failure to act would in some circumstances help the common enemy. Luther said that all Germany wanted was that during the transitional period before general disarmament came about she should be protected from bearing the general dangers of the League. Stresemann said that if there was a blockade or boycott Germany would not be able to help Russia. She was not asking for a change in the Covenant: she would be satisfied by a declaration on the lines of the provision of the Geneva Protocol that in considering measures against an aggressor a country's military and geographical situation must be taken into account, but extended to economic measures as well.

Chamberlain wound up by saying that if Germany participated in a conflict originating with an act of aggression by the Soviet Union, she would become allied with every other member of the League. 'Her strength would be their strength. Her weakness would be their weakness. Honour and their own interests would compel all the other nations to aid Germany and equip her, and those who had disarmed her would be the first then to rearm her'. Briand agreed that this was self-evident.[1]

The problem was then discussed in more private conversations. Hurst told the British delegation that he understood the Germans feared internal disorder if they allowed the passage of troops and might ask for the military clauses of the peace treaty to be relaxed so that they could raise more police. Chamberlain said that such talk was premature, and the Germans could be told that their country would certainly not be used as a line of communication if they could not keep order. But any appearance of a Holy Alliance directed against Bolshevism must be avoided.[2] Next day Chamberlain told Luther that the idea of a secret exchange of letters was unacceptable, and he thought it impossible that Germany should be allowed to remain neutral.[3] Hurst and Fromageot had a long discussion with Gaus, out of which came a draft of a note which the powers represented at the conference might address to the German Government, saying that they interpreted Article 16 as 'obliging each Member of the League to co-operate loyally and effectively in support of the Covenant and in resistance to any act of aggression to the extent which its geographical position and its military and economic situation permit'.[4]

During the trip on Lake Maggiore on 10 October Chamberlain tried to explain that the Germans were not alone in fearing the possible

1 Fourth meeting, 8 Oct. 1925.

2 British delegation meeting, 8 Oct. 1925, FO 840/1/6.

3 Chamberlain to FO, 10 Oct. 1925, C 12882/459/18, FO 371/10742. Soon after arriving at Locarno Briand remarked to Chamberlain that no Frenchman contemplated marching the French army across Germany to help Poland against the Soviet Union: Chamberlain to Tyrrell, 4 Oct., N 5714/710/38, FO 371/11022.

4 Minute by Hurst, 9 Oct. 1925, FO 840/1/6.

repercussions of action under Article 16, and spoke of British anxieties about conflict with the United States. Once in the League, he said, Germany would be able to discuss the application of the article and might find Britain working with her. 'Voilà', said Briand, 'une alliance qui se forme contre moi'. To Chamberlain's alarm Luther seemed to take this jest literally and spoke of Chamberlain having, as it were, suggested an alliance. He therefore explained that all he had done was to call attention to the fact that others besides Germany were worried about the consequences of Article 16, so that they might find themselves working together if the matter came before the Assembly again.[1] The boat trip resulted in a draft collective note, the so-called 'texte du bateau', the operative passage of which read: 'les obligations résultant dudit article pour les membres de la Société doivent être entendues en ce sens que chacun des États membres de la Société est tenu de collaborer loyalement et efficacement pour faire respecter le Pact et pour s'opposer à toute acte d'agression, dans une mesure qui ne soit pas hors de proportion avec sa situation militaire, et qui tienne compte de sa position géographique'.[2]

The discussion was resumed in the conference on 12 October. Despite the fact that the note gave the Germans all that they had publicly asked for, although not in the form of a note from the League, Stresemann said that it still meant a very serious situation for Germany, and he proceeded to develop the theme of disarmament. The German Government could only be satisfied with the note if they were convinced that the League, and the countries represented at the conference, were serious about disarmament.

Briand replied that there was no doubt that the League was taking disarmament seriously,[3] and that the idea corresponded with the general sentiments of France. One of the essentials, however, was that each member of the League should contribute to the forces needed to apply sanctions. If, say, twenty members, among them some of the most important, said that they could not take part the others would have to make up the difference and disarmament would be more difficult. France had already done a good deal, but public opinion was anxious: the German Government were not alone in having domestic difficulties.

1 Chamberlain to FO, 14 Oct. 1925, C 13052/459/18, FO 371/10742. No one made a record of the conversation on the boat trip and there are few even partial accounts.

2 Sixth meeting, 12 Oct. 1925. The translation in *Locarno-Konferenz,* No. 25, is of the text as amended at that meeting.

3 On 23 September the Assembly adopted a resolution asking the Council to make a preparatory study with a view to calling a disarmament conference.

Stresemann said that Briand seemed to be justifying the stabilisation of inequality in armaments. The Reichstag would certainly not concur: the German principle was an equality of armaments sufficient for each country. Briand replied that Stresemann had misunderstood him. What he had said was that if the League accepted the *non possumus* formula put forward by the Germans, this would be the result: it was not what he wanted. Chamberlain said that the Council had started work. His view had been that without security there could be no disarmament. The moment there was a sense of security the Allies were bound to work to the utmost for general disarmament.

Vandervelde said that the 'texte du bateau' went a good deal farther than the Geneva Protocol in allowing account to be taken of an individual country's position. The Belgian Government would support it, but he really disliked the exclusion of participation in economic sanctions. Chamberlain added that there must be no misunderstanding: he could not tell Parliament that the proposed note gave Germany a right to neutrality. As he understood it the Germans did not demand such a right, but asked that in a given case Germany's present position in the present European situation might be taken into account. No country could be asked to contribute beyond its capacity. Germany could not be asked to send troops which she did not possess, or were needed to preserve order at home. As for economic sanctions, he interpreted them in the sense of the Assembly resolution of 1921.

Luther agreed that Germany had never said that she wished to remain inactive in all cases. Now she wanted a new effort towards disarmament. She wished all members of the League to be in a state of armament which should be as small as possible but proportionate. Could the conference make some statement? The other delegates said that they would consider a declaration calling attention to the effect that what they had done ought to have on disarmament. But they were not empowered to discuss general disarmament at Locarno, and Chamberlain refused to consider the word 'proportionate'. The question of Germany's entry into the League was thus concluded.[1]

When the western arbitration treaties were discussed Vandervelde evidently abandoned his attempt to reintroduce arbitration as the final stage if the Council of the League failed to agree, so that the treaties followed the pattern agreed at the jurists' meeting. The path towards the eastern arbitration treaties was less smooth. Beneš had originally thought of a form quite different from the German model, but he had in September accepted a French suggestion that the two sets

1 Sixth meeting, 12 Oct. 1925. For the Assembly resolution of 1921, see p. 40, n. 2.

of arbitration treaties should be on the same pattern. However he wanted a non-aggression clause as well. It was presumably his inclusion of such a clause that gave Stresemann ground for later describing the Czechoslovak drafts as guarantee pacts, which Gaus rejected with a declaration that Germany would not discuss recognition of frontiers or renunciation of war.[1]

At the conference meeting on 13 October Fromageot reported that the eastern treaties were not ready, as further discussion of principles was required.[2] The difficulties, Chamberlain gathered, were the mention of frontiers and the renunciation of war. He offered his services and told Hurst to work to secure that war should be made impossible except in the conditions allowed in the west, and that it should be stated that the purpose was the avoidance of war.[3] The preambles to the treaties, in which statements of this kind would feature, were still not completed when Beneš and Skrzynski attended the conference meeting on 15 October to hear the discussion of the western arbitration treaties.[4] However they were ready for the final meeting the next day. The articles were identical with those of the Franco-German arbitration convention, with an additional one, analogous to Article 7 of the guarantee pact, reserving the rights and obligations of the parties as members of the League and those of the League itself. The preambles mentioned neither frontiers nor the renunciation of war, but spoke of the maintenance of peace, settlement of disputes without recourse to force, and respect for rights established by treaty. Stresemann later described them as a collection of platitudes.[5]

Almost as important, from the German's point of view, as the terms of the various treaties, were the concessions they wanted on the occupation and the control of their disarmament. The method chosen for dealing with these questions was to indicate at an early stage that

1 The negotiation of the arbitration treaties is not well documented. For Beneš's intentions see Beneš to Berthelot, n.d. [*c.*27 Jul. 1925] and 14 Sep.; Q d'O to Margerie, 22 Sep.; Beneš to Berthelot, 5 Oct., MAE, Grande Bretagne, Vols. 80, 83, 84. Stresemann gave brief accounts, emphasising German success, in speeches on 22 November and 14 December: *Vierteljahrshefte für Zeitgeschichte* 15 (1967), 415-36; *Akten zur deutschen auswärtigen Politik,* Series B, hereafter cited as *ADAP,* Vol. I.1 (Göttingen, 1966), 727-53, edited version in *Vermächtnis,* Vol. II, 231-44. See also Manfred Alexander, *Der deutsch-tschechoslowakische Schiedsvertrag von 1925 im Rahmen der Locarno-Verträge* (Munich and Vienna, 1970), Ch XL.

2 Seventh meeting, 13 Oct. 1925.

3 Chamberlain to Tyrrell, 14 Oct. 1925, FO 840/1/6.

4 Eighth meeting, 15 Oct. 1925.

5 Ninth meeting, 16 Oct. 1925; *ADAP,* Vol. I.1, 741.

discussion was desired, then to wait to see how the main negotiations went, and finally to press hard at the end when the pact was assured.[1]

A meeting of the French, British and German delegates to discuss German disarmament was held on 12 October. Stresemann began it by asking for a date to be fixed for the evacuation of the Cologne zone, setting out the points of disarmament on which the Germans wanted concessions, and raising the questions of League supervision and the future of German civil aviation. Briand replied that while it was certain that there would be changes if the pact went through, he had no power to deal with these questions at Locarno and the evacuation of Cologne depended on the execution of the peace treaty. He could not make promises outside the subject of the security pact or before it came into force. Chamberlain agreed that once security had been attained other things would follow; but he too was in no position to go into details now and would not make promises in advance or as a condition of the pact.

Luther said that he was going to be asked at home to show concrete results from the conference. Could they not find some formula that would enable him to meet accusations that he came home empty-handed? Briand replied that he could envisage going so far as to say in the Chamber that the occupation system must be reviewed in the light of the pact and certain changes would be made. But as for going home empty-handed, the Germans should look at what they had gained - the return of Germany to a footing of complete equality among the nations and in the League. Surely the German public could understand that? He was going to be reproached with weakening the position of France, and his domestic position might be less secure than Luther's.

Stresemann said that the points outstanding on disarmament were quite small, and the only thing the German people were thinking about was conditions in the Rhineland. Chamberlain repeated that evacuation of Cologne depended solely on German fulfilment of the Control Commission's requirements. He personally was anxious to hasten evacuation and avoid obstacles.[2]

In private conversations the Germans stressed the need for satisfaction

1 For early mention see memorandum by Luther, 7 Oct. 1925, 3123/D645137-43; Chamberlain to FO, 8 Oct., C 12881/459/18, FO 371/10742; Chamberlain to Luther, 8 Oct., FO 840/1/5; memorandum by Schubert, 9 Oct., 4509/E129175-82.

2 Chamberlain to FO, 13 Oct. 1925, C 13004/459/18, FO 371/10742; memorandum by Schubert, 12 Oct., 3123/D645168-80.

on evacuation and League supervision if the pact were to go through in Germany;[1] and in a meeting with the British, French and Belgian delegates on 15 October they battled hard to get a date fixed for the evacuation and then to get a favourable interpretation of Article 213 before Germany joined the League. They said that most of the requirements in the Allied note of June had been met, that Germany's disarmament was complete, and that the German people considered the continued occupation of Cologne unjustified. Briand repeated a promise already given to Luther, that he would press on his colleagues to the point of resignation the necessity for new conditions in the Rhineland. Chamberlain said that he would be delighted to leave Cologne the next day; but the points outstanding were not small, and in any case if the Germans thought they were so minor that it was foolish of the Allies to insist on them, it was even more stupid of the Germans not to carry them out and make evacuation possible. Luther said that he would not be able to carry the pact in the Reichstag until evacuation had taken place. The three Allied ministers replied that they had no mandate to settle the matter at Locarno, but if the Germans undertook to complete the remaining points and began to do so they would support a solution favourable to Germany.

Luther then turned to future League supervision and said that Germany could not join the League until it was settled. The Allied ministers replied that they had no power to discuss it: it was a matter for the Council and the Germans must not go on raising new demands. After a rather tense silence, followed by some argument over whether this was a new demand, Luther abandoned the point.[2]

This was the only conversation that produced a discordant note, causing Chamberlain to compare the Germans to a nagging old woman. On the whole, despite the often serious arguments, the atmosphere of the conference was constructive and the contrast with other meetings with German representatives in the postwar years made a deep impression on the British participants. After a few days at Locarno Lampson wrote home that the absence of chicanery was

1 Memorandum by Selby, 14 Oct. 1925; minute by Chamberlain, 14 Oct., FO 840/1/8; Chamberlain to FO, 14 Oct., C 13093/459/18, FO 371/10742; memoranda by Schubert, 14 and 15 Oct., 4509/E129612-21, E129656-59, E129660-64. Chamberlain and Lampson explained that the League scheme was in suspense, having been adjourned since March, and that the British interpreted Article 213 of the Treaty of Versailles as not allowing for permanent organs in Germany.

2 Chamberlain to FO, 16 Oct. 1925, C 13091/459/18, FO 371/10742; Chamberlain to FO, 17 Oct., C 13133/13120/18, FO 371/10759; Chamberlain to Tyrrell, 16 Oct., FO 840/1/9; memorandum by Schubert, 15 Oct., 4509/E129696-712; memoranda by Luther, 15 Oct., 3123/D645228-29; 4509/E129721-28.

amazing; soon Chamberlain wrote of the 'extraordinary' atmosphere; and at the end he was able not only to record his thankfulness at the success attained but to look back on the months of negotiation as 'so simple, so natural, so easy'.[1] The German delegates were less enthusiastic, but Schubert could write afterwards of an 'agreeable' atmosphere and of the 'frank and straightforward' tone of the conversations.[2] One of the lasting results of the conference was the impression made by Stresemann on Briand and Chamberlain, an impression of honesty and frankness which was to be an asset to him in future.

At the last meeting of the conference on the afternoon of 16 October, Chamberlain's sixty-second birthday, Mussolini appeared and the final protocol and the various instruments were initialled. The protocol stated that the conference had been held to seek by common agreement means for preserving the nations concerned from the scourge of war and for providing for the peaceful settlement of every kind of dispute that might arise between them. The delegates were convinced that the entry into force of the treaties would contribute to a moral relaxation of tension between nations, would help towards the solution of many political and economic problems, and, in strengthening peace and security in Europe, would hasten the disarmament provided for in the Covenant.

The identical treaties between France and Poland and France and Czechoslovakia did not form part of the Locarno settlement, but they were referred to in the final protocol. The main provision was that in the event of either party suffering from a failure to observe the undertakings arrived at with Germany the other, acting in application of Article 16 of the Covenant, would immediately lend aid and assistance if such failure were accompanied by a recourse to arms. If the Council of the League were unable to have its report on such a question accepted, and if either party were attacked without provocation, the other, applying Article 15(7) of the Covenant, would immediately lend aid and assistance. Compared with the previous French treaties with Poland and Czechoslovakia, the obligations in the new treaties were restricted and tied closely to the machinery of the League.[3]

1 Lampson to Tyrrell, 9 Oct. 1925, C 12984/459/18, FO 371/10742; Chamberlain to Tyrrell, 11 Oct., FO 840/1/7; Chamberlain to Tyrrell, 17 Oct., Chamberlain Papers, AC 6/1/623, printed in Petrie, *Life and Letters,* Vol. II, 287-90.

2 Schubert to Neurath, 23 Oct. 1925, 4509/E130032-39.

3 Ninth meeting, 16 Oct. 1925. All the instruments are printed in Cmd 2525 of 1925, *Final Protocol of the Locarno Conference, 1925 (and Annexes),*

From initialling to signature, October - December 1925

During the interval between the conclusion of the Locarno treaties and their signature attention focused less on the treaties themselves than on the immediate additional advantages that Germany might gain. Luther and Stresemann were attacked chiefly by the right wing in Germany despite D.N.V.P. membership of the Government. They therefore felt compelled to defend their work not as a gain for Germany in itself but as one that involved no renunciations, and to press for more concessions, to the point of wearying the British and French Governments with their importunity and calling down on Briand attacks from the right in France. How far this line corresponded with their real views it is hard to say precisely. Stresemann, it is clear, returned to Berlin well satisfied with the achievement of Locarno and regarded it as a considerable step forward in Germany's recovery of her position and freedom as a great power. Two major estimates that he gave of the Locarno policy and the possibilities that it opened up for the future differed in emphasis according to the audience addressed, but in both he stressed the security achieved in the west and the possibilities of future gains flowing from Germany's increasing political and economic weight.[1] As for renunciation Stresemann emphasised in both speeches that in renouncing war for the recovery of Alsace Lorraine Germany was not undertaking a political or moral obligation but was simply abandoning something that she was not in a position to use, but he admitted that he saw no prospect of recovering Alsace Lorraine by peaceful means and sought to turn his hearers' attention rather to economic expansion. In these speeches Stresemann played down the importance of the 'Rückwirkungen' in the Rhineland. For the purpose of securing parliamentary approval of the treaties he was aware of the importance of having immediate progress to show, but at least in his optimistic moments he was looking farther ahead.

Luther, although supporting the pact policy after initial hesitations, was less personally committed than Stresemann, and felt no need to be gracious about it.[2] He carried the chief responsibility for keeping the coalition together, and was more inclined than Stresemann to make

together with Treaties between France and Poland and France and Czechoslovakia, Locarno, October 16, 1925, and in *British and Foreign State Papers,* Vol. CXXI, 923-6; Vol. CXXII, 124-8, 287-8, 288-9.

1 Speech of 22 November, *Vierteljahrshefte für Zeitgeschichte* 15 (1967), 415-36; speech of 14 December, *ADAP,* Vol. I.1, 727-53. See also his letter to the ex-Crown Prince of 7 September, Stresemann Nachlass, 7138/H159871-75, incomplete in *Vermächtnis,* Vol. II, 553-5.

2 See Luther, *Politiker ohne Partei,* 398-401.

concessions to the Nationalist ministers. Equally he resented their resignation on 23 October, in refusal to accept Locarno, as much as or more than Stresemann. But this event did not free them from the need to pursue a 'national' line on the treaties. They had both been very anxious to get the Nationalists into the government in the first place and hoped that they would join another. A breach was therefore to be avoided. Thus they were more rather than less impelled to defend themselves against right-wing attacks by repeating that Germany had renounced nothing and was entitled to immediate benefits from the pact, even some that Stresemann had earlier denied any intention of seeking.[1] The defect of this line was not only that it was defensive and apologetic and obscured recognition of the gains actually made: it carried the risk that unless all the benefits were forthcoming quickly, which was unlikely, public opinion in Germany would become soured while western confidence in German intentions, necessary for the achievement of further gains, would in no way be strengthened.

The first task was to secure a date for the beginning of the evacuation of the Cologne zone. The Allied ministers had said at Locarno that the German Government should write to the Ambassadors' Conference undertaking to settle the remaining points of disarmament and give instructions for carrying them out, and they would support an early decision on evacuation. The German note was delivered on 23 October. It stated that the great majority of the demands made by the Allies in June had been met or were on the way to completion. On only a very small number had decisive progress not been made, but the Government hoped a satisfactory solution could be found if the Allies took account of German interests.[2]

While the details were being considered by their military advisers the Allied Governments were preparing for the political decision to accept German assurances and fix a date for evacuation to begin. Chamberlain was prepared to compromise on the remaining points of difficulty, arguing that the new spirit introduced into relations

1 See Turner, *Stresemann and the Politics of the Weimar Republic,* 213-7; Luther, *Politiker ohne Partei,* 386-94; Stresemann, *Vermächtnis,* Vol. II, 203-7; Stockhausen, *Sechs Jahre Reichskanzlei,* 181-5.

2 Cmd 2527 of 1925, *Correspondence between the Ambassadors' Conference and the German Ambassador at Paris respecting German disarmament, evacuation of Cologne zone and modification in the Rhineland régime, Paris, October-November 1925;* also *DDB,* Vol. II, No. 124 (without annexes). The points of difficulty were the organisation of the Schutzpolizei, the status of the Heeresleitung, prohibition of army training with certain weapons, the fortifications of Königsberg, and the 'patriotic' associations. See the British General Staff's comments in *DBFP,* Ser. IA, Vol. I, No. 28, n. 3. For the progress made in the summer and early autumn see Salewski, *Entwaffnung und Militärkontrolle,* 313-4.

with Germany indicated that peace could be better secured by mutual conciliation than by insistence on the fulfilment of all the June demands. He wanted to promise that evacuation would begin on 1 December, the date of the signature of the treaties.[1] Briand wished to avoid the appearance of bargaining and the risk of putting forward proposals which might not be wholly accepted, and was dubious about fixing a date before agreement had been reached with the Germans; but after some argument he deferred to Chamberlain on this point. The reply of the Ambassadors' Conference was sent to Hoesch on 6 November. It noted the progress made and asked the German Government to make immediate proposals for settling the points of difficulty, indicating the kind of measures on the police, the associations and the military command that were desired, rather than making specific demands. The Allied Governments, the note said, would be happy if the German reply enabled them to fix the date for starting the evacuation of the Cologne zone as 1 December.[2]

At the same time there was discussion of relaxations in the occupation régime of the second and third zones, such as a reduction in the number of Allied ordinances and the appointment of a Reich Commissioner to represent the German Government with the Inter-Allied High Commission. In this area German demands mounted and became increasingly embarrassing. On 26 October Chamberlain instructed D'Abernon to tell Luther and Stresemann that he knew the Germans would not be so foolish as to reject the treaty, but the Nationalists were doing their best to prove to opinion abroad that the Germany that mattered (a reference to a remark by Schubert at Locarno that they represented the best elements in the country) did not want peace. Chamberlain repeated the warning next day, saying that Briand's difficulties were being greatly increased and he himself was receiving 'most unfortunate reactions'.[3] Hoesch and Sthamer duly conveyed assurances that their Government were determined to carry through the pact, but within a few days Hoesch was again being instructed to press Briand on the occupation and evacuation, and Stresemann was saying that he hoped Briand would say something about shortening the period of occupation of the second and third zones.[4]

1 *DBFP,* Ser. IA, Vol. I, No. 50.

2 Op. cit. Nos. 59, 63, 70, 71; Cmd 2527 of 1925.

3 *DBFP,* Ser. IA, Vol. I, Nos. 26, 27, 32. Schubert's remark at Locarno reported in Chamberlain to FO, 14 Oct. 1925, C 13093/459/18, FO 371/10742.

4 *DBFP,* Ser. IA, Vol. I, Nos. 28, 31, 36, 43; AA to Hoesch, Sthamer, and Keller (Brussels), 27 Oct. 1925; Sthamer to AA, 28 Oct.; Hoesch to AA, 28 Oct., 3123/D645316-21, D644348-49, D644353-59; AA to Hoesch, 1 Nov., K1886/K465467-70.

This last request produced a fairly sharp reaction in London and Paris. Chamberlain telegraphed that he did not understand Stresemann's request for 'action' under Article 431 of the Treaty of Versailles. Throughout the negotiations of the spring and summer it had been made perfectly clear that the pact would not involve any change in the occupation clauses, and at the very outset the German Government had disclaimed any intention of asking for one. Great steps were being taken to grant alleviations but there was a limit, and if the Germans tried to push the Allies too far they might defeat their own object. Briand instructed de Margerie to say that the French Government had decided of their own accord to hasten the evacuation of Cologne and reduce the burdens of the occupation. But they would not abandon the essential disarmament questions still unsettled, nor allow Germany to raise the duration of the occupation, which had been no part of the pact negotiations, which constituted a guarantee of the execution of the peace treaty, and which was bound up with the question of reparations.[1] Stresemann still hoped that something could be said about future possibilities; but when this was refused Hoesch thought the limit of demands was being reached.[2]

German interpretations of the Treaty of Mutual Guarantee itself also caused concern. On 31 October Stresemann made a speech at Dresden in which he was reported as saying that Chamberlain had assured him that the entire British navy and army were at Germany's disposal if the French crossed the frontier. When asked to be careful about what he said Stresemann replied that he had been misquoted.[3] Then in a broadcast he said that Germany had not renounced Alsace Lorraine but only the possibility of recovering it by force. Stresemann was particularly anxious that Briand and Chamberlain should not refer to Alsace Lorraine in speeches because it was a central point of his argument with the Nationalists; but his own statements on the subject earned him a rebuke from Briand.[4]

In the first few days of November the Germans were pressing for an early announcement about the alleviations in the occupied territory,

1 *DBFP,* Ser. IA, Vol. I, Nos. 53, 56; Q d'O to Margerie, 3 Nov. 1925, MAE, Grande Bretagne, Vol. 86.

2 *DBFP,* Ser. IA, Vol. I, No. 66; Hoesch to AA, 5 and 6 Nov. 1925; memorandum by Stresemann, 8 Nov., 3123/D646419-22, D645400-03, D646451-56.

3 *DBFP,* Ser. IA, Vol. I, Nos. 48, 54; AA to Sthamer, 4 Nov. 1925, 3123/D645379. The misquotation was not serious.

4 AA to Hoesch, 4 Nov. 1925; Hoesch to AA, 5 and 6 Nov.; AA to Hoesch, 7 Nov., 3123/D645384, D645395-96, D646400-03; memorandum by Schubert, 7 Nov., 4509/E130227-28; memorandum by Stresemann, 8 Nov., 3123/D646451-56; memorandum by Léger, 5 Nov., MAE, Allemagne, Vol. 388; *DBFP,* Ser. IA, Vol. I, No. 69, n. 2.

without which, Stresemann said, the Government could not be reconstructed.[1] Chamberlain too was anxious for a decision despite his annoyance at the German appearance of bargaining and his concern at the reactions in France. The treaties were to be debated in Parliament and he needed to be able to announce the decisions and to name the date for the beginning of the evacuation of Cologne.[2] The German reply on disarmament was sent on 9 November. There followed a week of intensive negotiation on some points; but on 14 November the Ambassadors' Conference sent Hoesch a note on the alleviations in the occupation régime, including a prospective reduction in the number of troops - 'se rapprochant des chiffres normaux' - and a verbal declaration that the evacuation of the Cologne zone would begin on 1 December. This was made because the note on disarmament could not be ready before two important party meetings in Germany on 15 November: it followed in writing two days later.[3]

The German Cabinet met with the President on 16 and 18 November to discuss the outcome. Not all the ministers were satisfied, but most of them agreed that Locarno was a major breach in the Treaty of Versailles and opened the way for further dismantling. Gessler, the Reichwehr Minister, said that he would have preferred to wait to decide on the treaties until disarmament had been finally wound up, but he did not think that Germany had abandoned anything. In renouncing war in the west she was abandoning something that she did not have the means to undertake: it was like a man who had lost both legs saying that he had decided not to go dancing. Hindenburg grumbled that Germany's position was still quite unequal and Poland was still guaranteed by France. The Government must not forget the Soviet Union and must make sure that Germany's freedom of action was recognised. The Cabinet decided to recommend acceptance of the treaties to the Reichstag.[4] The Land Governments having accepted the treaties, they were approved by the Reichstag on 27 November by 292 votes to 174: the principle of entry into the League was approved by 275 to 183. The opposition consisted of the Communists and the

1 Op. cit. Nos. 49, 64, 69; AA to Hoesch, Sthamer, Neurath and Keller, 4 Nov. 1925; Sthamer to AA, 5 Nov.; Hoesch to AA, 5 Nov., 3123/D645380-81, D646407-09, D646419-22. The Government was not reconstructed until January.

2 *DBFP,* Ser. IA, Vol. I, Nos. 73, 75.

3 Notes in Cmd 2527 of 1925; *ADAP,* Vol. I.1, No. 1, n. 3. Hoesch had asked for an undertaking that the troops would be reduced to the prewar German figure: the French put in 'chiffres normaux' as deliberately vague but indicating a 'normal' situation: *DBFP,* Ser. IA, Vol. I, Nos. 192, n. 2, 203. For the final negotiations see Salewski, *Entwaffnung und Militärkontrolle,* 321-5.

4 Notes of Cabinet meetings, 16 and 18 Nov. 1925, 3243/D713972-99.

D.N.V.P., and two small parties. In addition to the government parties (D.V.P., Centre, D.D.P., and Bavarian People's Party) the Social Democrats voted in favour.

The House of Commons debated the treaties on 18 November. In his opening speech Chamberlain emphasised that, valuable as the agreements were, Locarno was even more important for the spirit which had produced them and was already at work. Locarno was not the end of the work of appeasement and reconciliation but its beginning. The greatest difficulty at the conference had been Germany's entry into the League, but the collective letter on Article 16 contained no more than what had been declared by the Assembly and was the common sense of the Covenant. In describing the Treaty of Mutual Guarantee Chamberlain laid stress on the importance of the demilitarised zone, but made it clear that for Britain to take action in advance of the Council the breach must be so serious as to give rise to danger if she delayed. He went on to say that without a *détente* on Germany's eastern frontier the work of Locarno would have been only half done; but there too security had been strengthened and war rendered more remote, and Locarno had already borne fruit in a Polish decision not to expel optants for German citizenship.[1]

Labour and Liberal speakers in the debate agreed that Locarno marked a great advance, and directed their criticism mainly at what had not been attempted, calling variously for general disarmament, more arbitration, Russian entry into the League, and settlements in south-east Europe. In answer to MacDonald Chamberlain declared that Locarno had not been organised for the purpose of uniting the west against the Soviet Union nor of detaching Germany from co-operation with her. In his winding-up speech Chamberlain said again that there was no foundation for any suspicion that the Government had at any time tried to engage any other countries in a league against the Soviet Union. In reply to complaints about failure to consult the Dominions, Chamberlain said that the Government had done their best to have a conference but none of the Dominions had been able to send a representative to London. He could not go to meeting after meeting of the League and say that Britain had no policy because the Government of the Empire had not been able to meet. The Dominions had been fully informed, their freedom had been safeguarded in the treaty, and it was hoped to discuss it fully at the next Imperial

1 *HC Deb.,* 5th ser., Vol. 188, cols 419-32. Chamberlain had asked Skrzynski to get his Government to show magnanimity over the optants: *DBFP,* Ser. IA, Vol. I, Nos. 6, 24, 57.

Conference.[1] The motion approving ratification of the treaty was adopted by 373 votes to 19.[2]

Even after the announcements about the evacuation of Cologne and alleviations in the second and third zones German ministers continued to express, publicly and privately, expectations of more concessions. At a dinner on 20 November Dufour Feronce told Chamberlain that his Government recognised that the promises made at Locarno had been fulfilled but there still remained many hopes and wishes, especially about reducing the period of the occupation, cutting forces, and relaxing restrictions on civil aviation. Chamberlain replied, good-humouredly but with serious intent, that the trouble about negotiating with Germans was that as soon as they got something they appeared to forget it. There really could not be more concessions now. He and Briand were willing to talk, but if questions of this kind were raised officially the answer would be no.[3] Then some passages in Luther's speech in the Reichstag debate on 23 November, as reported in the press, caused trouble. Luther was reported to have said that negotiations on civil aviation had begun (which was not the case) and that an assurance had been given at Locarno not only that Germany had an equal right to colonial mandates but that the right would be given practical recognition. He was in fact misquoted on this: what he said was that Germany's right to mandates had been recognised and it was expected that her claim would receive practical recognition. Even so there was reason to warn Dufour again that the western governments must not be faced with demands which could not be met.[4]

The death of Queen Alexandra, King George V's mother, and a change of government in Paris, reduced the opportunities for both festivities and long discussions on the occasion of the signature of the treaties. But the predicted size of the German delegation suggested that they thought they were coming for negotiations. Chamberlain

1 *HC Deb.,* 5th ser., Vol. 188, cols. 441-2, 519-29. None of the Dominions acceded to the Rhine pact. The New Zealand Government were prepared to do so, possibly also the Australian Government. The Canadian Government refused, and the South African Government would most probably have done so if asked to declare themselves. At the Imperial Conference of 1926 it was agreed that since not all were willing to adhere it was better that none should. CP 473(25), CAB 24/175; C 53(25), CAB 23/51; C 490, 696, 4881/1/18, FO 371/11247; CO 57768/25, CO 532/311; D 632/26, DO 35/1; D 7259/26, DO 35/4; E (I.R.26), 7th meeting, CAB 32/56; E 129, CAB 32/47.

2 In France and Belgium there were no parliamentary debates before the signature of the treaties: ratification was approved in 1926. In Poland and Czechoslovakia the treaties were approved before signature by parliamentary commissions, and their ratification by the parliaments later.

3 Dufour to AA, 21 Nov. 1925, 3123/D646558-63.

4 *DBFP,* Ser. IA, Vol. I, No. 116.

sent word that this would not be possible and it was not the moment for the Germans to ask for more.[1] In a moment of euphoria after the Reichstag vote Stresemann expounded to the French Chargé d'Affaires in Berlin his diplomatic programme for the next two years. First he would try to obtain by negotiation with France the earliest possible evacuation of the whole occupied territory. He was already in contact with the Belgian Government about the possible return of Eupen and Malmédy. He hoped to obtain mandates for some of the former German colonies. Finally there was the question of the Polish Corridor and Danzig: this was the biggest and most delicate problem but he was not unhopeful that it could be settled in the long run amicably and without depriving Poland of access to the sea. Laboulaye thought that despite warnings against raising new demands Luther and Stresemann did intend to bring up the question of early evacuation when they came to London. The Quai d'Orsay replied that the meeting was not for negotiations. In the future, if the loyal working of the Locarno agreements by both sides led to really cordial political and economic relations between France and Germany, and if the German Government made proposals for the early settlement of their reparation debt which, like security, was guaranteed by the occupation, then the French Government might discuss the matter. But meanwhile everyone should stick to the agreements reached, which were based on respect for the peace treaties.[2]

The Germans did not raise the larger questions in London, but after the treaties and agreements had been signed on the morning of 1 December Luther and Stresemann brought up the question of reducing the number of troops in the second and third zones to what they regarded as the 'chiffres normaux' referred to by the Ambassadors' Conference, namely 43,000, the number of German troops garrisoned in the same area before the war. They also had complaints about the interpretation of the principles agreed in the recent disarmament negotiations, and asked for early talks on air control. Chamberlain raised the subject of mandates and said that to avoid misunderstanding he must make it clear that the idea of Britain or any of the Dominions giving one up was out of the question. Luther replied that the matter would not be raised now but he could not say that it would never be raised. Chamberlain answered that a request for mandates would certainly be refused; and Briand added that the Italians felt that in any new distribution their country had first claim.[3]

1 Op. cit. No. 120.

2 Laboulaye to Q d'O, 28 Nov. 1925; Q d'O to Laboulaye, 29 Nov., MAE, Grande Bretagne, Vol. 87.

3 *ADAP*, Vol. I.1, No. 1; *DBFP*, Ser. IA, Vol. I, No. 122. The Italians protested

To Schubert Tyrrell repeated advice which Chamberlain had given to Dufour, that in future the Germans should sound the ground before asking for further alleviations, in order to minimise the risk of refusals. Lampson recommended that the German application for entry into the League should be sent soon: otherwise the impression would be created that they expected more concessions. Schubert said that they would have to wait for a moment that was suitable in relation to domestic problems; but he denied that there was any intention of making the application subject to further concessions.[1]

against Luther's reference to mandates: see op.cit. No. 121 and n. 3; *DDI*, Vol. IV, No. 186, n. 2.

1 *DBFP*, Ser. IA, Vol. I, No. 123; *ADAP*, Vol. I.1, Nos. 3-5.

6

DEFENCE POLICY AND ITS RELATION TO FOREIGN POLICY 1919 – 27

During the period covered by this study the connexion between foreign and defence policy was not close. Theoretically each has a strong bearing on the other, but in practice this was hardly the case. None of Britain's international engagements contained military commitments: avoiding them was a feature of policy on international security. Although there was plenty of disorder and minor threat in and on the borders of British-controlled territory there was no major threat to Great Britain or any part of the Empire, nor was it likely that the minor conflicts of other countries would seriously involve Britain. Those aspects of defence policy which did involve foreign policy considerations are examined in this chapter, together with its framework and general problems.

Principles and general problems, 1919 - 26

In the early 1920s, as before 1914, naval power was the key to imperial defence, although air power became a factor of some importance. The army reverted to its peacetime function of providing garrisons for territory under British control: its size was fixed not by comparison with that of any other country but by the needs of India and of overseas garrisons. No change in this system was suggested: possible future enemies could be hypothetically identified, and the basic requirements for expanding the army in case of a major war discussed, but little more. The size of the fleet, however, had at least since the 1880s been fixed by comparison with other major navies.[1] Soon after the war the yardstick had to be reconsidered, and before long a similar question arose for the air force.

Early in August 1919, when the Cabinet began to consider future policy and the state of the country, the service ministers, Long and Churchill, suggested that in order to fix the size of the armed forces their duties needed to be defined. As a result the Cabinet laid it down that in framing the service estimates it should be assumed that the British Empire would not be engaged in a major war during the next ten years, and an expeditionary force would not be needed: the main task of the military and air forces was to provide garrisons for India, Egypt,

1 Even if the British army had been primarily intended for continental warfare, to fix its size by comparison with a European conscript army would have been impracticable. For the meaning of the naval standard see E.L. Woodward, *Great Britain and the German Navy* (London, 1935), Appendix II.

and all other British-controlled territory. As for the navy, it was decided for the time being to make no change in the prewar standard.[1] The problem here was that before 1914 the United States had not been taken into account in framing the naval standard and Japan had been an ally. Although Britain ended the war far stronger than either in all classes of warship, and although the completion of ships under construction would only narrow the gap, the future of the Anglo-Japanese alliance was in doubt and the execution of the enormous building programme authorised in 1916 would by 1924 give the United States a substantial superiority in battleships and battle cruisers. To compete with the United States would be politically undesirable and financially ruinous; but to abandon British naval predominance, even over a country with which war was 'unthinkable', had serious implications for Britain's future. President Wilson had already at the peace conference shown himself willing to use the naval programme as an instrument of high policy: there were pressures in the United States in favour of building a navy second to none.[2] What was to be done?

The solution that emerged was to accept a one-power (instead of two-power) naval standard and to try to reach agreements on limiting naval building; but the first attempt to discuss the problem, in the autumn of 1919, failed because of Wilson's illness, and nothing more could be done during the remainder of his term of office.[3]

In June 1920 the Committee of Imperial Defence decided to examine the whole area of imperial defence anew.[4] When asked to provide material the Foreign Office, having listed Britain's treaty commitments, concluded that a statement of this kind was useless as a basis for defence policy since it did not answer the question of imperial responsibilities. 'For the last century the policy of His Majesty's Government has been inductive, intuitive, and quite deliberately opportunist, but through it all has run the dominant impulse of the defence of India'. To maintain this impulse for the next generation would mean increased commit-

1 WC 606A, 3 Aug. 1919; WC 616A, 15 Aug., CAB 23/15; Cabinet Finance Committee, 11 Aug., CAB 27/71.

2 For the immediate postwar situation and the 'naval battle of Paris' see Harold and Margaret Sprout, *Towards a New Order of Sea Power. American Naval Policy and the World Scene 1918-1922,* 2nd edn (Princeton, 1943), 50-87; Roskill, *Naval Policy,* 71-101.

3 See J. Kenneth McDonald, 'Lloyd George and the search for a post-war naval policy', *Lloyd George, Twelve Essays,* ed. A.J.P. Taylor (London, 1971), 191-222; Roskill, *Naval Policy,* pp. 214-19.

4 CID 133rd meeting, 29 Jun. 1920, CAB 2/3. The CID, which had been in suspense during the war, seldom met again on a full scale until 1922, its business being mainly conducted by the Standing Defence Sub-Committee chaired by Balfour. See Roskill, *Hankey,* Vol. II, 154-7.

ments: if it were abandoned the whole basis of foreign and colonial policy would have to be revised. On the other hand 'the events of the last twenty years have shown that we cannot be free to carry out our main objects, which are Imperial and Colonial, unless we are safe in Europe, and it will be many years yet before we can free ourselves from responsibility for Europe'.[1]

The General Staff found the possible European liabilities too indefinite, and too much dependent on political considerations, to be calculable; but the imperial ones that they could calculate seemed to require an increase, not a decrease, in the size of the army and the air force.[2] Hankey's secretariat summarised Britain's defence requirements as (a) to maintain superiority at sea over any combination of powers liable to be arrayed against the forces of the Empire; (b) to keep sufficient forces at home to maintain internal order, meet the Irish situation, and provide drafts and reinforcements for overseas garrisons; (c) to provide sufficient forces in the Middle East and India; (d) to garrison defended ports overseas; (e) to provide enough forces to fulfil obligations under the peace treaties; and (f) to have plans for the rapid expansion of the forces to meet any emergency. They pointed out that even though France was at present the only country which could attack the United Kingdom a scheme for home defence could not be entirely dispensed with, and asked whether it should be based on the possibility of France being the enemy or on the possibility of war with a revived Germany or Germany and Russia combined. Other questions suggested for consideration were: what was to be the naval standard; would it be British policy in future to support France, Belgium or the Netherlands against unprovoked German aggression; was the defence of India to be reconsidered; was the possibility of war with Japan to be taken into account in considering the Far East?[3]

The naval standard was the most urgent of these questions and was discussed at once: that of home defence was considered, in part, in the winter of 1921-2. That it would be British policy to support France and Belgium against German aggression was never seriously questioned even though no provision was to be made for doing so. The defence of India was reconsidered twice. The possibility of war with Japan was discussed at intervals throughout. The list of requirements did not produce matter for much argument. There was therefore little change in strategic assumptions during the ensuing years: the problems of defence policy were mainly matters of organisation and money - the latter, rather than

1 CID paper 251-B, 10 Jul. 1920, CAB 4/7.
2 CID paper 255-B, 27 Jul. 1920, CAB 4/7.
3 CID paper 257-B, 27 Sep. 1920, CAB 4/7.

any definition of 'sufficiency', generally determining the provision actually made.

The recession in 1921, when unemployment reached over 2 million, led to public demands for deflation and economy. In August the Government appointed a committee of business leaders under Sir Eric Geddes to examine the next year's estimates and recommend additional economies. In its first two reports, published early in 1922, the committee recommended savings of £75 million, of which £46½ million were to come from the services, and the creation of a Ministry of Defence to cut out overlapping between them. The Admiralty protested at once and a Cabinet committee was set up under Churchill's chairmanship to examine the defence spending recommendations. This committee did not advise setting up a Ministry of Defence, but suggested improvements in inter-service planning under the Committee of Imperial Defence. It recommended keeping the one-power standard, but its proposed savings on the naval estimates amounted to only about £2 million less than those of the Geddes Committee.[1]

Relations between the services were examined again in 1923. For two or three years after the war the R.A.F. had to battle for a separate existence. In essence the conflict was about different conceptions of the use of air power. Trenchard, the Chief of Air Staff and 'father' of the R.A.F., had a vision of strategic bombing and of the air force as the main defender of the United Kingdom which was hard to reconcile with maritime purposes, while most soldiers thought of aircraft primarily as a tactical weapon akin to artillery and many, both soldiers and civilians, thought of the air force as an economical means of policing turbulent tribesmen in the Middle East. Even when the threat that the R.A.F. would be reabsorbed into the army had been overcome the conflict went on between the R.A.F. and the navy. In March 1922 an enquiry into naval and air co-operation was decided on, but was not implemented until a year later when the C.I.D. appointed a sub-committee under Lord Salisbury to examine the co-operation and correlation of the three services.[2] In addition to considering the

1 See Roskill, *Naval Policy,* 230-3, 336-40. Total expenditure on the armed forces fell from £604 million in 1920 to £292.2 million in 1921, £189.5 million in 1922 and £111 million in 1923. It then remained at under £120 million a year until 1936. As a proportion of total government expenditure it was, even in 1921, considerably less than for any of the ten years before the war, and as a proportion of the national income it was thereafter slightly less. But with debt charges running at over ten times the prewar figure, and rising government expenditure on social items, the services remained a favourite target for economy. For the figures see H.R. Mitchell and Phyllis Deane, *Abstract of British Historical Statistics* (Cambridge, 1962), 398-400.

2 C 16(22), C 18(22), CAB 23/29; *HC Deb.,* 5th ser., Vol. 161, col. 35.

controversy about naval aviation the Salisbury Sub-Committee examined the assumptions on which defence planning should be based and the machinery required. They adopted as assumptions that home defence should be considered in relation to imperial defence, that in the oceans the primary responsibility rested on the navy, that in the narrow seas the navy was no longer solely responsible, and that while war with a great power was a remote contingency an adequate air force was essential to support British diplomacy.[1]

A compromise was reached on naval aviation, that continued to cause difficulty. On the machinery for defence planning the Salisbury Sub-Committee decided against a Ministry of Defence but also against abolishing the Air Ministry. They recommended making the Chiefs of Staff collectively responsible for tendering advice on defence to the government.[2] The Chiefs of Staff did not find this easy at first, or indeed always later, but the inauguaration of the Chiefs of Staff Committee was a step forward in providing for joint planning.

During his short period as chairman of the Committee of Imperial Defence in 1924 Haldane devoted some attention to co-ordination in defence thinking. At a meeting in the summer he pointed out that the different services were working on different political assumptions, and suggested that these should be re-examined.[3] But when, with the new government, Hankey suggested that Japan and France provided the best yardsticks for naval and air measures, Chamberlain replied that the less the Foreign Secretary knew about such assumptions the better. This confirmed that the yardsticks had little to do with the actual situation.[4] But a re-examination was called for not long afterwards by Churchill, who on entering office as Chancellor of the Exchequer proposed that the Committee of Imperial Defence should be asked to make a fresh appraisal of the dangers to which the Empire was exposed and to consider whether the ten-year rule should be extended or revised. The Admiralty, he considered, should be 'made to recast all their plans and scales and standards on the basis that no naval war against a first-class Navy is likely to take place in the next twenty years'.[5] At a meeting of the Committee Churchill said that the

1 CID Sub-Committee on Defence, 1923, 1st meeting, 15 Mar. 1923, CAB 21/260.

2 Cmd 2029 of 1924, *Report of the Sub-Committee of the Committee of Imperial Defence on National and Imperial Defence.* See Johnson, *Defence by Committee,* 193-8; Andrew Boyle, *Trenchard* (London, 1962), 467-91; Roskill, *Naval Policy,* 372-82; Roskill, *Hankey,* Vol. II, 336-41.

3 CID 187th meeting, 28 Jul. 1924, CAB 2/4.

4 Note by Hankey, 20 Nov. 1924, annexed to CID 187th meeting, CAB 2/4.

5 Churchill to Baldwin, 15 Dec. 1924, Baldwin Papers, D.1.3, Navy 2 (Vol. 2); Churchill to Chamberlain, 15 Dec., Chamberlain Papers, AC 51/66.

services had a right to expect from the government of the day a statement of the dangers against which they were to prepare. It would then be their duty to work out the means of meeting these dangers. This doctrine was not welcomed unanimously, the new First Lord of the Admiralty, Bridgeman, pointing out that governments had not been very successful in forecasting wars in the past and suggesting that it was better to take the line of insuring against reasonable risks.[1] But the Foreign Office advised that war with Japan was not to be expected in the next ten years, and after some discussion of how often the situation should be reviewed, the Committee recommended to the Cabinet that the policy of leaving to the Admiralty the responsibility for the naval defence of the Empire on the basis of the one-power standard should not be reversed or modified, but aggressive action by Japan against the Empire in the next ten years was not seriously to be apprehended: the Foreign Office should be responsible for giving warning of any change in the Far Eastern situation which would make a fresh review necessary.[2] This meant that so far as the Far East was concerned the ten-year rule was extended, but the basis of naval planning remained unchanged.

In the summer of 1926 the Chiefs of Staff produced their first annual review of defence policy. They were told by the Foreign Office that wars, quarrels and friction in any part of the world spelt loss to British commercial and financial interests, which was the reason why Britain intervened in almost every dispute and was one justification for maintaining the armed forces which enabled her to do so with authority; and that the more the nations of Europe became convinced of her readiness and ability to fulfil her guarantees the less would be the likelihood that she would be called upon to do so. They were told by Hankey to assume that at present there was no reason to anticipate a war among the great powers of Europe, that war with Japan in the next ten years was not to be expected, that war with France was inconceivable, and war with the United States was so improbable that no preparations need be made.[3]

Against this background the Chiefs of Staff stated the first principle of the system of imperial defence: the maintenance of sea communications, without which the various parts of the Empire, although able on the whole to keep order with their own forces or imperial garrisons, were in a larger emergency liable to defeat in detail, and on which

1 CID 193rd meeting, 5 Jan. 1925, CAB 2/4.

2 CID 198th meeting, 30 Mar. 1925, 199th meeting, 2 Apr., CAB 2/4; C 24(25), 6 May, CAB 23/50. See also below, p. 176.

3 CID paper 700-B, Jun. 1926, CAB 4/14; *DBFP,* Ser. IA, Vol. I, Appendix.

Britain depended for the essentials of life. 'The whole fabric is built upon the assumption of the command of the sea. Unless freedom and security of sea passage throughout are assured, the system breaks down'. Discussing Britain's ability to go to war, the Chiefs of Staff did not contest the Foreign Office view of the western guarantee but pointed out the limitations on basing defence policy on it: 'The size of the forces of the Crown maintained by Great Britain is governed by various considerations peculiar to each service, and is not arrived at by any calculations of foreign policy, nor is it possible that they ever should be so calculated'. Thus the expeditionary force and a limited number of R.A.F. squadrons, which constituted the only force available for immediate use in Europe or outside the Empire, was only available when the requirements of imperial defence allowed. The services could not make specific provision for European commitments apart from adopting such measures of training, organisation and equipment as would enable them to fight on the continent if required. It was most necessary to realise that the military basis on which foreign policy must ultimately rest for the fulfilment of continental commitments was the capacity of Britain and eventually (if they adhered to the Locarno treaty) the Dominions to mobilise all their resources for war. The despatch of the small expeditionary force could never be more than a pledge of Britain's readiness to fulfil her guarantees: the capacity to fulfil them would depend on having a framework for military expansion and preparation of the industrial mobilisation needed to keep a national army in the field.[1]

The Chiefs of Staff recommended, on naval policy, that the one-power standard for capital ships and aircraft carriers laid down in the Washington treaty should be maintained, and that all other types of ship should be kept at such strength as would ensure adequate security for British territory and freedom and security of sea passage to all parts of the Empire. On military policy they repeated that the size of the regular army was governed by the size of overseas garrisons, about half the army being at home and half abroad: an expeditionary force could only be organised from the units that were at home at any given time. The problem of defence, they were happy to note, was

1 According to the General Staff, in 1926 there existed for the expeditionary force a first contingent of one cavalry and three infantry divisions with a proportion of non-divisional units capable of mobilisation in two weeks, and a second contingent able to follow in four months. If more were required some of the Territorial Army might be sent overseas three or four months after the outbreak of hostilities but a steady flow of fully equipped divisions could not be despatched before six months from the date of mobilisation, and it would not be possible to maintain a force of twenty divisions until much later. In the case of a war of national effort conscription would have to be introduced before the Territorial Army was expanded: CID paper 269-C, May 1926, CAB 5/6.

immensely simplified by the assurance of a friendly France, which made the Rhine Britain's strategic land frontier, minimised the danger of air attack and secured the western Mediterranean. They recommended keeping up an air programme no smaller than the current one but thought that anti-aircraft defence could be postponed. In their detailed recommendations Singapore, the defence of the sea route to the east and the trade routes, and modernising the army in India, all took priority over home defence. In conclusion the Chiefs of Staff drew 'the earnest attention of the Committee of Imperial Defence to a consideration which has constantly impressed itself on our minds in the course of this enquiry, namely, the smallness of our defence forces when compared with the vast extent of our imperial responsibilities and commitments. We wish to place on record our view that the forces available for Imperial defence are now reduced to a minimum and are barely capable of dealing with the problems that are liable to arise either singly or simultaneously'.[1]

The Committee of Imperial Defence approved this review subject to a Cabinet decision on how far the country could afford to provide to meet its responsibilities. The Cabinet approved it as a general statement of defence policy but made no comment on the costs.[2] Expenditure on the army and navy was reduced again in 1927. No provision was made for equipment that would enable the army to fight in Europe, nor any study made of how it might be used. Whereas in the immediate postwar years informal contacts between the British and French General Staffs seem to have remained fairly close, once Britain undertook the commitment of Locarno the impossibility of holding staff talks with both France and Germany about the defence of each against the other meant that no plans were made for the implementation of the British guarantee. As the Chiefs of Staff pointed out in 1930, Britain was in a less favourable position to fulfil the guarantee than she had been, without any written undertaking, to go to the help of France and Belgium in 1914.[3] On the other hand the expeditionary force was not yet questioned. In July 1927 the War Office asked for, and received, confirmation of the decision that no European war was to be expected for ten years: their reason for asking was that equipment for both a continental and an eastern war could not be afforded, and providing for the latter was thought more urgent. A year later the Cabinet agreed that for the purposes of framing all the service

1 CID paper 701-B, 22 Jun. 1926, CAB 4/14.

2 CID 215th meeting, 22 Jul. 1926, CAB 2/4; C 49(26), 30 Jul., CAB 23/53.

3 In May 1928 the Chief of the Imperial General Staff stated that reserves, artillery and armoured fighting vehicles for the expeditionary force were seriously deficient: COS 247, CAB 53/21.

estimates it should be assumed that at any given date there would be no major war for ten years.[1]

Attempts during the 1920s to induce the Dominions to contribute to imperial naval defence was not very successful. At the Imperial Conference of 1921 the Admiralty put forward suggestions on the most useful ways in which they could build up their own forces - mainly cruisers and submarines - and develop naval bases.[2] Lee told the conference that it was doubtful whether Britain could afford even a one-power standard unless the Empire shared the cost and responsibility; but although the Prime Ministers agreed that 'equality in fighting strength with any other Naval Power' must be the minimum standard for the Empire, there was no agreement on sharing the cost. Hughes of Australia and Massey of New Zealand, to whose countries sea communications were vital, were anxious that the whole Empire should bear a proportionate share; Meighen of Canada said that his parliament would not approve any expenditure; Smuts suggested that the Dominions should contribute from their share of reparation receipts. The only resolution on which it proved possible to agree was an anodyne one recommending co-operation in providing for naval defence but stating that it was for the several parliaments to decide on methods and amounts. The Admiralty's proposals were held over until the position should be clear after the Washington conference.[3]

Cruisers and submarines were recommended again to New Zealand and Australia before the Imperial Conference of 1923, the Admiralty stressing that the task of the naval forces in the Pacific would be to delay and harass an enemy's attempt to seize Singapore before the main fleet could arrive. As in 1921 these two governments expressed willingness to co-operate, while Mackenzie King of Canada was concerned to emphasise the Dominions' independence. At the end the conference adopted resolutions suggesting that each part of the Empire should be responsible for its local defence, that provision be made to safeguard communications, that facilities be provided to ensure fleet mobility, and that naval strength equal to that of any

1 CP 207(27), CAB 24/168; C 41(27), CAB 23/53; CID 236th meeting, CAB 2/5; C 39(28), CAB 23/57. From 1930 the ten-year rule was increasingly questioned: it was abandoned in 1932: CID paper 1082-B, CAB 4/21; C 19(32), CAB 23/70.

2 The Admiralty had in the summer of 1918 proposed a single imperial navy. After that was rejected by the Imperial War Cabinet the former First Sea Lord, Jellicoe, visited several of the Dominions to advise them on building up their own naval forces. See Roskill, *Naval Policy*, 274-88.

3 E 4, CAB 32/6; E 14th, 16th meetings, CAB 32/2; E 26A, 26B, 26C, 31A meetings, CAB 32/4; Cmd 1474 of 1921, *Conference of Prime Ministers and Representatives of the United Kingdom, the Dominions, and India, held in June, July, and August 1921. Summary of Proceedings and Documents.*

other power should be maintained in accordance with the Washington naval treaty - all subject to the responsibility of the individual parliaments for deciding the nature and extent of their countries' effort.[1]

The conference of 1926 left matters much as before. Bruce stressed the concern of all for imperial defence, especially naval defence since it was doubtful whether any of the Dominions could defend itself so that all had an interest in seeing that the sea routes were kept open. Britain was primarily responsible but the Dominions should try to ensure that the burden was shared a little more equally: equality of status (as it had just been defined in Balfour's famous formula) carried with it, Bruce suggested, some responsibility for sharing the common burden. He and Coates of New Zealand undertook to see what their countries could contribute towards the cost of Singapore. The other Prime Ministers made no offers.[2] The conference reaffirmed the resolutions of 1923, expressed hopes for the further limitation of armaments, and commended the progress made on co-operation.[3]

Naval building and the Anglo-Japanese Alliance, 1920 - 22

Between 1919 and 1921 the question of naval building was bound up with relations with the United States and Japan, and further complicated by inter-imperial differences.[4] At the end of 1920, when the Admiralty asked for authority to lay down new capital ships, the Committee of Imperial Defence agreed that competition with Japan would be very expensive and with the United States ruinous, so that every possible step should be taken to prevent it.[5] Fears about competition reinforced doubts about the future of capital ships, a subject on which naval as well as civilian opinion was divided. However

1 CID papers 194-C, 195-C, 196-C, CAB 5/5; E 8th, 9th, 15th meetings, CAB 32/9; Cmd 1987 of 1923, *Imperial Conference, 1923, Summary of Proceedings;* Cmd 1988 of 1923, *Imperial Conference, 1923, Appendices to the Summary of Proceedings.*

2 E 9th, 9A, 9B, 9C, 12th meetings, CAB 32/46. Bruce quoted the following figures of defence expenditure per capita to reinforce his point: Great Britain, 1924-5, 48s.10d.; 1925-6, 51s.1d. Canada, 1924-5, 5s.8d.; 1925-6, 5s.10d. Australia, 1924-5, 25s.8d.; 1925-6, 27s.2d. New Zealand, 1924-5, 11s.5d.; 1925-6, 12s.11d. South Africa, 1924-5, 2s.9d.; 1925-6, 2s.6d. The New Zealand Government later contributed £1 million to the cost of Singapore.

3 Cmd 2768 of 1926, *Imperial Conference, 1926, Summary of Proceedings.*

4 See especially William Reynolds Braisted, *The United States Navy in the Pacific 1909-1922* (Austin, Texas, 1971); Michael G. Fry, *Illusions of Security. North Atlantic Diplomacy 1918-22* (Toronto, 1972); Ian R. Nish, *Alliance in Decline. A Study in Anglo-Japanese Relations 1908-23* (London, 1972). Together these supersede all earlier works on the subject.

5 CID 134th, 135th meetings, 14 and 23 Dec. 1920, CAB 2/3.

the case against them was rejected, and in July 1921 the Admiralty were given authority to construct four.[1] The prospect of naval competition between the United States and Japan increased doubts about the future of the Anglo-Japanese alliance, which had been under consideration since 1919. American resentment at the existence of the alliance was one factor here; others were the altered power structure in the Far East with the eclipse of Russia, the possible consequences of terminating the alliance, and Japan's policy in China. In the early months of 1920 the balance of departmental opinion in the Foreign Office tended towards continuing the alliance in some form that would not embarass relations with the United States, if such a thing could be found.[2] A step towards modification was taken when on British initiative the two governments informed the League of Nations that if the alliance were continued after July 1921 it would be in a form consistent with the Covenant. This step, it was hoped, would conciliate the United States. It failed to do so, and led to confusion later as to whether it constituted notice of termination.[3]

After a more intensive and higher level discussion a report was submitted to Curzon in January 1921. Its authors thought that the central problem was Japanese policy towards China. The question for Britain was whether her traditional policy - peace, the protection of her possessions and interests, the independence and integrity of China, and equal opportunity - was sufficiently like Japan's to make renewal of the alliance as an expression of common interests and principles practicable or desirable. The answer seemed to be no. Japan's policy was one of expansion, motivated by economic necessity; it was aimed at the control of China's resources and even at hegemony in the Far East and the Pacific, and was diverging increasingly from the principles on which British policy had long been based. If it were objected that non-renewal of the alliance would remove all restraint on Japan, it must be answered that the alliance had not been an effective brake and Chinese resentment at renewal would damage British interests. Moreover if the cardinal element of British policy was to cultivate close relations with the United States and secure American co-operation in maintaining world peace, renewal of the alliance in anything like its present form

1 C 60(21), CAB 23/26. For the capital ship enquiry see Roskill, *Naval Policy*, 221, 223-5.

2 See Nish, *Alliance in Decline*, 294-9.

3 The 1911 agreement was to remain in force for ten years. If neither party gave notice of termination twelve months before the end of this period the agreement would remain in force until twelve months after one or other party did denounce it. The Foreign Office legal advisers and the Law Officers held that the notification to the League constituted notice of termination: the Japanese Government held that it did not.

would be a serious obstacle. However the arguments against leaving Japan isolated and potentially hostile were strong. The report therefore suggested that the alliance be replaced if possible by a tripartite understanding with the United States and Japan without embarrassing commitments. Only if the United States would not enter such an arrangement should there be a new Anglo-Japanese agreement which conformed to the spirit of the League of Nations.[1]

This solution was very like the one eventually reached, but it took the best part of another year to achieve. The hope that British policy could be based on securing American co-operation in maintaining world peace was fading: it had never been held by some members of the Government, among them Curzon. But whilst American hostility to the Anglo-Japanese alliance was strong the prospects of discussing naval limitation improved. As the Imperial Conference of 1921 approached it became increasingly clear that the Dominions were divided, the Canadian Government anxious to work with the United States but blind to the strategic problem in the Pacific, the Australian and New Zealand Governments much more concerned about Japanese than about American hostility. On the eve of the conference the Cabinet favoured renewing the agreement in a modified form and asking the United States to call a conference of Pacific powers.[2]

At the Imperial Conference the divisions of opinion became even more clear, with Meighen and Hughes expressing diametrically opposed views. The immediate problem of the expiry of the Anglo-Japanese agreement was solved by the Lord Chancellor's advice that the notification to the League in 1920 did not constitute notice of termination. In the end it was agreed that the future of the alliance should be left open for the time being and that Curzon should ask the United States, Japanese and Chinese Governments whether they would join in a Pacific conference.[3] Almost simultaneously the United States Government made known their intention to call a disarmament conference in Washington. There followed some weeks of confusion as to whether there should be one conference or two, or whether preliminary talks on Pacific questions could be held; but owing to American refusal the idea was abandoned and on 11 August the

1 *DBFP,* Ser. I, Vol. XIV, No. 212. See Nish, *Alliance in Decline,* 310-13.

2 C 45(21), 30 May 1921, CAB 23/25. See Nish, *Alliance in Decline,* 324-32; Fry, *Illusions of Security,* 91-120. On 23 May the United States Senate passed the Borah resolution asking the President to invite Britain and Japan to a conference for the purpose of reducing naval armaments.

3 E 2nd, 6th, 8th, 9th, 10th, 11th, 12th, 13th meetings, CAB 32/2; C 56(21), CAB 23/26. See Nish, *Alliance in Decline,* pp. 333-40; Fry, *Illusions of Security,* 121-43.

formal invitations to a single conference in Washington were issued.[1]

The initiative in Pacific and Far Eastern affairs thus visibly passed to the United States, and it was exercised by that country throughout the Washington conference which met from November 1921 to February 1922.[2] But on a tripartite understanding Britain did take some initiative. Preliminary British formulae suggested an agreement to respect the parties' possessions in East Asia and the Pacific, to support the independence of China and the principle of equal opportunity, and to consult in case of danger. On his way across the Atlantic Balfour separated the Pacific and Chinese questions and produced a draft which, he wrote, was intended '(a) to enable the Americans to be parties to a tripartite arrangement without committing themselves to military operations; (b) to bring the existing Anglo-Japanese Alliance to an end without hurting the feelings of our Ally; (c) to leave it open to us to renew a defensive alliance with Japan if she should again be threatened by Germany or Russia; (d) to frame a Treaty which will reassure our Australasian Dominions; (e) to make it impossible for American critics to suggest that our Treaty with Japan would require us to stand aside in the case of a quarrel between them and Japan, whatever the cause of that quarrel might be'.[3] The treaty announced on 10 December (a quadruple one with France included) was mainly an American production, but it fulfilled most of these intentions except that of allowing for a new defensive alliance. The parties agreed to respect each other's rights in their island possessions in the region of the Pacific and to hold a conference if controversy arose between them on any Pacific question. If their rights were threatened by any other power they would communicate with one another as to the measures to be taken. The treaty was to remain in force for ten years, and on its ratification the Anglo-Japanese agreement was to terminate.

The American initiative was most obvious in the proposals for naval limitation, which Secretary of State Hughes put forward at the opening session and were the basis of the naval treaty signed on 6 February 1922. Balfour wrote at the end that Hughes's statement was conceived in a spirit of statesmanship which raised the whole level of debate and saved the lengthy technical discussions from being lost in petty disputations.[4] What enabled the statesmanship to be shown was

1 Nish, *Alliance in Decline,* 340-51; Fry, *Illusions of Security,* 143-53.

2 For the whole conference see Braisted, *United States Navy in the Pacific,* 567-653; Nish, *Alliance in Decline,* 354-82.

3 *DBFP,* Ser. I, Vol. XIV, Nos. 326, 405, 415.

4 Op. cit. No. 565.

the strength of the American position, the fact that only three countries were really involved, and the desire of all three to limit expenditure. There was thus a considerable degree of common interest and despite the talk of an inevitable American-Japanese clash there was no immediate conflict, especially as the Americans had decided not to challenge the Japanese position in Manchuria. The limitation agreed upon applied to capital ships and aircraft carriers only, and provided for equality in tonnage for the United States and Britain, Japanese tonnage three-fifths of each of theirs, and French and Italian rather more than half the Japanese. The treaty was coupled with a standstill on fortifications and naval bases in the western Pacific, which did not apply to the Japanese home islands, Hawaii or Singapore but provided, in Hankey's words, 'a great neutralised area separating America and Japan'.[1]

Chinese issues formed the subject of a declaration of principles in the Nine-Power Treaty, in which the parties undertook to respect the sovereignty, independence and integrity of China, to provide to her the fullest opportunity to develop a stable government, to establish and maintain the principle of equal opportunity, and to refrain from seeking special privileges. With a good deal of assistance the Chinese and Japanese delegations reached agreement on Shantung. Of the resulting treaty Balfour wrote that, with the Nine-Power Treaty, it was 'in complete harmony with the general policy of His Majesty's Government . . . and will provide the foundation of a solid and enduring peace in the regions of the Pacific and the Far East'.[2]

The outcome of the Washington conference did not greatly alter the situation in the Far East. The ending of the Anglo-Japanese alliance did not bring about an immediate reversal in relations between the two countries: it had never been effective in harmonising their relations in China. The naval treaty sanctioned Japanese predominance in the north-west Pacific; but Britain could not in any case afford to keep substantial naval power in the Pacific, Hong Kong was admitted to be indefensible against serious attack, and the United States Congress would probably not have approved expenditure on fortifying Guam in any event. A bone of contention between Britain and the United States was removed, but actual co-operation did not improve. The construction of a 'solid and enduring peace' in East Asia was to depend, more than on any treaty, on what kind of China emerged from the current turmoil.

1 Hankey to Lloyd George, 13 Jan. 1922, Lloyd George Papers, F/62/1/13.
2 *DBFP*, Ser. I, Vol. XIV, No. 585.

The home defence of Great Britain, 1921 - 25

By the end of 1921 the Air Staff were ready to press for a scheme of home air defence, and when the vulnerability of the British Isles to air attack was examined the strength of the French air force was much quoted. A report from the Chiefs of Staff and other service advisers began by saying that they had not taken political considerations into account: war with France could not be regarded as within the bounds of reasonable possibility but she had been taken as the basis of the enquiry because she was the nearest neighbour and had the most powerful air force in Europe. They had discussed air attack on its own, but it was unrealistic to assume that the other services would not be involved and the military as well as the political factors which would deter France from attacking ought to be borne in mind. Even on the narrow problem the report warned that the Air Staff's picture of the scale and effects of air attack was based on forecasts of the future effectiveness of air power rather than on experience. That picture was alarming, however: the Air Staff calculated that the French air force was able to drop 1,500 tons of bombs a month on Great Britain, and that attacks on this scale would dislocate the machinery for putting the country on a war footing and would probably make it necessary to move the seat of government to the north of England. They considered that if a continuous day and night attack were maintained indefinitely, 'railway traffic would be disorganised, food supplies would be interrupted, and it is probable that after being subjected for several weeks to the strain of such an attack the population would be so demoralised that they would insist on an armistice'. The Air Staff recommended that the establishment of the air force should be increased in order to provide the basis for an offensive as well as defensive organisation; and the sub-committee agreed that if the Government decided that defence against air attack was necessary, the air force at home should be enlarged.[1]

When the Committee of Imperial Defence discussed the report Balfour said that the question was very embarrassing. If the Air Staff's estimates were correct an enemy could strike a blow which would render the country almost powerless; but from the political point of view it was almost inconceivable that such an attack should come from France. The question was so important that there must be a special meeting with the Prime Minister.[2] Balfour then wrote a paper setting out the position as he saw it - largely accepting the Air Staff's

1 CID paper 106-A, 26 Apr. 1922, CAB 3/3. Meetings and memoranda of the sub-committee, CAB 16/39.

2 CID 137th meeting, CAB 2/3.

picture - and the possible courses of action. The first was 'to leave things as they are, and trust to the impossibility of the two Allies coming to blows. The objection to this course is that the impossible may after all occur; and that even if it does not occur, the mere fear of it may, in quite conceivable circumstances, greatly weaken British diplomacy and may put temptation in the way of French statesmen which they would find it hard to resist'. The second course was to expand the air force at home. This would be expensive, but could be done.[1]

Thus the service advisers' caution in using France merely as an example was discarded, France was taken as a possible enemy, and the problem of air defence was now being discussed with a mixture of realism and distaste, which hampered the provision of a proper scheme of defence against air attack from any quarter at a time when the basis could have been laid without great cost and fixed the Air Staff's mind on a most improbable enemy. Trenchard, however, was not anxious for a very rapid expansion. At the full-scale meeting of the Committee of Imperial Defence on 5 July, with Lloyd George in the chair and the Chancellor of the Exchequer present, he expounded two alternative schemes providing for six or for fifteen additional squadrons plus auxiliary squadrons. Lloyd George, who had adopted Balfour's view of the French threat, doubted whether either was enough since the French were said to have 220 squadrons.[2] After further meetings and discussions of cost the Committee agreed to recommend a scheme to provide 501 aircraft for home defence at a cost of £2 million a year. Further expansion was to be considered in the light of the financial situation in the following year and of the air policy of other countries. The Cabinet accepted the recommendation.[3]

When the problem was reconsidered in 1923 the Air Staff produced an alarming and exaggerated estimate of French air strength and of the weight of bombs that could be dropped on England. France was credited with a metropolitan air force of 946 aircraft, of which 600 were said to be capable of delivering 160 tons of bombs every twenty-four hours. This calculation was based on the assumption that each aircraft could make two sorties every twenty-four hours, that all reached their objectives, and that none was lost. In fact France had a first-line bomber strength of 320, with approximately the same number

1 CID paper 108-A, 29 May 1922, CAB 3/3.

2 CID 158th meeting, CAB 2/3.

3 CID papers 109-A, 111-A, CAB 3/3; CID 162nd, 163rd meetings, CAB 2/3; C 43(22), 3 Aug. 1922, CAB 23/30. See Basil Collier, *The Defence of the United Kingdom,* History of the Second World War, United Kingdom Military Series (London, 1957), Ch. I.

of fighters: the remainder were observation machines which the French did not regard as combat aircraft.[1] In addition, as the General Staff were quick to point out, the Air Staff ignored such considerations as French preoccupation with Germany.[2] Ministers, however, were impressed by the Air Staff's figures and agreed to recommend that the home defence air force should be built up to 600 first-line aircraft. Inevitably the fact that the French air force was being used as the yardstick became publicly known, and before the recommendation was accepted the Cabinet agreed that Salisbury should state in Parliament that talk of attack by France was deprecated and the Government could not conceive of anything worse than competition with her; but they would make necessary provision for defence and the strength of the R.A.F. would probably be increased.[3]

In the spring of 1924, when asked to comment on the implications of French control over the Rhineland, the Air Staff still talked in terms of French rather than continental air attack.[4] But in 1925 the problem of diverting shipping from the Channel in wartime was looked at in a wider context. In the first instance the Chiefs of Staff suggested that the necessity for diverting shipping would only arise in the case of war with France, and this was so unlikely to happen suddenly that early expenditure on preparations would not be justified.[5] Chamberlain gave it as his considered opinion that France would never risk war with Britain, or at any rate not until her population was as great as Germany's. France needed a strong friend on one side or the other, and Britain was really her sheet anchor notwithstanding her continental alliances. It was Hankey who pointed out that the shipping problem might also arise in case of war with Germany; and Chamberlain then said that he thought the moral of the report was that any future war should be kept as far away from the Channel as possible. The Chiefs of Staff were asked to prepare another paper which could be sent to the Dominions, to reinforce the argument for the western security pact.[6]

This second study began by stating that in the event of war with a nation occupying the continental coasts of the Channel Britain would be exposed to attacks on her sea communications and to serious danger

1 ND 4, ND 10, CAB 21/260. Actual French figures, from the Service Historique de l'Armée de l'Air, in Roskill, *Naval Policy,* 383, n.

2 ND 31, CAB 21/261.

3 Sub-Committee on National and Imperial Defence, 10th, 11th meetings, 16 May, 5 Jun. 1923, CAB 21/262; C 25(23), 9 May, CAB 23/45; C 32(23), CAB 23/46; *HL Deb.,* 5th ser., Vol. 54, cols. 83-8.

4 See above, p. 59 and n. 3.

5 CID paper 610-B, 7 May 1925, CAB 4/13.

6 CID 200th meeting, 22 Jun. 1925, CAB 2/4.

from the air. If France were the enemy, or an enemy power had control of France, shipping might have to be diverted from the Mediterranean as well. Britain would be immediately affected but the whole Empire would feel the indirect effects. Provided that the armed forces were maintained at proper strength, the Chiefs of Staff had no doubt that the nation would come through successfully, but the loss would be incalculable. From the defence point of view, therefore, foreign policy ought to be directed towards averting the possibility of such attack. The contingency of war with France was indeed remote; but the danger might arise

> if Germany (either with or without the support of Russia or other nations) were to gain successes commensurate with those obtained at the outset of the late war and, as a result, occupy the coasts of North France, Belgium or Holland. . .An advance which did not bring Germany so far as the coastline would be less dangerous since, in that event, whatever naval menace Germany might at that time be able to exert would not be accentuated and, so far as the aerial menace is concerned, the attacking aircraft would have to run the gauntlet of our own and our allies' air force and defences before approaching this country.
>
> From the point of view of defence, therefore, it is important that our foreign policy should provide, *inter alia,* first, for cordial relations with France and Belgium, and, second, that war shall be kept as far as possible from the English Channel, the Straits of Dover, and the southern shores of the North Sea.
>
> The above remarks are not directed primarily to the proposed Quadruple Pact, which, we are well aware, is based on considerations of wider policy than those with which we are dealing in the present Memorandum. In so much, however, as the proposed Pact fulfils the requirements of a sound national defence mentioned in the preceding paragraph, we welcome it from the point of view of defence policy. We do so, however, on the general understanding that the conclusion of agreements of this kind will not be regarded as justifying either a reduction of our defence forces below the level essential for the Empire's security or the relinquishment of the continuous study of the problems of Imperial Defence.[1]

Despite the warning in the last sentence the first result for defence policy of the Locarno treaties was a slowing down in the expansion of the home defence air force. At the end of 1925 the Cabinet agreed that completion of the programme could be postponed from 1929 to 1936.[2]

Singapore and the naval programme, 1925 - 26

The decision to develop a naval base at Singapore was taken in 1921 before the future of the Anglo-Japanese alliance and of capital ship limitation was known. The reason for it was that although there was no

1 CID paper 625-B, 3 Jul. 1925, CAB 4/13.

2 CP 421(25), 498(25), CAB 24/175; C 52(25), C 57(25), CAB 23/51.

expectation of keeping a large fleet in the Pacific in peacetime, a base with repair facilities and reserves of fuel was necessary if the fleet were to be able to operate there at all. There was no dockyard east of Malta capable of taking modern capital ships; Sydney was too far from a possible theatre of operations; Hong Kong was too vulnerable. The effect on Japan of developing a base in the Far East was considered, but it was argued that it would be less serious if the work were started soon and done gradually than if it were begun later when relations might be less good. In explaining the recommendation to the Cabinet Balfour said that the base would be needed even if the Anglo-Japanese alliance were renewed: they could not continue in a situation where it was impossible for whatever fleet it was decided to maintain to be used in the area where it was most likely to be needed. The Cabinet approved the development on the understanding that no considerable expenditure was likely for the next two years.[1]

Singapore was exempted from the standstill on fortifications and bases agreed at the Washington conference; but in the financial climate of 1922 there were proposals that it, and the creation of oil reserves for the navy, should be re-examined. Lee and Beatty, the First Sea Lord, explained that as a result of the Washington treaties the United States could no longer defend her interests in the western Pacific but Britain would have to try to defend them since she could not afford to see Japan seize the Philippines. This could only be done by the fleet, and although under the present fuel programme it would be able to reach Singapore in 1925 it would not be able to operate freely when it got there.[2] The Committee of Imperial Defence decided to recommend reaffirmation of the decision to develop the base at Singapore on the understanding that no considerable expenditure would be involved for the next two years. They recommended that completion of the fuel reserve on the route to the east could not prudently be delayed beyond 1931.[3]

Since no work had yet begun it was the idea of the base that remained a subject of contention. So far as the Dominions were concerned Australia and New Zealand, who were directly interested, disapproved the Labour Government's decision to abandon construction - a decision taken not as a result of strategic reappraisal but

1 CID paper 143-C, CAB 5/4. CID 140th, 141st meetings, 10 and 13 Jun. 1921, CAB 2/3; CP 3039, CAB 24/125; C 50(21), 16 Jun., CAB 23/26. See Roskill, *Naval Policy*, 289-91.

2 CID 161st meeting, CAB 2/3.

3 CID 168th meeting, CAB 2/3; C 11(23), 21 Feb. 1923, CAB 23/35. See Roskill, *Naval Policy*, 347-9. In February 1924 the date for completing the fuel reserve was put off to 1937: CID 181st meeting, CAB 2/4.

to serve the cause of international understanding and disarmament - whereas Smuts applauded it.[1] The news that Singapore was being reconsidered was welcomed in Japan, and after the decision was announced the British Ambassador, Eliot, wrote to MacDonald that it had had an excellent effect. Well-informed Japanese, he said, had not regarded Singapore as a threat but they had been hurt that their former ally had taken the first opportunity to create fortifications as near to Japan as the Washington treaty allowed, and had been angry at British statements that the base was needed on account of possible Japanese activity in the Pacific. Eliot could see no sign of an aggressive Japanese southward policy: even on the mainland Japanese intentions were, he thought, limited. The Japanese wanted a special position in north China and were anxious to extend their influence in Manchuria. In China proper they were chiefly interested in a preferential commercial position: they would prefer China to remain weak, but not so weak as to fall a prey to foreign powers. Eliot believed that the Japanese would for some time to come make considerable concessions rather than break away from the other powers.[2]

During the summer of 1924 Japanese-American relations were strained by the new United States immigration bill and the Japanese became, in Eliot's view, more assertive and more suspicious about reports of Anglo-American consultation over the civil war in China. No such consultation had taken place and the Foreign Office tried to soothe the Japanese suspicions; but they acknowledged that co-operation with Japan had become very difficult owing to the divergence between the two countries' interests in China.[3] It was suggested that MacDonald should speak to the Japanese Ambassador, but Parliament was dissolved before an opportunity arose. On entering office Chamberlain took up the suggestion and told the Ambassador that he desired close co-operation in Chinese affairs and would welcome Japanese views on a constructive policy. The Ambassador asked about Singapore and said that there would be anxiety in Japan if the new Government took up the project again. Chamberlain replied that if they decided to resume construction the Japanese must not think that it was with any

1 CID paper 192-C, CAB 5/5; C 14(24), C 15(24), C 21(24), CAB 23/47; R S (24), 1st and 2nd meetings, CAB 27/236; *HC Deb.*, 5th ser., Vol. 171, cols. 317-25. See Roskill, *Naval Policy*, 404-06, 419-22. The correspondence with the Dominion and Indian Governments was published in Cmd 2083 of 1924, *Singapore Naval Base. Correspondence with the Self-Governing Dominions and India regarding the development of Singapore Naval Base.*

2 Eliot to MacDonald, 3 May 1924, FO 800/219.

3 Eliot to FO, 12 Sep. 1924, F 3099/19/10, FO 371/10244; Eliot to MacDonald, 19 Sep., FO 800/219; FO to Eliot, 22 Sep.; minute by Wellesley, 26 Sep.; Eliot to FO, 28 Sep., 3 Oct,, 30 Oct., F 3099, 3281, 3245, 3582, 3638/19/10, FO 371/10244-5.

unfriendly intention towards them. Singapore was an essential link in the communications between Britain and Australia and New Zealand, and no British Government of any party could ever plan a deliberate attack on another country.[1]

The new Government soon decided in principle to proceed with Singapore, but the rate of development was to be examined again.[2] The question was then caught up in Churchill's attack on the naval programme and his proposal that the Committee of Imperial Defence should reappraise the dangers to which the Empire was exposed. The head of the Far Eastern Department in the Foreign Office, Wellesley, advised Chamberlain that Singapore was bound up with the problem of Japanese policy in China, which undeniably was to keep China weak and diminish the influence of other countries. The chief restraint on Japan was British and American influence, but it was not effective: American naval power had been eliminated from the western Pacific and if Singapore were abandoned British power would disappear too. The Japanese did not like the idea of the base but recognised that Britain had a right to build it. There was therefore a good deal to be said for undertaking the construction now when it did not represent a threat to Japan. On the other hand Wellesley regarded the chance of war in the Pacific as remote. Japan did not want to be politically isolated and at present had no alternative to some degree of co-operation with Britain and the United States: a combination with Russia and Germany was not inconceivable but was not at present on the horizon. Japan was not now in a position to make war on Britain, and it seemed almost inconceivable that she should wish to do so. The conflict of interests that existed in China was not of a kind likely to lead to war. In short, it would be unreasonable to regard Japan as an active enemy and to start building against her, but it was important to British interests that Japan should not be the only power with strength in the Pacific.[3]

Chamberlain repeated this advice to the Committee of Imperial Defence and suggested that something be done to assuage Japanese feelings, such as statements that the base was not directed against Japan and the two countries were still friends.[4] After further examina-

1 FO to Eliot, 14 and 21 Nov. 1924, F 3582, 3833/19/10, FO 371/10246. Chamberlain suggested to the United States Government that consultation on China was needed and they should take the initiative with the Japanese: FO to Howard, 14 Nov.; Chamberlain to Howard, 19 Nov.; FO to Howard, 25 Nov., 2 Dec.; Howard to Chamberlain, 3 Dec., F 3871, 3701, 3945, 3983, 4085/19/10, FO 371/10245-7.

2 CP 502(24), 534(24), CAB 24/169; C 64(24), CAB 23/49; *HC Deb.*, 5th ser., Vol. 179, col. 49. See Roskill, *Naval Policy*, 432.

3 Memoranda by Wellesley, 1 Jan. 1925, F 26, 27/9/61, FO 371/10958.

4 CID 193rd meeting, CAB 2/4. Bridgeman had already made a speech of the

tion of the proposed sites for the base and the programme of construction, the expenditure of £787,000 over the next three years on preparations for the floating dock was approved by the Cabinet: it was a modest start.[1] At the same time Chamberlain set out to Eliot the Government's policy on Singapore and towards Japan. The fleet, he wrote, must be able to go to the Far East, and therefore there must be a repair base. Singapore was at the centre of a vast area of British possessions and British trade, and 2,300 miles from Japan. He wanted to continue close friendship and co-operation with Japan: he could not believe that for the Japanese this must mean the disarmament of British naval power from Suez eastwards; for his part he would do anything he could to give expression to a sense of special friendliness.[2]

Churchill's campaign on naval building was, however, only just beginning. After an exchange of Cabinet papers between him and Bridgeman, naval estimates were presented to Parliament containing nothing for new construction: this was to be examined by another Cabinet committee.[3] To provide the basis for its work the Committee of Imperial Defence again considered naval policy with special reference to the possibility of war with Japan and the rate at which the Singapore base should be developed. The Foreign Office again advised that aggressive action by Japan such as might involve Britain in war in the Pacific was not seriously to be apprehended in the next ten years; but Chamberlain pointed out that this was not the same as saying that there was no need to make in the next ten years any preparations for a war later. He hoped that he would be able to repeat the same advice in three years' time, but he might then have to say that it would be advisable to be ready for war at the end of ten years. The Committee agreed that the one-power standard should be maintained and that preliminary arrangements to establish docking facilities at Singapore and develop oil fuel installations on the route to the east should proceed, but there was no need to make preparations involving additional expenditure for placing at Singapore a British battle fleet superior or at least equal to the Japanese sea-going navy. This decision was to be reviewed each year.[4]

kind suggested, and he and Baldwin made warm references to Japan in the House of Commons later: *The Times,* 17 Dec. 1924; *HC Deb.,* 5th ser., Vol. 180, col. 1590; Vol. 181, cols. 2525-9; Vol. 182, col. 136.

1 CP 124(25), CAB 24/171; C 12(25), 2 Mar. 1925, CAB 23/49, See Roskill, *Naval Policy,* 459-61; Gilbert, *Winston S. Churchill,* Vol. V, Chs. 4, 6.

2 FO to Eliot, 25 Feb. and 5 Mar. 1925, F 652, 595/9/61, FO 371/10958.

3 CP 39(25), 67(25), 71(25), CAB 24/171. See Roskill, *Naval Policy,* 445-9.

4 CID 198th, 199th meetings, CAB 2/4; C 24(25), CAB 23/50. See above, p. 160.

The Cabinet committee on the building programme, under Birkenhead, met from March to June 1925, most of the meetings being taken up by a ding-dong argument between Churchill and Beatty. Since their views could not be reconciled the Committee's report was signed only by the other members. When it was presented to the Cabinet Chamberlain was again asked whether he held that war with Japan was unlikely in the next ten years. He replied that he did, but could give no guarantee. The outcome was a modest five-year building programme and the appointment of a Treasury committee on economies in the fighting services.[1]

From time to time during 1924 there was talk in the United States of further limitation of naval armaments, but it did not originate from the Administration who were sceptical about the prospects for another conference. After the autumn elections, however, Howard reported that Hughes was anxious to see naval expenditure reduced and might call for a conference soon.[2] The British were ready to welcome a new conference in the hope that it might lead to further economy, and on 18 February 1925 the Cabinet approved, subject to Dominion concurrence, instructions to Howard so to inform Hughes.[3] However by the time the Dominion replies (generally welcoming the idea) were received the steam seemed to have gone out of the project in Washington, the Japanese had revealed doubts, and the French soon did so. Chamberlain then wrote to Howard that in view of this the despatch would probably not be sent. But if the new Secretary of State, Kellogg, asked for the British views he could say that the Government were prepared to discuss the size and armament of cruisers and destroyers, the armament of aircraft carriers, and the number, size and armament of submarines.[4] The Americans themselves dropped the idea of a conference, and it then became swallowed up for the time being in the preparations for the League of Nations discussion of disarmament.

1 NP (25), proceedings, CAB 27/273; report, CP 342(25), CP 357(25), CAB 24/174; C 37(25), C 38(25), C 39(25), CAB 23/50; *HC Deb.*, 5th ser., Vol. 186, cols. 2421-3. See Roskill, *Naval Policy,* 450-3. In May 1928 the First Sea Lord stated that numerically the required standard could be reached in 1936 provided the 1925 building programme was continued undiminished and capital ship replacements begun when international agreements allowed, although destroyers and cruisers would have to be kept in service longer than their fully efficient life; but the current rate of accumulation of the oil fuel reserve would not produce the total required within thirty years, and work on Singapore was in arrears: COS 141, CAB 53/14. Construction of the base was slowed down again in 1929.

2 Howard to Chamberlain, 22 Dec. 1924, A 77/49/45, FO 371/10636.

3 CP 87(25), CAB 24/171; C 9(25), CAB 23/49.

4 Chamberlain to Howard, 18 and 30 Mar. 1925, A 1478, 1462/49/45, FO 371/10736.

Already before the Assembly, on 23 September 1925, adopted the resolution asking the Council to make a preliminary study with a view to calling a disarmament conference, the Cabinet had decided to begin an enquiry into the problem.[1] By the time the Council in December adopted proposals for a preparatory commission the Cabinet, with a good deal of doubt as to the outcome, had decided that the Committee of Imperial Defence should study proposals and eventually draw up instructions for the British representatives.[2] The instructions drawn up in the spring of 1926 described the state of British armaments and the Government's attitude. The navy had been reduced as a result of the Washington treaties; further efforts to restrict submarines were desirable; but in view of the length and vulnerability of Britain's trade routes the Empire must have special treatment with regard to cruisers. The army was notoriously small in relation to its commitments and in comparison with those of other countries: it did not seem capable of reduction. The air force had been reduced to almost nothing after the war. It was now being built up again to a point of comparability with that of the nearest neighbour, but the Government would welcome any scheme which would give equality with other countries and were ready to consider specific arrangements with one or more European countries.[3]

The defence of India, 1922 - 27

The purposes for which the army in India was maintained were defence against external aggression and preservation of internal order, and in the early 1920s the latter loomed larger than the former. Even in 1919 and 1920, when Bolshevik incursion into the Caucasus, Persia and Afghanistan caused Curzon, in particular, great anxiety, the danger was seen as disorder and upheaval on the borders of India rather than as attack on India. Thus ministers were apparently satisfied with a statement in a report of June 1922 that in the financial and military circumstances it was not possible to base the defence of the frontier on any plan of campaign involving an advance in force to or towards Kabul. India was expected to pay normal defence expenditure from her own resources; but as before 1914, reinforcements in case of a war would have to come from Britain. The principle was also accepted that since India was, after the Montagu-Chelmsford reforms of 1919,

1 CP 365(25), CAB 24/174; C 41(25), CAB 23/50.

2 CID papers 628-B, 634-B, 641-B, 644-B, 647-B, 649-B, CAB 4/13; CP 454(25), CAB 24/175; C 52(25), C 57(25), CAB 23/51. CID 205th, 206th meetings, CAB 2/4.

3 CID paper 682-B, CAB 4/14; CID 212th meeting, CAB 2/4; C 19(26), CAB 23/52. See *DBFP,* Ser. IA, Vol. II, No. 2, n. 2. The early stages of the Preparatory Commission are discussed in Chapter 7.

launched on the long road towards self-government, the army in India would not be treated as though it were absolutely at the British Government's disposal for service overseas and should not be employed outside the Indian Empire, except in the gravest emergency, without consultation with the Governor-General in Council.[1]

It was not long, however, before requirements in India were considered again. Nicolson's characterisation of Russia as an Asian rather than a European problem has been mentioned,[2] and it was on the borders of India that in 1926 the problem seemed to become acute.[3] Reports of tension between the Soviet Union and Afghanistan, in particular, alarmed Birkenhead and Churchill. They said at a meeting of the Committee of Imperial Defence on 22 July that before long the Soviet Union might be operating on the Indian frontier, and they regarded conflict as inevitable. Churchill said that India could not be defended against Russia by military means but only by bringing into operation the great counterpoise of alliances and agreements: he regretted the loss of the Japanese alliance. Chamberlain was doubtful whether an attempt to extend British influence in Afghanistan might not make matters worse, and stressed that the Russians were more afraid of being attacked than likely to engage in open warfare.[4]

Tyrrell, in a memorandum written a few days later, agreed that 'Russia is the enemy' (whose chief weapon, however, was 'ruthless propaganda all over the world') and endorsed the opinion that Britain should act with Japan against 'Russian aggression'. But he also pointed out that reconstitution of the Anglo-Japanese alliance was impracticable and that war with the Soviet Union was impossible owing both to lack of means and to public opinion.[5] The Cabinet were not so alarmed as to take any immediate decisions, but agreed that Birkenhead should consult the Viceroy about the state of India's defences.[6] The answers to these enquiries were not encouraging, and in March 1927 at Birken-

1 CID papers 125-D, 130-D, CAB 6/4; CID 160th, 170th meetings, CAB 2/3. For the situation in 1919-20 see Ullman, *The Anglo-Soviet Accord,* Part III.

2 See above, p. 75.

3 To some extent also in China, where the Soviet political and military advisers were assumed to be fomenting the Canton Government's hostility to Britain, expressed in 1925-6 in an anti-British boycott which damaged British trade, and where the civil war situation in 1926-7 required the despatch of additional troops. But Chamberlain told the Cabinet on 13 December 1926 that the Kuomintang was not 'fundamentally Bolshevist' in character and his colleagues ought not to identify the two in their speeches: C 65(26), CAB 23/53.

4 CID papers 142-D, 143-D, 144-D, CAB 6/5; C 42(26), CAB 23/52; CID 215th meeting, CAB 2/4.

5 CP 303(26), CAB 24/181; *DBFP,* Ser. IA, Vol. II, No. 103.

6 C 49(26), 30 Jul. 1926, CAB 23/53.

head's instance the Committee of Imperial Defence set up a sub-committee to consider whether the integrity of Afghanistan was still as important a British interest as it had been thought in the early years of the century and, if it was, what could be done to defeat or reduce the risk of a Soviet incursion into the northern part of the country.[1] On the assumption that a Soviet takeover would have to be resisted, the General Staff calculated that the field army in India (four divisions and four cavalry brigades) would be quite inadequate. Nineteen divisions (five regular and fourteen Territorial Army) could be provided from Britain by the end of one year from the outbreak of war, but these were the total of the existing cadres and no more expansion, or replacements, would be possible without introducing conscription.[2] The forces in India were not only inadequate in numbers: they were seriously deficient in equipment. The General Staff reckoned that mobilisation of the field army would take nearly five months, chiefly owing to lack of standing transport. There were no anti-aircraft guns, no tanks, and no protection against gas; the signals were backward and gun ammunition was short. As for the air force, there were two bomber squadrons and four army co-operation squadrons, all equipped with wartime types of aircraft which could not fly high enough to cross the Hindu Kush.[3]

While on their side the Soviet leaders were announcing expectation of an attack by Britain, the sub-committee spent a number of meetings receiving advice on the situation in Afghanistan and on Soviet policy, and considering Birkenhead's questions. Sir Francis Humphrys, the British Minister in Kabul, and a former military attaché there, Major Dodd, advised that Afghanistan was not about to fall into Soviet hands and would now rather like some British support. Hodgson, returned from Moscow after the breach of diplomatic relations in May, advised that the Russians were obsessed by fear of encirclement and aggression but had neither the means nor the will to take aggressive action themselves. The Red Army and air force, he said, were improving and could without difficulty transport troops to Afghanistan; but while it might be said that for political reasons and in a military sense the army was strong for defence, for political and military reasons it was not a good weapon for aggression.[4]

1 CID paper 149-C, CAB 6/5; CID 223rd meeting, 17 Mar. 1927, CAB 2/5.

2 Defence of India Sub-Committee, DI 3A, DI 5, CAB 16/83. The field army was one of three components of the army in India: the others were the covering troops, intended to secure the concentration of the field army and keep the peace in the frontier area, and the internal security troops, intended to keep order in the interior.

3 DI 8, DI 9, 4 May 1927, CAB 16/83.

4 DI 2nd, 4th, 9th, 10th meetings, CAB 16/83. For the Soviet war scare in 1927 see Adam B. Ulam, *Expansion and Coexistence. The History of Soviet*

Meeting the deficiences in India was mainly a matter of who was to pay. Lord Reading, recently Viceroy, said that the only reason why the Russians might attack India was that it was British, and India could not be expected to bear the whole cost of putting the army on a footing to take part in a war on the scale contemplated. Sir Arthur Hirtzel of the India Office said that the net military expenditure of the Government of India had been reduced (from about three-eighths of total net revenue in the five years before the war to about five-sixteenths), but demand for civil expenditure was rising and shortage of money for the so-called 'nation-building' departments was largely responsible for the failure of reforms. Since 1917 the British Government, as well as the Government of India, had eliminated Russia as a factor in the defence problem: if she were to be restored as the main factor the Government of India would argue, as in the past, that no heavier obligation should be laid on them than that of being ready to do the minimum necessary before reinforcements arrived. The British ministers concerned, on the other hand, argued that Britain had to pay for maintaining the reinforcements, that improving efficiency need not cost much if economies were made elsewhere, and that the Exchequer should not be asked to contribute.[1]

As for what else could be done, study showed that there was very little means of putting pressure on the Soviet Union anywhere else. The Chiefs of Staff, assuming that in such a war Britain would have no allies (which they regarded as the most probable as well as the most difficult case), concluded that naval operations such as raids in the Baltic and the Black Sea and air operations from Iraq or from ships, might possibly distract the Soviet Union but would not reduce by one man the number of troops she could despatch to or deploy in Afghanistan. All that needed to be said about the army was that operations conducted by the British Empire against European Russia would have no effect whatever on the situation in Asia. If other powers did become involved the one which from a military point of view would be the most useful was Japan, but even she could not prevent the Soviet Union from concentrating on the borders of Afghanistan the largest force which could be maintained by the existing communications.[2] A study of possible economic pressure produced equally negative results: the Soviet Union was self-sufficient

Foreign Policy 1917-1967 (New York and London, 1968), 162-7; John Erickson, *The Soviet High Command* (London, 1962), Chapter 10.

1 DI 6th, 7th, 13th meetings, CAB 16/83.

2 DI 16, CAB 16/83. Sir Denys Bray, Foreign Secretary to the Government of India, when asked by Churchill whether the Anglo-Japanese alliance had been a great relief to the Government of India, replied that it had not; but the Anglo-Russian agreement of 1907 had been: CID 223rd meeting, CAB 2/5.

in food; the few vital raw materials which she needed to import could be bought in neutral countries; necessary machinery could be supplied by Germany or the United States; cutting off credit by Britain alone would be ineffective; closing the British market to Soviet exports would cause difficulty but no more. In short, the British Empire and the Soviet Union were practically independent of each other so far as vital necessities were concerned, and a British blockade was most unlikely to be effective. The possible effect of a blockade in which all the Soviet Union's European neighbours joined, as in the case of coercive action by the League, was not studied at all.[1]

Eventually the sub-committee reported that although the Soviet Union, if she decided on aggressive action, must be regarded at least numerically as a first-class power, Afghanistan had not fallen under her influence and Hodgson's view that she was not at present going to take aggressive action was accepted. The danger to India was therefore not imminent. This they thought fortunate, since the army and air force in India were not capable of filling the role assigned to them in the Chief of the Imperial General Staff's plan for an advance into Afghanistan, since it was clear that no operations elsewhere could have important results, and since even intervention by Japan could not affect Soviet operations against India through Afghanistan. All the same the sub-committee thought that any substantial Russian encroachment into Afghanistan would be as dangerous to India and general British interests as in the past; and they were satisfied that provided the Empire made the necessary effort it would be possible, not to prevent a temporary Russian occupation of northern Afghanistan but to turn them out as a result of a more or less prolonged war. They therefore proposed to reaffirm that Britain's obligation to defend the independence and integrity of Afghanistan was unimpaired and if necessary she would declare war on the Soviet Union. The General Staff had been told not to count on conscription being introduced during the first year of such a war, but to assume that enough volunteers would be forthcoming. The Government must consider how the deficiencies in the forces in India could be remedied, since the Government of India could not be expected to bear the whole cost. Recommendations were made on political action (such as help with communications) that could be taken to keep Afghanistan friendly.[2]

These recommendations were accepted by the Cabinet in February 1928, and the sub-committee remained in being to receive progress

1 DI 34, CAB 16/83.

2 CID paper 158-D, 19 Dec. 1927, CAB 6/5; CID 232nd meeting, 26 Jan. 1928, CAB 2/5.

reports on the defence of India. [1] Thus the phantom of Soviet military aggression in Asia provided a stimulus to improving the capacity of the forces in India. But at a time when political and communal difficulties in India were increasing, the start of 'indianisation', while politically desirable, exposed the Indian Army, in the War Office's view, to the risk of deterioration in efficiency to the point where it might not be reliable in actual warfare or even for the maintenance of internal order. [2] The cost of making good any such deficiency was bound to fall on Britain.

1 CP 26(28), CAB 24/192; C 11(28), CAB 23/57.
2 CID paper 160-D, 1 Jan. 1928, CAB 6/5.

7

THE CONSEQUENCES OF LOCARNO 1926 – 27

In a number of statements on British foreign policy made during 1926 Locarno was treated as the end of postwar troubles and the beginning of a new era in Europe, with the return of Germany to the comity of nations and the inauguration of an international spirit which might spread throughout the continent. Thus speaking at the Imperial Conference just over a year after the initialling of the treaties, Chamberlain said: 'The Locarno settlement is at once the sign and the cause of a new spirit in Europe. We hope that it marks the end, or the beginning of the end, of the fear and distrust which found expression for so long in a policy of threats and sanctions on one side and sullen resentment on the other'.[1] Papers prepared for the conference by the Foreign Office were even more optimistic. The disputes arising from the execution of the Treaty of Versailles were said to be virtually at an end. The policies of France and Germany had taken a new turn: no one in either country believed it possible to return to the old days, and few wished to do so. Locarno might prove an all important step on the road to general disarmament. The effect was spreading among other countries: arbitration treaties had become the fashion and it was not fantastic to hope that in the next few years the existing alliances might be replaced by mutual non-aggression agreements between former enemies. Locarno was in large measure a British achievement and was recognised as such by the other parties. As a result: 'British friendship is cultivated, British counsel asked, British aid sought, and as in the days of Castlereagh, Great Britain stands forth again as the moderator and peacemaker of the new Europe created by the Great War'.[2]

Official optimism of this kind was at least in part put on for public consumption. In private it was less complete; and even in public the need for effort to foster the new spirit was often emphasised. But at least the statements identified the areas where, if it was real, the new spirit would have to show itself.

German disarmament and the Rhineland, 1926 - 27

During the negotiations of October-November 1925 on the points of German disarmament that must be settled, the Allies undertook

1 E 118, CAB 32/47; E 2nd and 3rd meetings, CAB 32/46; *DBFP*, Ser. IA, Vol. II, Appendix.

2 E 117, CAB 32/47; *DBFP*, Ser. IA, Vol. I, No. 1.

that the Military Control Commission would be withdrawn as soon as the remaining tasks were completed. The Germans were anxious to see the Control Commission wound up, but for them the timing of its withdrawal was connected with entry into the League and the opportunity to discuss future supervision.[1] At the beginning of February 1926 they suggested that the Commission should be withdrawn in return for the Reichstag's approval of the application for membership of the League. But after the fiasco at Geneva in March they no longer desired early withdrawal lest they be confronted by the League supervision scheme of 1924. Since execution of the outstanding points was by no means complete in the summer there was little prospect of early withdrawal unless the Allies decided to make further concessions on policy grounds. The Foreign Office were doubtful whether League investigation could ever be applied, but to meet French anxiety about the demilitarised zone Chamberlain suggested to Briand that in due course the Germans might be asked whether they would accept some permanent organ in the Rhineland as part of a larger settlement.[2] When in August the Ambassadors' Conference sent Hoesch a note calling for the early execution of the points still delayed, the British refused to agree to a statement that if results were not obtained the Control Commission would remain. Lampson would have liked to tell the French that Britain was unwilling to continue control after September whatever happened.[3]

After Germany entered the League in September and the Locarno treaties came into force, both the British and the Germans were eager to see the work of the Control Commission wound up by the end of the year. The remaining points of difficulty were the organisation and size of the Schutzpolizei, the definition of war material in German legislation on import and export, the state of fortifications on the eastern frontier, and legislation forbidding military activity by the nationalist associations. Final negotiations began on 20 November but had not been concluded by the time that the Foreign Ministers met at the League Council in December. After seeing Briand on his way to Geneva Chamberlain was hopeful of agreement; and from his first conversation with Stresemann he concluded that they would be 'very clumsy' if they could not arrange for the early end of control and the entry into force of the League scheme.[4] While the representatives

1 For the German position see Salewski, *Entwaffnung und Militärkontrolle,* 329-32. For the negotiations of the spring and summer, op. cit. 332-42; documents in *DBFP,* Ser. IA, Vols. I-II and *ADAP,* Vol. I.1.

2 *DBFP,* Ser. IA, Vol. I, Nos. 210, n.2, 236.

3 Op. cit. Vol. II, Nos. 115, 120, 121, 124, 127, 130, 139, 178; minute by Lampson, 5 Aug. 1926, C 8689/436/18, FO 371/11289.

4 *DBFP,* Ser. IA, Vol. II, Nos. 318, 326.

in Paris continued to wrestle with fortifications and war material, the ministers at Geneva discussed League control and supervision in the demilitarised zone. Certain German doubts about the League scheme were considered, but no one showed any wish to examine it *de novo*. Stresemann now preferred to avoid discussion, believing that time would work in Germany's favour.[1] On supervision in the Rhineland Briand admitted that Article 213 of the Treaty of Versailles did not provide for permanent or special organs, but he suggested that German agreement to some unobtrusive organisation which could observe and report any infraction of demilitarisation might, by calming French fears, facilitate an earlier end to the occupation. Stresemann did not commit himself and left it to Schubert to raise objections.[2]

After further discussions on the disarmament questions it was agreed that the Control Commission would be withdrawn on 31 January 1927, leaving only some experts in Berlin. If by that date the remaining questions had not been settled they would be referred to the Council of the League. Since neither side was keen to do this, agreement was reached in time.[3] The final stages were not held up by the revelations about German-Soviet military collaboration, made in the *Manchester Guardian* and taken up by the Social Democratic press in Germany. The disclosures seem to have caused no stir in British official quarters. A certain amount had always been known about the collaboration; now it appears to have been regarded as a thing of the past; and the conviction prevailed that in any case Germany could not be kept subject to control.[4] There seems to have been no further discussion of a special organ in the Rhineland until the autumn of 1928. The final report of the Control Commission, deposited with the League and detailing the extent to which the military clauses of the peace treaty had and had not been executed, was never published.[5]

Another aspect of German disarmament wound up after some months of negotiation was the control of aviation. The Aeronautical Commission of Control had been withdrawn from Germany in 1922 and replaced by a set of regulations known as the 'nine rules' and by a Committee

1 *ADAP,* Vol. I.2, No. 198.

2 Op. cit. Nos. 233, 234, 237, 240, 242, 244; *DBFP,* Ser. IA, Vol. II, No. 333.

3 *DBFP,* Ser. IA, Vol. II, Nos. 352-5 and Ch. III, *passim; ADAP,* Vol. I.2, Nos. 251, 254, 257, 258, 260, 261; Vol. IV, Nos. 7-86, *passim;* Salewski, *Entwaffnung und Militärkontrolle,* 358-71; John P. Fox, 'Britain and the Inter-Allied Military Commission of Control', *Journal of Contemporary History* 4 (1969), No. 2, 143-64.

4 *DBFP,* Ser. IA, Vol. II, Nos. 334, 415; Vol. III, Nos. 20, 24; *ADAP,* Vol. I.2, Nos. 158, 270.

5 For a summary see Salewski, *Entwaffnung und Militärkontrolle,* 375-8.

of Guarantees, which was in turn to be reconsidered when the Cologne zone was evacuated. At the end of November 1925 the German Government proposed that the committee and the nine rules should be replaced by German legislation prohibiting the construction of military aircraft and any links between civil aviation and the military or naval authorities. The Allies agreed to abandon restrictions on German civil aviation, but insisted on legislation to prevent or limit, as far as possible, the development of high-powered aircraft unsuitable for commercial purposes and flying training for military or naval personnel.

The Reichswehr were extremely loath to accept any limitation on personnel learning to fly, but eventually gave way in order to secure the advantages for civil aviation. An agreement was finally signed on 22 May 1926. Among other things the German Government undertook to forbid the construction or import of military-type aircraft and gliders, and all military flying instruction. The number of army and naval personnel allowed to fly (apart from 36 who already held licences) would be allowed to rise by stages to 36 at the beginning of 1932. When the requisite German ordinances had been issued the Committee of Guarantees was abolished on 1 September.[1] The Air Ministry were satisfied that under this agreement Germany could not become an air menace: only, they said, if she were again allowed a military air force would the position be different.[2]

During the months between the evacuation of the Cologne zone and Germany's entry into the League the main problem about the occupied Rhineland was the number of Allied troops; but the possibility of shortening the period of occupation was mentioned from time to time. The Germans pressed continually for substantial reductions in numbers; the French military authorities were resistant to change; the British were conscious that a promise to reduce numbers had been given, but their own contingent was now so small that further withdrawals would reduce it to no more than a token force and would make no substantial difference. They were aware of the need to strengthen Stresemann's hand against the Nationalists but doubtful of the outcome if his support among the government parties was as weak as he alleged, and were conscious that Briand's position was not strong either. Part of the trouble was of the German Government's own making, in that they had allowed and even encouraged exaggerated expectations during the campaign for the acceptance of the treaties. During January 1926

1 See *DBFP,* Ser. IA, Vol. I, Nos. 125-500; Vol. II, Nos. 29-152; *ADAP,* Vol. I.1, Nos. 25-220, *passim.*

2 Hoare to Cecil, 14 Dec. 1926; Cecil to Hoare, 17 Dec.; Hoare to Cecil, 23 Dec., Cecil Papers, BL Add. MS 51083.

they tried to secure a promise of reductions to the 'chiffres normaux' - as interpreted by them - before the Reichstag vote on sending the application for League membership, but had to be content with a statement by Briand that the occupying powers were examining the position with a view to reducing the troops to the lowest possible number as soon as the treaties came into force.[1]

After the failure at Geneva in March both the Germans and the British raised the question of troop reductions again, Stresemann stressing that what was needed to impress German opinion was a substantial withdrawal rather than piecemeal small ones. On each occasion, down to August, Briand replied that reductions were in progress and he was doing his utmost; but he also complained that the Germans were not doing their part in carrying out the Locarno policy.[2] Similar complaints went to Berlin from Chamberlain, who for example wrote on 1 February that the Germans were exposing him and Briand to the charge that they were being duped into making all the possible concessions piecemeal while the German Government did nothing, and again on 23 April that the German authorities in the occupied territory seemed unable to realise what was needed for the execution of Stresemann's great idea, to have 'no regard for the public opinion which other Governments have to consult, and, apparently, no gratitude or even appreciation of what, by great personal effort, has already been secured for them'.[3]

At the same time, however, Chamberlain raised with Crewe the question of the future of the occupation. The Labour M.P. Arthur Ponsonby had asked a question in the House of Commons about the declaration by Wilson, Clemenceau and Lloyd George of 16 June 1919, that if before the end of the occupation period Germany gave proofs of good will and satisfactory guarantees to ensure the fulfilment of her obligations the Allies would be ready to agree among themselves for the earlier termination of the occupation. Chamberlain wrote that until Germany was in the League there could be no question of hastening the end of the occupation, but once the Locarno treaties were in force it would become an increasingly obvious anomaly, with which great play

1 *DBFP,* Ser. IA, Vol. I, Nos. 183, 189, 191, 202, 206, 214, 216; memorandum by Lampson, 15 Jan. 1926, C 566/44/18, FO 371/11297; *ADAP,* Vol. I.1, Nos. 36, 37, 43, 46, 48, 59, 60, 62, 78, 81, 87; Margerie to Q d'O, 4 Feb., MAE, Rive gauche du Rhin, Vol. 83.

2 *DBFP,* Ser. IA, Vol. I, Nos. 386, 395, 487, 505; Vol. II, Nos. 107, 112, 113, 132, 135; *ADAP,* Vol. I.1, Nos. 182, 184, 228, 252, 277, 280, 290, 291; Vol. I.2, Nos. 3, 4, 7.

3 *DBFP,* Ser. IA, Vol. I, Nos. 231, 232, 236, 432, 455, 469; Chamberlain to D'Abernon, 23 Apr. 1926, C 4703/481/18, FO 371/11301.

would probably be made in Britain. He was anxious to take the initiative cautiously before this happened.[1]

Chamberlain thought that Briand and Berthelot favoured shortening the occupation. This was the case, but they saw it as part of a further settlement to which Germany would make a contribution. After the German attempt to raise the matter at the end of November 1925 had been repelled, the earliest mentions came from the French side, generally connected with the idea of mobilising part of the German reparation obligation.[2] At the end of February Briand, in the Chamber of Deputies, referred to Article 431 of the Treaty of Versailles as requiring evacuation before 1935 if Germany fulfilled her obligations.[3] He told Crewe on 6 May that once Germany was in the League the matter of the occupation was bound to come up; and a fortnight later Berthelot mentioned it to Hoesch, with the mobilisation of reparation obligations, as topics for a conversation between Briand and Stresemann.[4]

On 26 June Stresemann set out to the Foreign Affairs Committee of the Reichstag his intention of invoking Article 431 to raise the end of the occupation once Germany was in the League Council and the Control Commission was withdrawn. He said that he did not intend to suggest revision of the Dawes Plan, but Germany would be willing to anticipate annuities in order to secure evacuation. Once the Control Commission was wound up the obligations referred to in Article 431 could only be reparations, and Stresemann contended that the requirement was not that Germany should have completed payment but only that she should have ensured payment of the annuity for the current year.[5]

The Foreign Office legal advisers did not think that this interpretation was correct. They held that whereas Article 429 meant that Germany need only be up to date with her obligations for the first and second zones to be evacuated, Article 431 meant that she must have fulfilled all her obligations if the occupation were to be ended before the fifteen years. But policy was another matter. This, according to Chamberlain, demanded that 'we should use every effort first to diminish the number of troops, secondly to shorten the period of occupation. Once we have set to work on the policy of reconciliation

1 *DBFP,* Ser. IA, Vol. I, Nos. 438, 487; see *HC Deb.,* 5th ser., Vol. 194, cols. 1186-8

2 *ADAP,* Vol. I.1, Nos. 2, 8, 15; memoranda by Seydoux, 2 Dec. 1925, MAE, Allemagne, Vol. 398.

3 *Journal officiel, Chambre des députés,* Jan.-Feb. 1926, 978.

4 *DBFP,* Ser. IA, Vol. I, No. 505; *ADAP,* Vol. I.1, No. 225.

5 *DBFP,* Ser. IA, Vol. II, No. 93.

embodied in the twofold provisions for a guarantee against aggression and of voluntary acceptance of existing obligations by joining the League and signing the Covenant, we ought not to need the occupation and its continuation by keeping up the old state of mind hinders instead of helping the new policy. But to get France to move will be most difficult . . . It is however to be hoped that French statesmen will see that for success in dealing with the economic difficulties of France they require political factors which can only be produced by general appeasement and by a spreading conviction in Europe and elsewhere that the danger of new quarrels is finally averted for our time at least'.[1]

Whatever interpretation Stresemann put on Article 431, he was aware that in practice some extra inducement to France would be needed to secure an end to the occupation. Although authoritative German opinion was divided about the possibility and desirability of mobilising reparation obligations, he was prepared to discuss with Briand some financial operation as part of a settlement in which the French would agree to end the occupation and return the Saar territory, and consent to a Belgian-German deal on Eupen and Malmédy.[2]

This last question had been under discussion for some months semi-officially between Schacht, the President of the Reichsbank, and Delacroix, a former Belgian Prime Minister who was now Belgian representative on the Reparation Commission and trustee of the German railway bonds which formed part of the security for the reparation debt. The occasion was a financial crisis in Belgium, for the solution of which a large amount of foreign exchange was required. At the end of July the Germans offered a total payment of 60 million dollars, half of which would be a credit repayable over ten years, on condition that a political agreement was reached over the retrocession of Eupen and Malmédy. Some members, at least, of the Belgian Government were prepared to accept the German terms provided that Britain and France agreed. The Foreign Office at this stage were non-committal; but the French Cabinet, after discussion with Belgian ministers, decided on 18 August to oppose the transaction because it would jeopardise reparation payments and create an undesirable precedent in breaching the territorial settlement of the peace treaties.[3]

1 Minutes on C 8960/778/18, FO 371/11508; *DBFP*, Ser. IA, Vol. II, No. 153.

2 *ADAP*, Vol. I.2, Nos. 11, 37, 55; Margerie to Q d'O, 17 Jul. 1926, MAE, Allemagne, Vol. 389; Q d'O to Margerie, 12 Aug., Rive gauche du Rhin, Vol. 86; Laboulaye to Q d'O, 23 Aug., Allemagne, Vol. 398.

3 Q d'O to Herbette (Brussels), 18 Aug. 1926, MAE, Belgique, Vol. 70. For a fuller account of the negotiations see my article 'Thoiry revisited', *Durham University Journal* 67 (1975), 205-18.

France was herself undergoing a financial crisis in 1926, due more to internal than to external causes but marked by a serious fall in the value of the franc. Several different Ministers of Finance failed during the first half of the year to get reforms accepted by the Chamber, and on 17 July Briand resigned as president of the council. Herriot was entrusted with office but failed to form a government and gave up after two days. Finally on 23 July Poincaré formed a ministry, taking the finance portfolio himself and giving that of foreign affairs once again to Briand. Poincaré at once began to introduce financial reforms: he was also disposed to take up the question of commercialising German obligations, partly to provide alternative help for Belgium and partly to help the French franc. In the last part of August and the first half of September Poincaré argued that an emission of reparation bonds was possible and did not require German consent; but Briand maintained that American consent was unlikely unless France ratified her war debt funding agreement (signed in April but not yet presented to the Chamber) and that German consent both was necessary and would have to be paid for with political concessions.[1] It was against this background that Briand prepared to meet Stresemann at Geneva.

The Thoiry meeting, September 1926

The failure in March 1926 to secure Germany's entry into the League was due to confusion over the claim of other countries to permanent seats on the Council as well, while the German Government insisted that their country should enter alone.[2] The composition of the Council was discussed during the summer and by the date of the Assembly meeting in September a solution was found, satisfactory to all except Spain and Brazil. On 8 September the Assembly voted to admit Germany to the League, and then voted to allocate her a permanent seat on the Council. Two days later the German delegation took their seats amid loud applause and were greeted by Briand in one of his most eloquent speeches.

Within a fortnight the world press was full of reports that Briand and Stresemann had provisionally agreed on a grand settlement, by which the occupied territory would be evacuated in 1927, the Saar territory returned to Germany, and Eupen and Malmédy ceded by Belgium, in return for German payments of between 370 and 400 million gold

1 Memoranda and correspondence, 19 Aug.-15 Sep. 1926, MAE, Allemagne, Vol. 398; Belgique, Vol. 71.

2 Full accounts in Walters, *History of the League of Nations,* Vol. I, 316-27; *Survey of International Affairs, 1926.* 1-78; Spenz, *Die diplomatische Vorgeschichte des Beitritts Deutschlands zum Völkerbund,* 127-68. Documents in *DBFP,* Ser. IA, Vols. I-II and *ADAP,* Vols. I.1-I.2.

marks and support for the marketing of about 1,500 million gold marks' worth of railway bonds. Understanding and co-operation between France and Germany, the real fruit of Locarno, seemed to be realised. It has generally been supposed that the bargain was genuine and that the reasons why it came to nothing were that Briand found himself too far ahead of French opinion and the financial arrangements proved impossible. French accounts of the Thoiry meeting have never altogether supported this interpretation: the French archives throw some fresh light on the subject but still do not entirely answer the question whether the expectation of a bargain was based on a misunderstanding.

Before leaving for Geneva Stresemann told his ministerial colleagues that he doubted whether large-scale negotiations with France would be possible while Poincaré was in power; but at Geneva Hoesch and then Stresemann gathered that Briand wanted to discuss a general solution which could be put into effect by stages and was prepared to talk about the Saar and the occupation.[1] Immediately before the meeting with Briand the German delegation agreed that if a general settlement seemed possible repurchase of the Saar mines could be offered and the immediate evacuation of the second and third zones asked. If Briand asked for more, mobilisation of railway bonds could be discussed and a maximum of 1,500 gold marks' worth offered. Stresemann should say that Germany expected a free hand in the negotiations with Belgium. If it appeared that a general solution was not possible, Stresemann would concentrate on improvements in conditions in the Rhineland, reduction of troops, and withdrawal of the Control Commission.[2]

Briand and Stresemann lunched and spent the afternoon of 17 September together at Thoiry. The German and French accounts of the conversation differ a good deal.[3] According to Stresemann, Briand began by saying that he wished to discuss a general solution of all questions between France and Germany, and asking whether Germany would be forthcoming in the economic sphere. He was thinking of the return of the Saar territory and the end of the occupation. Stresemann said that he had found great opposition in Germany to a realisation

1 *ADAP,* Vol. I.2, Nos. 72, 82 and n. 2.

2 Op. cit. No. 95.

3 Stresemann dictated a short note on the conversation on 17 September and a longer account three days later. He gave a verbal account to the Cabinet on 24 September. Professor Hesnard, who acted as interpreter, seems to have written three memoranda, two of which were used by Briand's biographer: the third, in the archives of the Quai d'Orsay, is printed in *Durham University Journal* 67 (1975), 216-8. *ADAP,* Vol. I.2, Nos. 88, 94, 105; Stresemann, *Vermächtnis,* Vol. III, 14-23 (edited version); Suarez, *Briand,* Vol. VI, 215-27; MAE, Allemagne, Vol. 398. Hesnard's memoranda are not complete records.

of railway bonds, and he thought it could only be overcome if the occupation were to be ended in one year. Agreement had been reached on a figure of about 300 million gold marks for the Saar mines: he did not think that the world market could absorb, or Germany pay interest on, more than 1,500 million gold marks' worth of bonds. The whole transaction would produce for France a capital sum of 1,050 million gold marks. The French accounts suggest that it was Stresemann who first mentioned concrete matters, but make no mention of the Saar and the occupation. There is other evidence from the French side that they were discussed;[1] but the absence of a French version on these points is unfortunate.

According to Stresemann he then asked about the end of military control. Briand replied that Stresemann should get the outstanding points settled. He defended French officials against Stresemann's charge of quibbling over details and described graphically how he had given instructions to concentrate on the main questions. The soldiers would obey if they were given clear orders. But he was worried about the nationalist associations in Germany. The French military authorities accused him of ignoring what was going on: why did the German Government not suppress activities like military training by the Stahlhelm? Stresemann said that the Stahlhelm had no military significance and was not supported by the Reichswehr, and he defended the attitude of Gessler and Seeckt.

Next Stresemann, according to his account, said that if they agreed about the occupation, the Saar, and military control, they must understand one another about Eupen and Malmédy. Briand said that the Belgians had behaved foolishly and the timing was all wrong. But when Stresemann asked whether France objected in principle, Briand replied that if the general problem were solved Eupen and Malmédy would be solved too.

Finally Briand said that there had been disagreements about the occupied territory and he wanted to point out what had been done. Almost everything the Germans had asked for at Locarno had been completed. The French had given up nearly a quarter of the buildings requisitioned and the number of troops had been significantly reduced. Stresemann replied that Briand himself had said that the 6,000 men now being withdrawn were not enough; but he could refrain from talking about reductions if they had the prospect of complete evacuation. He then asked about supervision after the withdrawal of the Control Commission. Briand answered that the League's right to investigate must be secured, but no one was thinking of using it against

1 Suarez, *Briand,* Vol. VI, 228-9; *DBFP,* Ser. IA, Vol. II, Nos. 234, 238.

a member of the Council. But he earnestly begged Stresemann to pay attention to the Reichswehr: he had the impression that they were doing things Stresemann did not know about, and their policy must not be allowed to suffer. Stresemann replied that he understood but he did not think the matters were serious.

Apart from the French omission to mention the occupation and the Saar, the main difference between Stresemann's and Hesnard's accounts is one of tone, which is important for the question whether there was a misunderstanding or whether Briand committed himself too far. Hesnard's notes convey the impression of a general friendly exploration of a number of topics and possibilities: Stresemann's accounts - especially as summarised in the record of the Cabinet meeting on 24 September - suggest something very like the heads of an agreement. Briand obviously talked expansively: it is impossible to tell how far Stresemann took his generous expressions literally, but he does seem to have taken some of them more seriously than was wise, and to have fallen into one of the fits of optimism in which he saw great things within easy reach. But a careful reading even of Stresemann's record indicates that Briand made no specific promises.

Both agreed that they had not committed their governments and the suggestions would have to be examined by experts. As soon as this process began the obstacles to the financial proposals became obvious. Studies undertaken by the Germans indicated that it would not be possible to pay for the Saar mines by means of reparation annuities, and reparation experts agreed that marketing railway bonds would need the consent of all the creditors and American support.[1] Informal enquiries about Poincaré's earlier proposal to approach the United States Government revealed that American consent would depend on French ratification of the debt agreement and the British Government refused support.[2] The Treasury quickly recorded their objections to the 'Thoiry Scheme'. While admitting that in theory there was much to be said for converting the reparation debt into a commercial one that would engage Germany's credit, they pointed out the practical difficulties. In the first place the total debt was too large to be commercialised without being written down much more drastically than anyone had contemplated so far. Secondly the Dawes bonds were not suitable for marketing: until the annuities reached their maximum in 1928 it was impossible to say whether the security was good enough, so any issue now would have to be at a heavy discount. In

1 *ADAP,* Vol. I.2, Nos. 113, 114, 115, 137, 144, 145.

2 Correspondence, 24 Sep.-15 Oct. 1926, MAE, Allemagne, Vols. 398-9; *DBFP,* Ser. IA, Vol. II, Nos. 228, 252, 256.

time these difficulties might disappear, but that of getting a sufficiently large block of bonds absorbed without compromising all other receipts from Germany appeared insurmountable. It might seem invidious, the Treasury conceded, for Britain to oppose attempts by France to meet her financial difficulties, especially if Germany, who had nothing to lose by giving away other people's money, encouraged her; but still such a policy ought to be discouraged. Repurchase of the Saar mines would bring advantages to both sides, and the Eupen and Malmédy deal fell outside the treaty arrangements. One or other might be financed but the two together would involve a payment of £25-30 million in priority over reparations, and this would be bound to affect the Dawes Plan.[1]

Chamberlain was anxious not to seem to be 'destroying for selfish reasons so promising a development in Franco-German relations',[2] and the Treasury objections were not sent to the French Government. There was no need to do so, since the French were now aware that American consent to marketing the bonds was unlikely; and as the need for immediate financial help diminished with the success of Poincaré's emergency measures it began to be said that the interest on the proceeds of selling bonds to foreign investors was not much for Germany to pay for the evacuation of the Rhineland. The Germans had by the middle of October made little progress with their studies, and Stresemann was recommending to his colleagues that they should abstain from making any proposals.[3] It was thus not easy to see how the Thoiry idea could be carried farther. The French began to think about other possible counterparts for evacuation, such as new German political assurances in the east, or a loan. The Germans would not contemplate any political concessions, especially in the east; and they feared that the United States Government, who would not approve any direct credits to France as long as the debt agreement was not ratified, would object to a German loan which would in effect be passing on American money.[4] After some further inconclusive discussion between Hoesch and Briand both sides in November tacitly dropped the Thoiry programme.[5]

It is probable that at Thoiry Briand had in mind no precise plan for

1 CP 333(26), 27 Sep. 1926, CAB 24/181; conclusion in *DBFP*, Ser. IA, Vol. II, No. 237, n. 5.

2 Minutes, 9 and 12 Oct. 1926, on C 10779, 10930/10060/18, FO 371/11331.

3 *ADAP*, Vol. I.2, No. 144.

4 Memorandum, 8 Oct. 1926, MAE, Allemagne, Vol. 399; *ADAP*, Vol. I.2, Nos. 142, 154, 159.

5 Memorandum, 28 Oct. 1926, MAE, Allemagne, Vol. 399; Margerie to Q d'O, 3 Nov., Allemagne, Vol. 400; *ADAP*, Vol. I.2, Nos. 161, 167, 175, 177, 178.

achieving his aim of Franco-German reconciliation but simply wished to explore possible steps towards it. It is clear that it was not he but Poincaré who pushed the idea of mobilising the railway bonds and that Briand was better advised about the obstacles. Stresemann was no more certain than Briand about the financial proposal, but he was determined to explore every means of achieving his aim in the west. It is impossible to be sure how the different conceptions of what happened at Thoiry arose. Almost certainly the press gave unwarranted precision to the conversation; but in so far as Stresemann himself appears to have thought that an outline agreement had been reached, the different personalities of the two ministers may have been responsible.[1] The possibility of a future bargain on the occupation was not excluded by this failure, but a week after the withdrawal of the Control Commission Crewe remarked that no plan for early evacuation seemed practical politics from the French point of view. Great concessions on German disarmament had been made and a first line of defence abandoned. It would be extremely difficult for France to give up the last concrete pledge of security until the German Government gave repeated and unmistakable proofs of pacific intentions or some new compensation of value was found.[2]

The Polish and Russian factors, 1925 - 27

Whereas Stresemann's aim in the west was to secure German territory and sovereignty, his aim in the east was revision of the territorial provisions of the peace treaty; and his policy of understanding with France was directed towards both. Far therefore from introducing an element of stability and reconciliation into German-Polish relations as Chamberlain hoped, Locarno stimulated German hopes of recovering lost territory, not indeed by military means but by political and economic pressure.

An opportunity appeared for a time to be offered by a serious financial and economic crisis in Poland. In the autumn of 1925 the Polish Government asked for British financial advice and for help from the Bank of England and the Federal Reserve Bank of New York. They received a non-committal reply saying that since an American economic adviser was about to visit Warsaw it seemed premature to send anyone else, and that it was undesirable that foreigners should hold any of the capital of the Bank of Poland.[3] The Poles then seem to have considered

1 This was suggested by Seydoux in a memorandum of 23 Oct. 1926, MAE, Allemagne, Vol. 399.

2 *DBFP*, Ser. IA, Vol. III, No. 7.

3 Roberts (Warsaw) to FO, 11 Nov. 1925; Bank of England to Polish Legation, 29 Dec., N 6314, 7159/43/55, FO 371/10998.

asking for experts to investigate the whole economy. Treasury officials thought that Poland might have to approach the League of Nations for a financial scheme similar to those which had been applied to Austria and Hungary; and the Governor of the Bank of England, who was concerned with the general stabilisation of European financial systems, was believed to favour an international effort to the extent of discouraging piecemeal offers.[1]

In any international effort German participation would obviously be desirable since Germany was Poland's principal trading partner and an important source of capital, and was heavily involved in Poland's international economic transactions. Since the middle of 1925 the two countries had been in a state of trade warfare.[2] In his speeches of 22 November and 14 December on the results of Locarno Stresemann looked forward to promoting Germany's political demands on Poland in return for co-operation in financial help. The principal target for German efforts was British financial circles, especially the Bank of England. At the end of the year the Auswärtiges Amt prepared a case to be put to the British. Germany, Dirksen wrote, would welcome an international operation to sort out Poland's finances but it must be accompanied by a political settlement. The only possible permanent solution would be the return of Danzig, the return of the Corridor as far south as a line from Schneidemühl to Thorn, some smaller rectifications farther south (not including Posen), and Upper Silesia and parts of central Silesia.[3] But in April the Auswärtiges Amt admitted that Germany was not yet strong enough to secure the full solution: an attempt to settle the frontier question now would at best produce partial results, and these would prejudice the chance of a full solution later. On the other hand Germany must not, by refusing to participate in an international effort, incur the charge of sabotaging it: she must therefore try to postpone a definitive rehabilitation of Poland. If the League undertook reconstruction it would become involved in the territorial arrangements; and an additional reason for resisting Polish claims to a Council seat was that as a member of the Council Poland could hardly be subjected to international financial control.[4]

From their contacts with the Bank of England the German Embassy in London believed that Norman, although doubtful about involvement in political questions, was prepared to consider connecting Polish

1 Niemeyer to Lampson, 10 Feb. 1926; Niemeyer to Max Muller, 29 Mar., N 639, 1463/41/55, FO 371/11760-1; *ADAP*, Vol. II.1, Nos. 26, 116.

2 See Harald von Riekhoff, *German-Polish Relations 1918-1933* (Baltimore and London, 1971), Ch. VII.

3 *ADAP*, Vol. II.1, No. 21.

4 Op. cit. No. 150.

stabilisation with a German-Polish settlement.[1] But when Schacht visited London at the end of May he found the Governor much less ready to couple the two questions, and received warnings about the bad impression that would be caused if Germany refused to take part in helping Poland.[2] The German Minister in Warsaw, too, advised that refusal to participate would not help Germany's cause. Rauscher did not believe that Poland would ever surrender territory voluntarily, and did not share Dirksen's hope that Britain would put pressure on her to come to terms with Germany.[3]

The Foreign Office were not involved in the German approaches to the Bank of England. Such mention as there was of the possibility of frontier revision and British pressure was in very general terms and the reaction generally discouraging.[4] At last on 12 August, and as if it was his own idea, Norman suggested to Lampson that the idea of Germany buying back Eupen and Malmédy might be applied to the Corridor as well. Lampson said that he thought it would be most unwise to start talking about the Corridor. He did not take Norman's remarks very seriously, but Chamberlain did so sufficiently to instruct Lampson to repeat the discouraging advice.[5]

Even if, as the German reports suggest, there was a change in Norman's position in the spring, there is nothing to connect it with Pilsudski's *coup d'état* in Poland in May. Any theory that this event changed British policy towards Poland must rest on the assumption that the *coup* was welcomed and that Pilsudski was expected to be more pro-British than the weak parliamentary régime. Such an assumption is, however, unfounded. In the first place, while the Foreign Office certainly wanted better German-Polish relations their attitude to any discussion of frontier revision was discouraging before and after the *coup*, and Skrzynski's disappearance from office was regretted. In the second place, far from having supported Pilsudski in 1919-20, the British had very strongly distrusted him and his policy in the early days of the republic. Thirdly, the Soviet conviction to the contrary

1 *ADAP,* Vol. II. 1, Nos. 72, 97, 116.

2 Op. cit. No. 213.

3 Op. cit. Vol. II.2, Nos. 1, 2, 3, 8, 13.

4 D'Abernon to FO, 3 Mar. 1926, N 1034/228/55, FO 371/11768; minute by Collier, 4 Jun., N 2591/41/55, FO 371/11763; *ADAP,* Vol. I.1, No. 173; Vol.II.1, No. 208.

5 *DBFP,* Ser. IA, Vol. II, No. 143; minutes on C 9013/234/18, FO 371/11280. For the whole episode see Riekhoff, *German-Polish Relations,* 256-63; Korbel, *Poland between East and West,* 197-200. Sir Henry Clay, *Lord Norman* (London, 1957), 258-60, gives only a brief account of the Polish financial problem and says nothing about the political aspect.

notwithstanding, they were not pursuing an anti-Soviet coalition which Pilsudski might have been thought willing to join.[1]

The Polish economic position improved in the summer of 1926, thanks to *de facto* devaluation and increased coal exports during the long miners' strike in Britain. In the autumn the German Government decided to resume negotiations on a trade agreement and other matters, although they continued to try to block an international loan to Poland. In November officials in the Auswärtiges Amt acknowledged that frontier revision was far distant. There were only three possible sources of help for Germany, Zechlin wrote: Britain and the United States, the Soviet Union, and France. Britain had long been regarded as the best hope, because British opinion had been the first in western Europe to recognise the 'impossible' nature of the Corridor. But the hope of enlisting British support for a combination of frontier revision with financial reconstruction had come to nothing; and although Britain might welcome changes which contributed to pacification without upsetting the balance of power, she was unlikely to take any initiative. At present Germany could not conduct a foreign policy without or against Britain, but little was to be hoped for from her in the Polish question. The most popular possibility for a solution was German-Soviet collaboration. The two countries certainly had a common interest in altering the Polish frontiers; but in other respects (notably Lithuania) their interests were not the same and in practice even a Soviet military victory over Poland would not help German interests so long as a German-French understanding had not been reached. France in fact held the key to German aims in the east, and an understanding with her must lead to one about the east as well. It was a very large problem, but if there were no further cause of direct dispute between the two countries collaboration between them might in time enable Germany's interests to be satisfied.[2]

Stresemann did not regard the Soviet Union as an ally for the destruction of Poland, but any hint of a Polish-Soviet *rapprochement* was treated with great suspicion and in general the Soviet Union was

1 For a Foreign Office view of Pilsudski's *coup* see *DBFP*, Ser. IA, Vol. I, No. 529. The allegation that Britain engineered the *coup* is discussed in Polonsky, *Politics in Independent Poland*, 514-17. Pilsudski's assumption of power also gave rise to rumours that a new Polish attack on Lithuania was being planned, and later that Britain would support compensation for Poland in Lithuania in return for the surrender of Danzig to Germany. The German Government assured the Soviet Government that no such approaches had been made to them; and when at Geneva in December 1926 Stresemann mentioned Chicherin's fears, Chamberlain replied that 'this silly report' was unfounded: *ADAP*, Vol. II.2, Nos. 60, 65, 127, 137, 148, 163; *DBFP*, Ser. IA, Vol. II, No. 323.

2 *ADAP*, Vol. II.2, No. 140: see also Nos. 134, 145.

not to be let go. The negotiations for a political agreement were resumed after the Locarno conference at the Soviet request.[1] Although the Germans maintained that the western powers' letter on Article 16 was entirely satisfactory in safeguarding Germany's position and ought to remove the Soviet objections, the Russians professed themselves unconvinced. The negotiations therefore consisted in the main of Soviet attempts to induce Germany to commit herself to neutrality in case of a war in which the Soviet Union was involved even as the aggressor, and German attempts first not to have a treaty at all but only some kind of declaration not mentioning neutrality, and then to confine a neutrality undertaking to cases where the Soviet Union was the victim of unprovoked aggression, coupled with a promise not to join in an economic boycott in peacetime. The Germans were throughout prepared to give assurances about Article 16. They also spared no effort to deter the Russians from signing even an arbitration treaty with Poland.

In the last week of February 1926 the German Government approved drafts of a short treaty and a protocol which corresponded fairly closely to the texts eventually signed. Stresemann did not intend to sign until Germany was safely in the League, but meanwhile an agreement was concluded for a credit to the Soviet Union of 300 million marks. The setback at Geneva, however, and the almost simultaneous Polish refusal of a non-aggression pact with the Soviet Union unless the Baltic States were included, decided the Germans that the treaty must be signed without further delay. The final stage of the negotiation was complicated. By telling the western powers that a treaty was in prospect the Germans committed themselves to signing something; but they secured themselves against the charge of repeating the surprise of Rapallo, and to some extent against far-reaching Soviet amendments. The Russians battled to the last to secure undertakings that Germany would remain neutral in a war provoked by the Soviet Union and would not join in economic action at any time; and they put forward proposals for new military collaboration. Finally they accepted compromise proposals which, the Germans believed, secured the principle of their draft while removing words to which the Russians objected.

The British and French Governments were informed of the prospect of the treaty on 31 March. Both expressed anxiety about the compatibility of a promise of neutrality with the obligations of the Covenant.[2] Chamberlain and Briand agreed that it was impossible to prevent the treaty; but Chamberlain asked the Germans to take steps

1 A full account is given in Rosenbaum, *Community of Fate,* 188-219.

2 *DBFP,* Ser. IA, Vol. I, Nos. 384, 391, 392, 397, 398, 400, 409, 410; *ADAP,* Vol. II.1, Nos. 99, 100, 104, 108, 109, 110, 113.

to reassure Poland, and Briand hoped that signature might be delayed until the French Senate had approved the Locarno treaties.[1] However on 14 April *The Times* reported that what it described as a new Reinsurance Treaty was imminent, so the chance of postponing signature was removed. The Germans complained about the leak, but it probably came from them and it was not altogether to their disadvantage. Less than ever could they afford to let the negotiations fail, but their chance of resisting excessive Soviet demands was strengthened.

Eastern European countries were a good deal alarmed by the news of the treaty. Beneš suggested that the German Government should be asked officially how its terms were to be reconciled with the procedures of the League.[2] The Poles were not easily soothed, and Schubert did not improve matters by accusing them of intrigue against Germany.[3] This 'intrigue' consisted mainly of having discussed a non-aggression pact with the Soviet Union, even though it was the Poles who had turned it down. In suggesting to the western governments that the possibility of a Polish-Soviet agreement and the actual signature of a new Polish-Rumanian treaty had been their reasons for deciding on the German-Soviet treaty, the Germans professed fear of Polish rather than of Soviet policy. They also professed - and felt - some fear of a Franco-Soviet *rapprochement* resulting from the debt negotiations recently started in Paris.[4]

The Russians told the French Ambassador in Moscow that their reason for pursuing a treaty with Germany was that their initiatives for a Franco-Polish-Soviet agreement on the Polish-Soviet frontier, and for non-aggression pacts with all countries except Rumania, had been turned down in Paris. But Briand replied that only vague suggestions had been made, which he had answered by saying that he would be interested to hear specific proposals but negotiations must begin with a settlement of the debt and property questions. He would still be interested in an agreement safeguarding the Polish eastern frontier, but could not contemplate anything that would conflict with the Covenant.[5]

The German-Soviet treaty and an exchange of notes on Germany's

1 *DBFP*, Ser. IA, Vol. I, Nos. 412, 414, 415, 418, 420, 421, 423; *ADAP*, Vol. II.1, Nos. 119, 121, 124.

2 *DBFP*, Ser. IA, Vol. I, Nos. 429, 435, 437, 441, 443, 447, 449; *ADAP*, Vol. II.1, Nos. 155, 167, n. 3; Vol. III, No. 120.

3 *DBFP*, Ser. IA, Vol. I, Nos. 450, 459; *ADAP*, Vol. II.1, No. 157.

4 *DBFP*, Ser. IA, Vol. I, Nos. 392, 401, 407, 409, 415, 435, 445, 454, 464.

5 Herbette (Moscow) to Q d'O, 5, 6 and 8 Apr. 1926; Q d'O to Herbette, 10 Apr., MAE, Russie, Vol. 333; Herbette to Q d'O, 13 and 15 Apr.; Q d'O to Herbette, 19 Apr.; memorandum by Berthelot, 10 May, Russie, Vol. 359.

obligations under the Covenant were signed in Berlin on 24 April and published two days later.[1] Knowledge of the exact terms did not allay anxiety abroad. It was decided not to ask for formal explanations, but Gaus gave verbal explanations to Fromageot and Hurst. Gaus repeated that the treaty could not override the Locarno treaties or the Covenant, and explained that in the German view the neutrality stipulation and the undertaking not to join in an economic boycott were applicable only when the Soviet Union was the victim of unprovoked aggression (although the term was not used) and when Articles 16 and 15(7) of the Covenant did not arise. The statement that Article 16 did not oblige Germany to take any action without her own consent accorded with the Assembly resolution of 1921: Germany had not undertaken that she would never vote the Soviet Union to be an aggressor.[2]

On the effects of the Treaty of Berlin one of the best informed German experts on the Soviet Union, Schlesinger, wrote early in July that Soviet policy was bound to affect Germany's position. At a time when she was virtually the only link between Russia and Europe Germany must try, in her own interest, both to prevent the Soviet Union from following a policy that would endanger her existence and to prevent the threat to Soviet survival from becoming acute. Schlesinger believed that this threat really came from Britain. He shared Soviet fears that Britain had the means to cause other states to conduct an active anti-Soviet policy on her behalf even if for domestic reasons she could not conduct one herself.[3] In fact the Foreign Office had very little to do with relations between the Soviet Union and her neighbours, and Chamberlain's policy of indifference lasted throughout 1926. Before Chicherin visited Paris in November 1925 the French were told that Chamberlain would consider a suggestion of a meeting;[4] and the Foreign Office discussed a change of policy in view of the fact that other countries were improving their relations with the Soviet Union and moves might be expected to include her in the pacification of Europe and perhaps to admit her to the League. But Chicherin did not ask for a meeting and there was no sign of Soviet readiness to fulfil the conditions, laid down for the resumption of talks for a settlement, of an improved attitude on debts and claims and an end to anti-British activities. So when the Soviet Chargé d'Affaires made enquiries about talks he was given the same answer as before.[5]

1 German texts in *ADAP,* Vol. II.1, No. 168; translation in *British and Foreign State Papers,* Vol. CXXV, 738-41.

2 *ADAP,* Vol.I.1, No. 227, annex 2.

3 Op. cit. Vol. II.2, No. 32.

4 *DBFP,* Ser. IA, Vol. I, No. 46, n. 4.

5 Op. cit. Nos. 46, 65, 142, 150, 181.

By the spring the Foreign Office were again considering the desirability of a settlement; but the domestic political pressure for a breach increased. Chamberlain had resisted it in the winter, recommending to his Cabinet colleagues not to make speeches that would confirm Chicherin's fears, and having the London Chamber of Commerce informed that the Government were prepared to consider a settlement and did not favour abrogation of the trade agreement. Even when the transfer of Soviet funds to support the General Strike increased the demands for a breach, Chamberlain stated in the House of Commons that the Government did not intend to break off relations; and he told the Soviet Chargé d'Affaires that he wanted to avoid a rupture.[1] No important element in the situation changed thereafter; but in May 1927 the pressure from the Conservative Party and some members of the Government finally overcame the opposition of Chamberlain and his advisers.[2] Had the breach of relations really been the prelude to an anti-Soviet coalition Schlesinger's fears about Germany's position would have been justified; but it proved to have little international significance.

The pursuit of settlements in other parts of Europe, 1925 - 27

The hope expressed in Britain before and after Locarno that pacification in western Europe would spread to other sensitive parts of the continent did not bear fruit in the ensuing year. The chief obstacle to Locarno-type settlements in central and south-east Europe was the fact that the lesser peace treaties were secured by a preponderance of power on the side of the victors. They therefore lacked an incentive to make concessions; and the smaller defeated countries, being unable to upset the settlement on their own, had nothing to offer directly and possibly much to gain from fomenting causes of insecurity and seeking outside patronage. Much therefore depended on the attitude of the major powers, and since at this time Germany could not offer much help to revisionists and Britain would undertake no responsibilities, Italian policy in the Balkans and the Danubian area, and Italian relations with France, were the most important factors.

At Geneva in June 1925 Chamberlain and Briand agreed to try to enlist Italian co-operation in dealing with the recurrent troubles in the Balkans. They gave Scialoja a message to Mussolini saying that they believed the great powers ought to keep an eye on the area and exchange

1 *DBFP,* Ser. IA, Vol. I, Nos. 278, 416, 504; Vol. II, Nos. 31, 52, 55, 56, 60, 61, 62, 71, 80, 90, 103, 176; *HC Deb.,* 5th ser., Vol. 197, cols. 769-77.

2 *DBFP,* Ser. IA, Vol. III, Chs I-II; G. Gorodetsky, *The Precarious Truce* (London, 1977), 211-31; F. Stambrook in *International Review of History and Political Science,* 6 (1969), No. 3, 109-27.

views, and hoped Mussolini would lend his personal support. From the French point of view this was a watering down of a suggestion of Franco-Italian conversations about extending the western pact by an agreement on Austria and central and south-east Europe; but even this mild proposal of co-operation seems to have been unwelcome in Rome. The message somehow got 'lost', and although Chamberlain gave a copy to Torretta in August Mussolini was still in no hurry to reply.[1] Chamberlain referred to the message in his one conversation with Mussolini at Locarno and again suggested exchanges of views if the three governments thought a dangerous situation was arising or united action might be salutary. Mussolini was non-committal, and noticeably reticent about Albania; and his reply to the June message, eventually delivered in the last week of October, was equally vague.[2] However the Italian Government did co-operate over the serious Greco-Bulgarian frontier incident of 19 October, which went to the Council of the League.

In his conversation with Mussolini Chamberlain suggested that a pact of mutual guarantee might be possible in central Europe, and he advised Beneš to consider a pact between the Little Entente countries and Austria and Hungary; but here too the Italian attitude seemed likely to be unhelpful.[3] Chamberlain wished all concerned at least to be made aware that Britain would welcome and support any proposal aiming at extending the principle of agreements between former victors and former enemies, and had a despatch to this effect sent to the British representatives in the central European capitals and in Rome.[4] The first reactions were not very encouraging. Mussolini was again non-committal. The Hungarians said that their grievances must be met before relations with their neighbours could improve. The Prime Minister, Count Bethlen, indicated in December that he might consider an arbitration treaty with Czechoslovakia; but shortly afterwards the discovery of a conspiracy in Hungary to counterfeit French banknotes for political use in central Europe set relations back.[5] The British

1 Memorandum by Nicolson, 4 Jun. 1925; Chamberlain to FO, 10 Jun.; Chamberlain to Torretta, 12 Aug., C 8327, 7815, 7915/251/62, FO 371/10695; Q d'O to Massigli (Geneva), 9 Jun.; Massigli to Q d'O, 9 Jun., MAE, Grande Bretagne, Vol. 77; Q d'O to Besnard (Rome), 17 Aug., Italie, Vol. 84.

2 Chamberlain to FO, 17 Oct. 1925, C 13128/459/18, FO 371/10743; minute by Lampson, 24 Oct.; message from Mussolini, C 13711, 13838/251/62, FO 371/10695; Romano Avezzana to Briand, 23 Oct., MAE, Italie, Vol. 84; *DDI*, Vol. IV, No. 166.

3 Kennard (Belgrade) to Nicolson, 19 Jun. 1925, C 8497/251/62, FO 371/10695; Chamberlain to FO, 17 Oct.; Kennard to FO, 22 Oct., C 13131, 13384, 13385, 13386/13131/62, FO 371/10701; *DDI*, Vol. IV, No. 164.

4 *DBFP*, Ser. IA, Vol. I, No. 39.

5 Op. cit. Nos. 84, 137; Graham to FO, 6 Nov. 1925; Barclay (Budapest) to FO, 6 Nov.; minute by Lampson, 11 Nov.; FO to Barclay, 3 Dec., C 14262,

Minister in Vienna thought that the Austrians would not be interested in a security pact because it might prejudice the chance of union with Germany, and on account of the south Tirol.[1]

Despite Yugoslav fears about Italian policy Kennard, the British Minister in Belgrade, thought early in 1926 that it might be possible to get a pact committing the Balkan countries to a pacific policy.[2] Crewe and Graham were instructed to consult the French and Italian Governments about encouraging a system of comprehensive arbitration treaties between the countries of central and south-east Europe, but then the despatch was withdrawn.[3] At almost the same time, as a result partly of an Italian suggestion of a new treaty with Yugoslavia and partly of long-standing discussion of a Franco-Yugoslav treaty, the French and Yugoslavs proposed a tripartite agreement with Italy to secure the territorial settlement in the region. This suggestion smacked too much of an alliance of the victors to meet with British approval. Chamberlain, who was pursuing a specially friendly relationship with Italy despite or even because of his awareness that Mussolini might become dangerous, was anxious to see an improvement in Franco-Italian relations; but instead of welcoming a proposal that might have contributed to this end he echoed Mussolini's objection that it was contrary to the Locarno spirit. Mussolini's refusal to contemplate French participation in any combination in the Adriatic was founded on Italian ambitions in the area and a desire to reduce French influence in central and south-east Europe, not on devotion to the spirit of Locarno. He succeeded not only in killing a tripartite pact but in delaying conclusion of a Franco-Yugoslav treaty until the summer of 1927.[4] Briand's deference to Mussolini's wishes on this occasion did

14270, 14474, 15697, 15814, 15962/13131/62, FO 371/10701. For the forged currency affair see *Survey of International Affairs, 1926,* 178-90.

1 *DBFP,* Ser. IA, Vol. I, No. 119.

2 Op. cit. No. 166; Kennard to FO, 16 Dec. 1925; Kennard to Howard Smith, 17 Dec.; Kennard to FO, 23 Dec.; Lampson to Graham, 30 Dec., C 16338, 16372, 16607/276/92, FO 371/10794; minute by Lampson, 22 Dec., C 16521/251/62, FO 371/10695; Kennard to Lampson, 24 Dec., C 16693/13131/62, FO 371/10701; Kennard to Lampson, 7 Jan. 1926, C 420/308/62, FO 371/11239.

3 FO to Crewe and Graham, 22 Jan. 1926; Crewe to FO, 28 Jan.; Graham to FO, 29 Jan., C 840, 1114, 1170/308/62, FO 371/11239.

4 MAE, Italie, Vol. 120; Yougoslavie, Vol. 70; *DBFP,* Ser. IA, Vol. I, Nos. 263, 291, 300, 329; Kennard to Howard Smith, 23 Feb. 1926; Howard Smith to Kennard, 1 Mar., C 2673/1618/62, FO 371/11242; *DDI,* Vol. IV, Nos. 237, 240, 249, 250, 262, 263, 266, 269, 271, 273, 278, 283. At the end of 1923 the Italians had themselves suggested a tripartite agreement but withdrew the proposal when the Yugoslav Government showed themselves ready for direct negotiations for a settlement on Fiume; MAE, Italie, Vols. 118-19; Yougoslavie, Vol. 69. For Italian policy in 1925-6 see Alan Cassels, *Mussolini's Early Diplomacy* (Princeton, 1970), 315-47; Carrocci, *La Politica estera dell'Italia fascista,* Chs. IV-VII.

not help to improve French relations with Italy, which on the contrary deteriorated. Much as Chamberlain regretted this fact, he continued to favour the expansion of Italian influence across the Adriatic and was not much disturbed by the extensive Italian control over Albania achieved in 1926. The Foreign Office viewed with equanimity the French misgivings about the decline of their position in central Europe.[1]

In the Baltic area negotiations for non-aggression treaties, collective pacts and the like were repeatedly hampered by the conflicting interests and suspicions of almost all the countries involved.[2] The British Government played no part other than general statements, in reply to enquiries, that they favoured any arrangement anywhere that would tend to promote peace and a feeling of security, but any agreements reached must not conflict with the terms and obligations of the Covenant.[3] The terms of the Soviet-Lithuanian treaty signed in September 1926 corresponded closely to those of the Treaty of Berlin; but one of the reasons for the failure of the Soviet negotiations with the other Baltic States was Finnish insistence on fidelity to the Covenant.

General disarmament, 1926 - 27

The Preparatory Commission for the Disarmament Conference began its first session on 18 May 1926. The bulk of its work falls outside the period covered by this study, but even the first stage suggested certain conclusions about its future. From the first the British resisted all attempts to link reduction of armaments with further guarantees of security or procedures for assistance under Article 16. Their attitude was explained in the instructions given to Cecil; and when at an early meeting of the drafting committee the French delegation proposed a study of procedures Cecil objected and the French Government were asked for an explanation.[4] A substitute was found in a Belgian proposal to improve Council procedures for rapid meetings when a danger of war arose, and no more was said about Article 16 for the time being.[5] The Preparatory Commission had by no means completed its work by the time of the Assembly meeting of 1926, but it was then

1 *DBFP,* Ser. IA, Vol. II, Nos. 74, 88, 126.

2 See Korbel, *Poland between East and West,* 189-208; X.J. Eudin and H.H. Fisher, *Soviet Russia and the West, 1920-1927* (Stanford, 1957), 280-2.

3 See for example *DBFP,* Ser. IA, Vol. I, Nos. 83, 417; FO to Vaughan (Riga), 29 Jan. and 1 Jun. 1926, N 300, 2222/124/59, FO 371/11723-4.

4 *DBFP,* Ser. IA, Vol. II, Nos. 2, 14, 16, 19, 20, 21, 28, 35, 47.

5 *DBFP,* Ser. IA, Vol. II, Nos. 44, 53, 83, 187, 196, 320; Vol. III. Nos. 15, 47; *ADAP,* Vol. I.1, Nos. 236, 239, 242.

instructed to hasten so that if possible the disarmament conference could be called before the next Assembly. With many doubts the British Government decided to put forward a draft convention. The French also put forward a draft: intensive discussion brought agreement on some points but left others unreconciled, so that the Commission's report contained a number of alternatives, and no figures.[1] The problem of naval limitation was made worse by the failure of the separate naval conference in the summer of 1927.

Surveying the scene after the Preparatory Commission adjourned in April 1927 Cadogan, one of the Foreign Office officials permanently attached to the British delegation to the League of Nations, was inclined to think that the attempt not only had achieved very little but had been misguided. The League, he wrote, had discovered between 1920 and 1922 that general reduction or limitation of armaments was impossible in the absences of security. It had then pursued general security and had found it impossible. Locarno had been a 'brilliant start' on the alternative path towards security through regional agreements; but there had been no sequel and there seemed to be no prospect of a series of regional arrangements which would create a general feeling of security sufficient to lead to a general reduction of armaments. But since 1925 the feeling that something must be done about disarmament had grown into an obsession: the wheel had come full circle and security had dropped out of sight. Cadogan thought that the meeting of the disarmament conference would be only the beginning of the difficulties and dangers, for it was then that figures would have to be filled in. Even supposing that agreement could be reached on the basis of what each country regarded as the minimum necessary for its safety, that would not constitute reduction of a kind to satisfy Germany. Cadogan had no proposal as to how the negotiations should be continued, other than delay. He would have preferred to seek regional disarmament in areas where security had been achieved.[2]

Cecil, naturally, did not concede that little had been achieved, and he argued that even if the disarmament conference produced only a very modest initial reduction it would mark a step forward by setting up a definite machinery. He also maintained that delay was impossible, precisely because of the German difficulty: and it would not go away, because the Allies were bound by the Covenant, the Treaty of

1 *DBFP*, Ser. IA, Vol. III, Nos. 10, 37; C 15(27), CAB 23/54. Texts of the draft conventions in Cmd 2888 of 1927, *League of Nations. Preparatory Committee for the Disarmament Conference. Report of the British Representative to the Secretary of State for Foreign Affairs.*

2 *DBFP*, Ser. IA, Vol. III, Nos. 200, 300.

Versailles and their own statements to promote a scheme of general disarmament.[1]

Whether the German obligation to remain disarmed depended legally on the Allies' obligation to formulate and carry out a scheme of general disarmament was not a simple question;[2] but it was certainly true that the German difficulty had already arisen and that the British Government, thanks to League opinion and not least to Cecil, had committed themselves to the general reduction of armaments. Their feet were set on the boulder-strewn road from which, as the next six years were to show, there could be no turning whatever happened to security. Cadogan's idea that the Locarno powers might be able to agree on limitation of armaments as between themselves was not a practicable alternative. It was presumably based on an assumption not only that Locarno had solved the problem of western European security but also - contrary to all the evidence - that France no longer feared Germany. Although the French Government in 1927 carried out their long-promised intention of reducing the term of military service to one year, no reduction of armaments to which France would agree would have met the German case.[3]

1 *DBFP,* Ser. IA, Vol. III, No. 202.

2 Op. cit. Nos. 326, 508.

3 For French military reorganisation and thinking in 1926-7 see Judith M. Hughes, *To the Maginot Line. The Politics of French Military Preparation in the 1920's* (Cambridge, Mass., 1971), Ch. 5; Jon Jacobson, *Locarno Diplomacy. Germany and the West 1925-1929* (Princeton, 1972), 105-13. For the aims of German disarmament policy at the time see *ADAP,* Vol. I.1, No. 144.

CONCLUSION

In 1927 the world was more secure than it had been in 1920, but those who professed to see a new age dawning were victims of their rhetoric. Although the precise causes of the subsequent breakdown of security could not all have been foreseen at that date, the general causes had been present since the end of the war and the sources of trouble were not hard to identify. No single country could have solved all the underlying causes of insecurity, even if it had wished or tried to dictate peace to the world: the question is whether British policy could have been more effective than it was.

For the League of Nations, despite British hopes that it could solve underlying problems and reconcile differences, British governments made no sacrifices; but neither did they reveal such scepticism as they felt. Doubting whether sanctions could ever be enforced, they refused to undertake any more general obligations; but they did not share their doubts with the electorate until the attempt had been made. They used more or less internationalist language without commitment, and in the end got the worst of both worlds.

In the Far East few options were open. Even at the height of her power Britain had never professed to exercise leadership there single handed. Now the region's security depended less than ever on her and more on the United States, a Japan in search of autonomy, and a China in the throes of long-drawn-out revolution. To harmonise or mediate between these forces was well beyond Britain's capacity, Singapore was an earnest of her intention to protect her interests and exert influence, but even this task proved more than she could combine with others nearer home.

It was with regard to European security that there was an obvious alternative to the policies followed. Locarno was not the worst of both worlds, but was not enough. In so far as it improved relations and all the main parties gained from it, it was a success. The gains for Germany were considerable. By the time the treaties were signed the object for which Stresemann made his security offer had been achieved. Within the next eighteen months it had been made exceedingly unlikely that the state of German armaments would ever again be investigated. The hope of an early complete evacuation of the Rhineland proved vain, but before he died Stresemann secured a promise of accelerated evacuation and an improved reparations plan: these fell short of German desires but were no small achievement. The gain for France was a relaxation of fear for her own safety and a formal assurance of British support in case of need: a secondary gain was a reduction of the risk that her strength would be over-taxed by a German-Polish quarrel. The gain for Britain was release from constant involvement in Franco-German friction.

For Germany's eastern and south-eastern neighbours, especially Poland, any gain from the Locarno settlement depended almost entirely on a change in German policy. And even in western Europe, if Locarno were to prove more than a temporary surcease a much greater reconciliation of aims as well as of words was needed. 'L'esprit de Locarno est composé de plusieurs esprits fort differents,' wrote Henri de Jouvenel in 1932.[1] It is perhaps too easy with hindsight to dismiss as wishful thinking the optimism that, in Britain, made up so large a part of the spirit of Locarno, or to regard it as a wilful exaggeration of Britain's contribution. But even without exploring the question of popular illusion and the discrepancy between public oratory and private reservations, it is clear that there was over-optimism and a false estimate of German motives. Had the objectives of Stresemann's policy been more frankly faced, the rejoicings might have been more tempered and the expectations more realistic.

For Stresemann's policy was to secure even more far-reaching treaty revision and the restoration of Germany as the greatest power in Europe. Understanding with France was a means to this end, not an end in itself. But Germany's revival was bound to make her much stronger than France, both economically and militarily. Stresemann hoped that France could be brought to acquiesce in this change of relative power; but he did nothing, perhaps in the political circumstances in Germany could do nothing, to make it seem palatable for France or safe for others.

Locarno set the seal for France on the change from an active to a passive defence of the peace settlement. Had her collaboration in Germany's revival been secured, the implications for Britain of such a continental *bloc* might not have been altogether favourable. But on the other hand some peaceful territorial revision in east central Europe might have followed. There was in Britain little objection in principle to such revision: many Frenchmen too were willing to envisage it, but not if it meant further accretion of strength to an unreconciled Germany. What terms might have been devised that could have induced Poland willingly to part with territory are hard to imagine: without her genuine assent a solution concerted and imposed by the great powers would still have left a nucleus of insecurity on Germany's eastern frontier. Propaganda and economic pressure, Stresemann's substitute for the

1 Henri de Jouvenel, *La Paix française* (Paris, 1932), 181.

risky game of an alliance with the Soviet Union, were ineffective and even counter-productive. Whether he would have continued to believe that revision could be achieved by these means, and whether he would have continued to rely on them alone once Germany's strength was greater, are speculative questions. Most authorities are inclined to give Stresemann himself the benefit of the doubt;[1] but his domestic position was not strong and he did nothing to prepare the German people for a rational discussion of the claim against Poland. Of no other possible Foreign Minister of the republic could one give a more confident reply: only a dictator was able to put the claim into cold storage for a few years. The Polish problem was moreover not the only one. There was Austria as well, and Czechoslovakia; and beyond them the Danubian basin and the Balkans where Mussolini was keeping trouble brewing and where a revived Germany would certainly look again for political as well as economic influence. Annelise Thimme, in her short study of Stresemann, wrote that whereas in the negotiations for the security treaty each country had something to contribute, once it was signed Germany had no more to give and could only demand.[2] This may be a true statement of what was actually possible for Weimar Germany: if so, it shows how little Locarno did to solve the problem of European security.

No doubt those in Britain who expressed misgivings in private hoped that by the time Germany recovered her strength she would be so tied to the west by interest and the habit of co-operation that her revival would not jeopardise the security of others. But the question was not discussed, nor was any positive policy evolved for dealing with the other great dissatisfied power, the Soviet Union. It is tempting to debate whether the disasters of the 1930s could have been prevented if British governments and the British people had decided that the answer to postwar problems and their own limited means was the alternative policy of alliance and close co-operation with France, not to hold Germany down but to convince the German people that their reduced territorial circumstances must be accepted. Such acceptance need not have implied inferiority, but would have been the only lasting basis for Franco-German reconciliation. As the foregoing story has shown, however, it was too difficult for Britain to choose such a policy. Virtually everything told against it: postwar fatigue, the reaction against the experience of long-drawn-out continental warfare, suspicion of France, lack of obvious necessity, and the fact that although the retreat from empire was beginning Britain still was - and certainly still regarded herself as - a great imperial power whose chief interests lay outside Europe. Awareness that

1 See Riekhoff, *German-Polish Relations,* Chs IX and XII, especially 263-71.

2 Annelise Thimme, *Gustav Stresemann* (Hanover and Frankfurt, 1957), 111.

only if she were safe in Europe could she be free to carry out her imperial tasks may have been more widely spread since 1914, but the implications had not sunk into the national consciousness and the practical difficulties of providing for imperial and European interests would have been formidable in any event.

Britain's defence policy was certainly unsuited to her position. The role of producer of security is necessarily expensive, and she did not even spend enough to ensure the security of her own territory and interests. It was natural that under the assumption of the ten-year rule the general pressure for economy should be felt most heavily by the armed services, but whether it need have gone so far or have been reinforced by so much 'moral disarmament' is another matter. It may well be debated whether the position reached by 1932, when 'the whole of our territory in the Far East, as well as the coastline of India and the Dominions and our vast trade and shipping, lies open to attack', could have been avoided without damage to the economy and the country's eventual capacity, whether it was necessary to reduce armaments to well below the standard of that Article 8 of the Covenant which Cecil so frequently invoked,[1] or whether a larger premium earlier could have insured against the situation in which defence weakness became a major factor in foreign policy. But even in this field circumstances told against a European alliance: it appeared to involve giving - and spending - more than Britain needed to receive so long as France, by defending herself, shielded the British Isles against an insecure continent. Thus the choice was evaded; pragmatism became a cloak for unwillingness to think about the unpleasant; and the British people were allowed to nurture their illusions of peace. In the end they decided that they must use force to uphold what remained of the territorial settlement in eastern Europe. Had they been willing to promise more earlier, the cost might have been less.

1 See COS 295, review of defence for 1932, CAB 53/22; CP 64(34), first report of the Defence Requirements Committee, CAB 24/247.

BIBLIOGRAPHY

1. *Unpublished sources*
2. *Published Sources*
3. *Biographies, diaries, memoirs, collections of papers*
4. *Contemporary works*
5. *Later works*
6. *Articles*

1. *Unpublished Sources*

Great Britain, Government archives. Public Record Office

Cabinet
Conclusions CAB 23; Memoranda CAB 24; Conferences of Ministers CAB 23; Cabinet Committees CAB 27

Committee of Imperial Defence
Minutes CAB 2; Memoranda CAB 3, CAB 4, CAB 5; Sub-Committees CAB 16, CAB 34

Chiefs of Staff Committee CAB 53

Imperial Conferences CAB 32

International Conferences, 1921-24 CAB 29

Washington Conference, 1921-22 CAB 30

Genoa Conference, 1922 CAB 31

Hankey Papers CAB 63

Foreign Office
Political correspondence FO 371; Private Papers FO 800; Locarno Conference, British Delegation FO 840/1

Colonial Office
Correspondence, Canada CO 42; Correspondence, New Zealand CO 209; Correspondence, Dominions CO 532; Correspondence, South Africa CO 551

Dominions Office
Correspondence, Dominions DO 35

Great Britain, private collections

Birmingham, University Library : Austen Chamberlain Papers

Cambridge, University Library : Baldwin Papers; Crewe Papers; Templewood Papers

Edinburgh, National Library of Scotland : Haldane MSS

London, House of Lords Library : Bonar Law Papers; Lloyd George Papers

London, British Library : Balfour Papers; Cecil of Chelwood Papers; D'Abernon Papers

London, India Office Library and Records : Curzon Papers

London, Public Record Office : MacDonald Papers

France, Ministère des Affaires Étrangères

Archives des Affaires Étrangères : Amérique 1918 - 1929; Europe 1918 - 1929; Papiers Herriot

Germany, Foreign Ministry archives

Büro des Reichsministers

Kabinett-Protokolle	Serial 3242
Reparationsfragen	3243
Londoner Konferenz 1924	3398
England	2368
Frankreich	2406
Russland	2860
Polen	2945
Belgien	3015
Österreich	3086
Tschechoslowakei	3086
Verhandlungen mit den Allierten über einem Sicherheitspakt, etc.	3123
Völkerbund	3147

Büro des Staatssekretärs

Die Durchführung des Sachverstandigengutachtens, etc.	4492
Die Räumung der ersten Zone	4504
Sicherheitsfrage, etc.	4509
Russland-Polen-Randstaaten, etc.	4556
Rückwirkungen der Garantiepaktverhandlungen auf die Deutsch-Russische Beziehungen	4562
Privatbriefe	4567
Anschlussfrage	4576
Politische Angelegenheiten der Kleinen Entente, Ungarns und des Balkans	4582
Völkerbund	4584
England, ganz geheim	4597

Abteilung IIA
Sicherheitsfrage K1885
Politische Beziehungen Frankreichs zu Deutschland K936
Politische Beziehungen der Tschechoslowakei zu Deutschland L417

Abteilung II. Besetzte Gebiete
Räumung der I. Zone 9518
Sicherheitspakt K1886

Abteilung II. F-M
Die künftige Völkerbundskontrolle auf Grund des Artikels 213 9856

Abteilung III
Politische Beziehungen Englands zu Deutschland K1976

Abteilung IV
Politische Beziehungen Polens zu Deutschland L557

Geheimakten 1920-1936
Frankreich. Politische Beziehungen Frankreich Deutschland 5881
England. Allgemeine auswärtige Politik K125, K1825
England. Politische Beziehungen Englands zu Deutschland L1555, K126
Polen. Staatsfinanzen in Allgemeinen K160
Polen. Politische Beziehungen Polens zu Deutschland K170
Russland. Politische Beziehungen Russlands zu Deutschland K281
Russland. Sicherheitspakt K288
Russland Handakten. Präambel Vorgänge 6698
Russland Handakten. Sicherheitsfrage 6698

Referat Völkerbund
Lokarnovorverhandlungen K2338
Lokarno-Vertrag K2339
Länderakten. Deutschland L1837

2. *Published Sources*

Great Britain

Foreign Office *British and Foreign State Papers.* London 1841-
Documents on British Foreign Policy 1919-1939. Series I, IA. London 1946-

Command Papers
1921: Cmd 1474
1922: Cmd 1621, 1627, 1667, 1737, 1742
1923: Cmd 1812, 1938, 1943, 1987, 1988

1924: Cmd 2029, 2083, 2169, 2184, 2191, 2200, 2270, 2273
1925: Cmd 2301, 2368, 2429, 2435, 2458, 2468, 2525, 2527
1926: Cmd 2768
1927: Cmd 2888

The Parliamentary Debates. House of Commons. 5th series
The Parliamentary Debates. House of Lords. 5th series

Belgium

Ministère des Affaires Etrangères. *Documents diplomatiques relatifs aux réparations. Du 26 décembre 1922 au 27 août 1923.* Brussels 1923

Ministère des Affaires Etrangères et du Commerce Exterieure. *Documents diplomatiques belges 1920-1940. La Politique de sécurité extérieure.* Brussels 1964 -. Vols. I-II

France

Ministère des Affaires Etrangères. *Documents diplomatiques. Demande de moratorium du gouvernement allemand à la Commission des Réparations (14 novembre 1922), Conference de Londres (9-11 décembre 1922), Conférence de Paris (2-4 janvier 1923).* Paris 1923

——— *Documents diplomatiques. Documents relatifs aux notes allemandes des 2 mai et 5 juin sur les réparations (2 mai-3 août 1923).* Paris 1923

——— *Documents diplomatiques. Réponse du gouvernement français à la lettre du gouvernement britannique du 11 août 1923 sur les réparations, 20 août 1923.* Paris 1923

——— *Documents diplomatiques. Documents relatifs aux négociations concernant les garanties de sécurité contre une agression de l'Allemagne, 10 janvier 1919-7 décembre 1923.* Paris 1924

Journal Officiel de la République Francaise. Débats et documents parlementaires

Germany

Auswärtiges Amt. *Akten zur deutschen auswärtigen Politik 1918-1945.* Series B, 1925-1933. Göttingen 1966-

Bundesarchiv. *Akten der Reichskanzlei, Weimarer Republik,* Boppard 1968-

Deutsche Demokratische Republik. Ministerium für Auswärtigen Angelegenheiten. *Locarno-Konferenz 1925. Eine Dokumentensammlung.* Berlin 1962

Italy

Ministero degli Affari Esteri. *I Documenti diplomatici italiani.* Settima serie. Rome 1953-

League of Nations

Monthly Summary. Geneva 1921-
Official Journal. Geneva 1920-
Records of the First [etc.] *Assembly.* Geneva 1920-
Resolutions and Recommendations adopted by the Assembly at its Second [etc.] *Session.* Geneva 1921-

United States

Department of State. *Conference on the Limitation of Armament.* Washington 1922.
——— *Papers Relating to the Foreign Relations of the United States.* Washington 1862-

U.S.S.R.

Ministerstvo inostrannykh del. *Dokumenty Vneshnei Politiki S.S.S.R.* Moscow 1959-
——— *Lokarnskaya Konferentsiya.* Moscow 1959
Royal Institute of International Affairs. *Soviet Documents on Foreign Policy,* ed. Jane Degras. Vols I-II. London 1951-2

3. *Biographies, Diaries, Memoirs, Collections of Papers*

Amery, L.S. *My Political Life.* Vol. II. London 1953
Birkenhead, Earl of. *F.E. The Life of F.E. Smith, First Earl of Birkenhead.* London 1959
Blake, Robert. *The Unknown Prime Minister.* London 1955
Boyle, Andrew. *Trenchard.* London 1962
Cecil of Chelwood, Viscount. *A Great Experiment.* London 1941
——— *All the Way.* London 1949
Chamberlain, Austen. *Down the Years.* London 1935
Chastenet, Jacques. *Raymond Poincaré.* Paris 1948
Churchill, Randolph S. *Lord Derby, 'King of Lancashire'.* London 1959
Clay, Sir Henry. *Lord Norman.* London 1957
D'Abernon, Viscount. *An Ambassador of Peace. Lord D'Abernon's Diary.* 3 vols. London 1929, 1930
Dawson, R. MacGregor. *William Lyon Mackenzie King. A Political Biography.* Vols. I-II. Toronto 1958, 1963

Dugdale, Blanche E.C. *Arthur James Balfour.* London 1936
Edwards, Cecil. *Bruce of Melbourne.* London 1966
Fénaux, Robert. *Paul Hymans.* Brussels 1946
Gessler, Otto. *Reichswehrpolitik in der Weimarer Zeit.* Stuttgart 1958
Gilbert, Martin. *Winston S. Churchill.* Vols. IV-V. London 1975, 1976
Görlitz, Walter. *Gustav Stresemann.* Heidelberg 1947
Graham, W.R. *Arthur Meighen.* 2 vols. Toronto 1960, 1963
Hamilton, Mary Agnes. *Arthur Henderson.* London 1938
Hancock, W.K. *Smuts.* Vols. I-II. London 1962, 1968
Hardinge of Penshurst, Lord. *Old Diplomacy.* London 1947
Herriot, Edouard. *Jadis.* Vol. II. Paris 1952
Hirsch, Felix. *Stresemann.* Göttingen 1964
Hubatsch, Walther. *Hindenburg und der Staat.* Göttingen 1966
Hutchison, W. Bruce. *Mackenzie King. The Incredible Canadian.* Toronto 1952
Hymans, Paul. *Mémoires,* edd. Frans van Kalken and John Bartier. Brussels 1958
Jones, Thomas. *Whitehall Diary,* ed. Keith Middlemas. Vol. I. London 1969
Kessler, Harry Graf. *Tagebücher 1918-1937.* Frankfurt 1961
——— *Walther Rathenau, sein Leben und sein Werk.* Berlin 1928
Laroche, Jules. *Au Quai d'Orsay avec Briand et Poincaré.* Paris 1957
Lee, Viscount. *"A Good Innings." The Private Papers of Viscount Lee of Fareham,* ed. Alan Clark. London 1974
Loucheur, Louis. *Carnets secrets, 1908-1932,* ed. Jacques de Launay. Brussels and Paris 1962
Luther, Hans. *Politiker ohne Partei.* Stuttgart 1960
Marquand, David. *Ramsay MacDonald.* London 1977
Maurice, Major-General Sir Frederick. *Haldane.* Vol. II. London 1939
Meier-Welcker, Hans. *Seeckt.* Frankfurt 1967
Middlemas, Keith, and Barnes, John. *Baldwin. A Biography.* London 1969
Miquel, Pierre. *Poincaré.* Paris 1961
Nicolson, Harold. *Curzon: The Last Phase 1919-1925.* London 1934
Parmoor, Lord. *A Retrospect.* London 1936
Paul-Boncour, J. *Entre deux guerres.* Vol II: *Les Lendemains de la victoire 1919-1934.* Paris 1945
Persil, Raoul. *Alexandre Millerand.* Paris 1949
Petrie, Sir Charles. *The Life and Letters of the Right Hon. Sir Austen Chamberlain.* 2 vols. London 1939, 1940
Poincaré, Raymond. *Histoire politique. Chroniques de quinzaine.* 3 vols. Paris 1920, 1921
Pusey, Merlo J. *Charles Evans Hughes.* 2 vols. New York 1951, 1963

Rabenau, General Friedrich von. *Seeckt. Aus seinem Leben 1918-1936.* Leipzig 1940
Riddell, Lord. *Lord Riddell's Intimate Diary of the Peace Conference and After, 1918-1923.* London 1933
Ronaldshay, Earl of. *The Life of Lord Curzon.* London 1926
Rosen, Friedrich. *Aus einem diplomatischen Wanderleben.* Wiesbaden 1959
Roskill, Stephen. *Hankey, Man of Secrets.* Vol. II. London 1972
St-Aulaire, Comte de. *Confession d'un vieux diplomate.* Paris 1953
Schmidt, Paul Otto. *Statist auf diplomatischer Bühne 1923-1945.* Bonn 1949
Snowden, Viscount. *An Autobiography.* London 1934
Soulié, Michel. *La Vie politique d'Edouard Herriot.* Paris 1962
Stern-Rubarth, Edgar. *Three Men Tried. . . .* London 1939
Stockhausen, Max von. *Sechs Jahre Reichskanzlei.* Bonn 1954
Stresemann, Gustav. *Vermächtnis. Der Nachlass in drei Bänden,* ed. Henry Bernhard. 3 vols. Berlin 1932, 1933
Suarez, Georges. *Briand. Sa vie, son oeuvre.* Vols. V-VI. Paris 1952
——— *Herriot, 1924-1932.* Paris 1932
Thimme, Annelise, *Gustav Stresemann,* Hanover and Frankfurt 1957
Young, Kenneth. *Arthur James Balfour.* London 1963

4. *Contemporary Works*

Archimbaud, Léon. *La Conférence de Washington.* Paris 1923
Bardoux, Jacques. *Le Socialisme au pouvoir. L'Experience de 1924. Le Dialogue J. Ramsay MacDonald-Edouard Herriot.* Paris 1930
——— *Lloyd George et la France.* Paris 1923
Beneš, Eduard. *Five Years of Czechoslovak Foreign Policy.* Prague 1924
Bergmann, Carl. *Der Weg der Reparationen.* Frankfurt 1926
Brunet, René. *La Société des Nations et la France.* Paris 1921
Bywater, Hector C. *Navies and Nations. A review of Naval Developments since the Great War.* Boston 1927
——— *Sea Power in the Pacific.* Boston 1921
Caillaux, Joseph. *Où va la France? Où va l'Europe?* Paris 1922
Castex, Capitaine de frégate Raoul Victor Patrice. *Synthèse de la guerre sous-marine.* Paris 1920
Dalton, Hugh. *Towards the Peace of Nations. A Study in International Politics.* London 1928
Dewey, A. Gordon. *The Dominions and Diplomacy: the Canadian Contribution.* London 1929
Djourovitch, Djoura. *Le Protocole de Genève devant l'opinion anglaise.* Paris 1928

Fabre-Luce, Alfred. *La Crise des alliances. Sur les relations franco-britanniques depuis la signature de la paix.* Paris 1922

——— *Locarno sans rêves.* Paris 1927

Fischer, Louis. *The Soviets in World Affairs.* London 1930

Fisk, Harvey E. *The Inter-Ally Debts.* New York 1924

Headlam-Morley, Sir James. *Studies in Diplomatic History.* London 1930

Ichihashi, Yamato. *The Washington Conference and After.* Stanford 1928

Lichtenberger, Henri. *Relations between France and Germany.* Washington 1923

Linnebach, Karl. *Die Entmilitarisierung der Rheinlande und der Vertrag von Locarno.* Berlin 1927

MacDonald, J. Ramsay. *Foreign Policy of the Labour Party.* London 1923

——— 'Protocol or Pact', in *International Conciliation,* No. 212, September 1925

Miller, David Hunter. *The Drafting of the Covenant.* New York and London 1928

Mills, J. Saxon. *The Genoa Conference.* London 1922

Moulton, Harold G. and Lewis, Cleona. *The French Debt Problem.* New York 1925

Moulton, Harold G. and McGuire, Constantine E. *Germany's Capacity to Pay.* New York 1923

Moulton, Harold G. and Pasvolsky, Leo. *World War Debt Settlement.* New York 1926

Noel Baker, P.J. *The Geneva Protocol.* London 1925

Pinon, René. *Chroniques du ministère Poincaré.* 2 vols. Paris 1923, 1924

Rheinbaben, Werner Freiherr von. *Von Versailles zur Freiheit. Weg und Ziele der deutschen Aussenpolitik.* Hamburg 1927

Roques, Paul. *Le Contrôle militaire interallié en Allemagne.* Paris 1927

Royal Institute of International Affairs. *Survey of International Affairs.* London 1927-

Selle, Georges. *Une crise de la Société des Nations.* Paris 1927

Sering, Max. *Deutschland unter dem Dawes-Plan.* Berlin 1928

Smogorzewski, Casimir M. *La Pologne, l'Allemagne et le 'Corridor'.* Paris 1929

Strupp, Karl. *Das Werk von Locarno.* Berlin 1926

Temperley, H.W.V., ed. *History of the Peace Conference of Paris.* 6 vols. London 1920-24

Tirard, Paul. *La France sur le Rhin. Douze années d'occupation rhénane.* Paris 1930

Williams, Roth [K. Zilliacus]. *The League, the Protocol and the Empire.* London 1925

5. *Later Works*

Albrecht-Carrié, René. *France, Europe and the two World Wars.* Geneva 1960

Alexander, Manfred. *Der deutsch-tschechoslowakische Schiedsvertrag von 1925 im Rahmen der Locarno-Verträge.* Munich and Vienna 1970

Anderle, Alfred. *Die deutsche Rapallo-Politik.* Berlin 1962

——— *Rapallo und die friedliche Koexistenz.* Berlin 1963

Bachofen, Maja. *Lord Robert Cecil und das Völkerbund.* Zürich 1959

Blücher, Wipert von. *Deutschlands Weg nach Rapallo.* Wiesbaden 1951

Bonnefous, Georges and Edouard. *Histoire politique de la Troisième République.* Vols. III, IV. Paris 1959, 1960

Bournazel, Renata. *Rapallo: naissance d'un mythe.* Paris 1974

Braisted, William Reynolds. *The United States Navy in the Pacific 1909-1922.* Austin, Texas 1971

Brebner, John Bartlett. *North Atlantic Triangle: the Interplay of Canada, the United States and Great Britain.* New York 1945

Bregman, Aleksander. *La Politique de la Poland dans la Société des Nations.* Paris 1932

Bretton, Henry L. *Stresemann and the Revision of Versailles.* Stanford 1953

Breuning, E.C.M. 'Germany's Foreign Policy between East and West'. D. Phil. thesis, Oxford 1965

Brügel, J.W. *Tschechen und Deutschen 1918-1938.* Munich 1967

Campbell, F. Gregory. *Confrontation in Central Europe. Weimar Germany and Czechoslovakia.* Chicago 1975

Carr. E.H. *A History of Soviet Russia. The Bolshevik Revolution.* Vol. III. London 1953

Carrocci, Giampiero. *La Politica estera dell'Italia fascista 1925-1928.* Bari 1969

Carsten, F.L. *The Reichswehr and Politics 1918-1933.* Oxford 1966

Carter, Gwendolen M. *The British Government and International Security. The Role of the Dominions.* Toronto 1947

Cassels, Alan. *Mussolini's Early Diplomacy.* Princeton 1970

Castellan, Georges. *Le Réarmement clandestin du Reich.* Paris 1954

Chaput, Rolland A. *Disarmament in British Foreign Policy.* London 1935

Charvet, Jean Felix. *L'Influence britannique dans la S.D.N.* Paris 1937

Chastenet, Jacques. *Histoire de la Troisième République.* Vol. V. Paris 1960

Collier, Basil. *The Defence of the United Kingdom.* History of the Second World War: United Kingdom Military Series, ed. J.R.M. Butler. London 1957

Craig, Gordon A. and Gilbert, Felix, edd. *The Diplomats.* Princeton 1953

Crowley, James B. *Japan's Quest for Autonomy.* Princeton 1966
D'Ombrain, Nicholas. *War Machinery and High Policy. Defence Administration in Peacetime Britain 1902-1914.* London 1973
Dorpalen, Andreas. *Hindenburg and the Weimar Republic.* Princeton 1964
Dorten, J.A. *La Tragédie rhénane.* Paris 1945
Dyck, Harvey Leonard. *Weimar Germany and Soviet Russia 1926-33: A Study in Diplomatic Instability.* London 1966
Erickson, John. *The Soviet High Command.* London 1962
Eudin, Xenia Joukoff, and Fisher, Harold H. *Soviet Russia and the West 1920-1927. A Documentary Survey.* Stanford 1957
Eyck, Erich. *A History of the Weimar Republic.* 2 vols. Cambridge, Mass. 1962, 1964
Felix, David. *Walther Rathenau and the Weimar Republic. The Politics of Reparations.* Baltimore and London 1971
Freund, Gerald. *Unholy Alliance.* London 1957
Fry, Michael G. *Illusions of Security. North Atlantic Diplomacy 1918-22.* Toronto 1972
Gatzke, Hans W. *Stresemann and the Rearmament of Germany.* Baltimore 1954
Gescher, Dieter Bruno. *Die Vereinigte Staaten von Nordamerika und die Reparationen 1920-1924.* Bonn 1956
Gordon, Harold J. *The Reichswehr and the German Republic.* Princeton 1957
Gorodetsky, Gabriel. *The Precarious Truce. Anglo-Soviet Relations 1924-27.* London 1977
Hankey, Lord. *Diplomacy by Conference.* London 1946
Helbig, Herbert. *Die Träger der Rapallo-Politik.* Göttingen 1958
Hérisson, Charles D. *Les Nations anglo-saxonnes et la paix.* Paris 1936
Hilger, Gustav, and Meyer, Alfred G. *The Incompatible Allies.* New York 1953
Holtje, Christian. *Die Weimarer Republik und das Ostlocarno-Problem 1919-1934.* Würzburg 1958
Howard, Michael. *The Continental Commitment.* London 1972
Hughes, Judith M. *To the Maginot Line. The Politics of French Military Preparedness in the 1920's.* Cambridge, Mass. 1971
Iriye, Akira. *After Imperialism. The Search for a New Order in the Far East 1921-1931.* Cambridge, Mass. 1965
Jacobson, Jon. *Locarno Diplomacy. Germany and the West 1925-1929.* Princeton 1972
Johnson, Franklin Arthur. *Defence by Committee. The British Committee of Imperial Defence 1885-1959.* London 1960
Jordan, W.M. *Great Britain, France, and the German Problem 1918-1939.* London 1943

Jouvenel, Bertrand de. *D'une guerre à l'autre.* Vol. I. Paris 1940

Jouvenel, Henri de. *La Paix française.* Paris 1932

Kennedy, Malcolm D. *The Estrangement of Great Britain and Japan.* Manchester 1969

Kieft, David Owen. *Belgium's Return to Neutrality. An Essay in the Frustrations of Small-Power Diplomacy.* London 1972

Klein, Fritz. *Die diplomatische Beziehungen Deutschlands zur Sowjet-Union 1917-1932.* Berlin 1952

Korbel, Josef. *Poland between East and West.* Princeton 1963

Laubach, Ernst. *Die Politik der Kabinette Wirth 1921-22.* Lübeck 1968

Linke, Horst Gunther. *Deutsch-sowjetische Beziehungen bis Rapallo.* Cologne 1970

Lloyd George, David. *The Truth about Reparations and War Debts.* London 1932

Louis, Wm Roger. *British Strategy in the Far East 1919-1939.* London 1971

Lyman, Richard W. *The First Labour Government.* London 1957

McCallum, R.B. *Public Opinion and the Last Peace.* London 1944

Maxelon, Michael-Olaf. *Stresemann und Frankreich. Deutsche Politik der Ost-West-Balance.* Düsseldorf 1972

Medlicott, W.N. *British Foreign Policy since Versailles.* 2nd edn. London 1968

Mitchell, B.R. and Deane, Phyllis. *Abstract of British Historical Statistics.* Cambridge 1962

Nelson, Harold I. *Land and Power. British and Allied Policy on Germany's Frontiers 1916-1919.* Toronto and London 1963

Nollet, General Charles. *Une expérience de désarmament. Cinq ans de contrôle militaire en Allemagne.* Paris 1932

Northedge, F.S. *The Troubled Giant. Britain among the Great Powers 1916-1939.* London 1966

Nish, Ian. *Alliance in Decline. A Study in Anglo-Japanese Relations 1908-23.* London 1972

Polonsky, Antony. *Politics in Independent Poland 1919-1939.* Oxford 1972

Post, Gaines. *The Civil-Military Fabric of Weimar Foreign Policy.* Princeton 1973

Riekhoff, Harald von. *German-Polish Relations, 1919-1933.* Baltimore 1971

Rosenbaum, Kurt. *Community of Fate, German-Soviet Diplomatic Relations 1922-1928.* Syracuse 1965

Rosenfeld, Gunter. *Sowjetrussland und Deutschland 1917-22.* Berlin 1960

Roskill, Stephen. *Naval Policy between the Wars.* Vol. I: *The Period of Anglo-American Antagonism 1919-1929.* London 1968

Royal Institute of International Affairs. *Survey of British Commonwealth Affairs.* Vol. I: *Problems of Nationality 1918-1936,* by W.K. Hancock; Vol. II: *Problems of External Policy 1931-1939,* by Nicholas Mansergh. London 1937, 1952

Salewski, Michael. *Entwaffnung und Militärkontrolle in Deutschland 1919-1927.* Munich 1966

Sasse, Heinz Gunther. *100 Jahre Botschaft in London.* Bonn 1963

Schuker, Stephen A. *The End of French Predominance in Europe. The Financial Crisis of 1924 and the Adoption of the Dawes Plan.* Chapel Hill, N.C. 1976

Schwoebel, Jean. *L'Angleterre et la sécurité collective.* Paris 1938

Seeckt, Generaloberst Hans von. *Deutschland zwischen West und Ost.* Hamburg 1933

Selsam, J. Paul. *The Attempts to form an Anglo-French Alliance 1919-1923.* Philadelphia 1936

Spenz, Jürgen. *Die diplomatische Vorgeschichte des Beitritts Deutschlands zum Völkerbund 1924-1926.* Göttingen 1966

Sprout, Harold and Margaret. *Towards a New Order of Sea Power. American Naval Policy and the World Scene 1918-1922.* 2nd edn. Princeton 1943

Steiner, Zara S. *The Foreign Office and Foreign Policy 1898-1914.* London 1969

Thimme, Roland. *Stresemann und die deutsche Volkspartei 1923-25.* Lübeck 1961

Turner, Henry A. *Stresemann and the Politics of the Weimar Republic.* Princeton 1963

Ulam, Adam B. *Expansion and Coexistence. The History of Soviet Foreign Policy 1917-1967.* New York and London 1968

Ullman, Richard H. *Anglo-Soviet Relations, 1917-1921.* Vol. III: *The Anglo-Soviet Accord.* Princeton 1972

Vinson, John Chalmers. *The Parchment Peace. The United States Senate and the Washington Conference 1921-1922.* Atlanta 1955

Vondracek, Felix Hohn. *The Foreign Policy of Czechoslovakia 1918-1935.* New York 1937

Walsdorff, Martin. *Westorientierung und Ostpolitik. Stresemanns Russlandpolitik in der Locarno-Ära.* Bremen 1971

Walters, F.P. *A History of the League of Nations.* London 1952

Wandycz, Piotr S. *France and her Eastern Allies 1919-1925.* Minneapolis 1962

Weill-Raynal, Etienne. *Les Réparations allemandes et la France.* Paris 1947

Weidenfeld, Werner. *Die Englandpolitik Gustav Stresemanns.* Mainz 1972

Wheeler, Gerald E. *Prelude to Pearl Harbor. The U.S. Navy and the Far*

East 1921-1931. Columbia, Miss. 1963

Winkler, H.J. *The League of Nations Movement in Great Britain 1914-1918.* New Brunswick, N.J. 1952

Wolfers, Arnold. *Britain and France between Two Wars.* New York 1940

Woodward, E.L. *Great Britain and the German Navy.* London 1935

Zimmermann, Ludwig. *Deutsche Aussenpolitik in der Ära der Weimarer Republik.* Göttingen 1958

——— *Frankreichs Ruhrpolitik. Von Versailles bis zum Dawesplan,* ed. Walther Peter Fuchs. Göttingen 1971

Zimmern, Sir Alfred. *The League of Nations and the Rule of Law.* London 1936

Zsigmond, L. *Zur deutschen Frage 1918-1923.* Budapest 1964

6. *Articles*

Artaud, Denise. 'A propos de l'occupation de la Ruhr', *Revue d'histoire moderne et contemporaine* 17 (1970), 1-21.

Asada, Sadao. 'Japan's 'Special Interests' and the Washington Conference', *American Historical Review* 67 (1961), 62-70.

Burks, David D. 'The United States and the Geneva Protocol of 1924: "A New Holy Alliance"?' *American Historical Review* 64 (1958-59), 891-905.

Carlton, David. 'Disarmament with guarantees: Lord Cecil 1922-1927', *Disarmament and Arms Control: an International Journal,* 1965, 143-64.

——— 'Great Britain and the League Council crisis of 1926', *Historical Journal* 11 (1968), 354-64.

Carsten, F.L. 'The Reichswehr and the Red Army 1920-1933', *Survey. A Journal of East and West Studies* 44-5 (1962), 114-32.

Cassels, Alan. 'Mussolini and German nationalism, 1922-25', *Journal of Modern History* 35 (1963), 137-57.

Castellan, Georges. 'Reichswehr et Armée Rouge 1920-30', *Les Relations germano-soviétiques 1933-39,* ed. J.B. Duroselle, Paris 1954.

Cook, Ramsay. 'J.W. Dafoe at the Imperial Conference, 1923', *Canadian Historical Review* 41 (1960), 19-40.

——— 'A Canadian account of the 1926 Imperial Conference', *Journal of Commonwealth Political Studies* 3 (1965), 50-63.

Crowe, Sybil Eyre. 'Sir Eyre Crowe and the Locarno Pact', *English Historical Review* 87 (1971-2), No. 342, pp. 49-74.

Davies, Norman. 'Lloyd George and Poland, 1919-20', *Journal of Contemporary History* 6 (1971), No. 3, pp. 132-54.

Erdmann, Karl Dietrich. 'Deutschland, Rapallo und der Westen', in *Vierteljahrshefte für Zeitgeschichte* 11 (1963), 105-65.

Fox, John P. 'Britain and the Inter-Allied Military Commission of Control, 1925-26', *Journal of Contemporary History,* 4 (1969), No. 2, 143-64.

Fry, M.G. 'The North Atlantic Triangle and the abrogation of the Anglo-Japanese alliance', *Journal of Modern History* 39 (1967), 46-64.

Galbraith, John S. 'The Imperial Conference of 1921 and the Washington Conference', *Canadian Historical Review* 29 (1948), 148-52.

Gasiorowski, Zygmunt J. 'Beneš and Locarno: some unpublished documents', *Review of Politics* 20 (1958), 209-24.

——— 'Polish-Czechoslovak relations, 1918-1922', *Slavonic and East European Review* 35(1956-57), 172-93.

——— 'The Russian overture to Germany of December 1924', *Journal of Modern History* 30 (1958), 97-117.

——— 'Stresemann and Poland before Locarno', *Journal of Central European Affairs* 18 (1958-9), 25-47.

——— 'Stresemann and Poland after Locarno', *Journal of Central European Affairs* 18 (1958-9), 292-317.

Gatzke, Hans W. 'Russo-German military collaboration during the Weimar Republic', *American Historical Review,* 63 (1957-58), 565-97.

——— 'Von Rapallo nach Berlin. Stresemann und die deutsche Russlandpolitik', *Vierteljahrshefte für Zeitgeschichte* 4 (1956), 1-29.

Geigenmuller, Ernst. 'Botschafter von Hoesch und die Räumungsfrage', *Historische Zeitschrift,* 200 (1965), 606-20.

Glenny, M.V. 'The Anglo-Soviet Trade Agreement, March 1921', *Journal of Contemporary History,* 5 (1970), No. 2, 63-82.

Hirsch, Felix. 'Stresemann in historical perspective', *Review of Politics,* 15 (1953), 360-77.

Johnson, Douglas. 'Austen Chamberlain and the Locarno agreements', *University of Birmingham Historical Journal* 7 (1961), 62-81.

——— 'The Locarno Treaties', *Troubled Neighbours. Franco-British Relations in the Twentieth Century,* ed. Neville Waites. London 1971.

Kollman, Erich C. 'Walther Rathenau and German foreign policy: thoughts and actions', *Journal of Modern History* 24 (1952), 127-42.

Larner, Christina. 'The Amalgamation of the Diplomatic Service with the Foreign Office', *Journal of Contemporary History* 7 (1972), 107-26.

Lower, A.R.M. 'Loring Christie and the genesis of the Washington Conference of 1921-1922', *Canadian Historical Review* 47 (1966), 38-48.

Luther, Hans. 'Stresemann und Luther in Locarno', *Politische Studien* Jg. 8, Heft 84, April 1957.

McDonald, J. Kenneth. 'Lloyd George and the search for a post-war naval policy, 1919', *Lloyd George. Twelve Essays,* ed. A.J.P. Taylor. London 1971.

Morgan, R.P. 'The political significance of German-Soviet trade negotiations, 1922-5', *Historical Journal,* 6 (1963), 253-71.

Nish, I.H. 'Japan and the ending of the Anglo-Japanese alliance', *Studies in International History, Essays presented to W.N. Medlicott,* ed. K. Bourne and D.C. Watt. London 1967.

Orde, Anne. 'Thoiry revisited', *Durham University Journal* 67 (1975), No. 2, 205-18.

Rosen, Edgar R. 'Mussolini und Deutschland 1922-1923', *Vierteljahrshefte für Zeitgeschichte* 5 (1957), 17-41.

Schieder, Theodor. 'Die Entstehungsgeschichte des Rapallo-Vertrags', *Historische Zeitschrift* 204 (1967), 545-609.

Sharp, Alan J. 'The Foreign Office in eclipse 1919-22', *History* 61 (1976), 198-218.

Stambrook, F.G. ' 'Das Kind' - Lord D'Abernon and the origins of the Locarno Pact', *Central European History* 1 (1968), No. 3, 233-63.

——— 'The Foreign Secretary and foreign policy. The experiences of Austen Chamberlain in 1925 and 1927', *International Review of History and Political Science* 6 (1969), No. 3, 109-27.

Steiner, Zara, and Dockrill, M.L. 'The Foreign Office reforms 1919-1921', *Historical Journal* 17 (1974), 131-51.

Tate, Merze, and Foy, Fidele, 'More light on the abrogation of the Anglo-Japanese alliance', *Political Science Quarterly* 74 (1959), 532-54.

Thimme, Annelise. 'Gustav Stresemann, Legende und Wirklichkeit', *Historische Zeitschrift* 181 (1956), 287-338.

——— 'Stresemann als Reichskanzler', *Die Welt als Geschichte* 17 (1957), 9-25.

Turner, Henry A. 'Eine Rede Stresemanns über seine Locarno-politik', *Vierteljahrshefte für Zeitgeschichte* 15 (1967), 415-36.

Venkataramani, M.S. 'Ramsay MacDonald and Britain's domestic and foreign relations 1919-1931', *Political Studies,* 8 (1960), 231-49.

Vinson, J. Chal. 'The drafting of the Four Power Treaty of the Washington Conference', *Journal of Modern History,* 25 (1953), 40-7.

——— 'The Imperial Conference of 1921 and the Anglo-Japanese alliance', *Pacific Historical Review* 31 (1962), 257-66.

Watt, D.C. 'Imperial defence policy and imperial foreign policy, 1911-1939; a neglected paradox?' *Journal of Commonwealth Political Studies* 1 (1961-63), 266-81.

Winckler, Henry R. 'The emergence of a labor foreign policy in Great Britain, 1918-1929', *Journal of Modern History* 28 (1956), 247-58.

INDEX

Note. Details of individuals' careers are given only for the period dealt with in this work.